Lab Manual

Module H

HOLT McDOUGAL

HOUGHTON MIFFLIN HARCOURT

Acknowledgements for Covers

Cover Photo Credits

Light echo in space (bg) ©NASA/ESA/Hubble Heritage Team (STScI/AURA); *pacific wheel* (l) ©Geoffrey George/Getty Images; *snowboarder* (cl) ©Jonathan Nourok/Photographer's Choice/Getty Images; *water droplet* (cr) ©L. Clarke/Corbis; *molecular structure* (r) ©Stockbyte/Getty Images

Printed in the U.S.A.

ISBN 978-0-547-59325-8

4 5 6 7 8 9 10 0982 20 19 18 17 16 15 14 13 12
4500364970 A B C D E F G

Contents

INTRODUCTION

TEACHER LAB SAFETY

STUDENT LAB SAFETY

Unit 1 Matter

Unit 2 Energy

Unit 3 Atoms and the Periodic Table

Unit 4 Interactions of Matter

Unit 5 Solutions, Acids, and Bases

Using Your *ScienceFusion* Lab Program

Your *ScienceFusion* Lab Program is designed to include activities that address a variety of student levels, inquiry levels, time availability, and materials. In this Lab Manual, you will find that each student activity is preceded by Teacher Resources with valuable information about the activity.

Activity Type: Quick Lab

Each lesson within each unit is supported by two to three short activities called Quick Labs. Quick Labs involve simple materials and set-up. The student portion of each Quick Lab should take less than 30 minutes. Each Quick Lab includes Teacher Resources and one Student Datasheet.

Activity Types: Exploration Lab, Field Lab, and S.T.E.M. Lab

Each unit is supported by one to four additional labs that require one or more class periods to complete. Each Exploration, Field, and S.T.E.M. Lab includes Teacher Resources and two Student Datasheets. Each Student Datasheet is targeted to address different inquiry levels. Below is a description of each lab:

- **Exploration Labs** are traditional lab activities. The labs are designed to be conducted with standard laboratory equipment and materials.
- **Field Labs** are lab activities that are partially or completely performed outside the classroom or laboratory.
- **S.T.E.M. Labs** are lab activities that focus on Science, Technology, Engineering, and Math skills.

Inquiry Level

The inquiry level of each activity indicates the level at which students direct the activity. An activity that is entirely student-directed is often called Open Inquiry or Independent Inquiry. True Open or Independent Inquiry is based on a question posed by students, uses experimental processes designed by students, and requires students to find the connections between data and content. These types of activities result from student interest in the world around them. The *ScienceFusion* Lab Program provides activities that allow for a wide variety of student involvement.

- DIRECTED Inquiry is the least student-directed of the inquiry levels. Directed Inquiry activities provide students with an introduction to content, a procedure to follow, and direction on how to organize and analyze data.
- GUIDED Inquiry indicates that an activity is moderately student-directed. Guided Inquiry activities require students to select materials, procedural steps, data analysis techniques, or other aspects of the activity.
- INDEPENDENT Inquiry indicates that an activity is highly student-directed. Though students are provided with ideas, partial procedures, or suggestions, they are responsible for selecting many aspects of the activity.

Each Quick Lab includes one Student Datasheet that is written to support the inquiry level indicated on the Teacher Resources. Each Exploration Lab, Field Lab, and S.T.E.M. Lab includes two Student Datasheets, each written to support an inquiry level. In addition, the Teacher Resources includes one or more modification suggestions to adjust the inquiry level.

Student Level

The *ScienceFusion* Lab Program is designed to provide successful experiences for all levels of students.

- BASIC activities focus on introductory content and concepts taught in the lesson. These activities can be used with any level of student, including those who may have learning or language difficulties, but they may not provide a challenge for advanced students.
- GENERAL activities are appropriate for most students.
- ADVANCED activities require good understanding of the content and concepts in the lesson or ask students to manipulate content to arrive at the learning objective. Advanced activities may provide a challenge to advanced students, but they may be difficult for average or basic-level students.

Lab Ratings

Each activity is rated on three criteria to provide you with information that you may find useful when determining if an activity is appropriate for your resources.

- **Teacher Prep** rating indicates the amount of preparation you will need to provide before students can perform the activity.
- **Student Setup** rating indicates the amount of preparation students will need to perform before they begin to collect data.
- **Cleanup** rating indicates the amount of effort required to dispose of materials and disassemble the set-up of the activity.

Teacher Notes

Information and background that may be helpful to you can be found in the Teacher Notes section of the Teacher Resources. The information includes hints and a list of skills that students will practice during the activity.

Science Kit

Hands-on materials needed to complete all the labs in the Lab Manual for each module have been conveniently configured into consumable and non-consumable kits. Common materials provided by parents or your school/district are not included in the kits. Laboratory equipment commonly found in most schools has been separately packaged in a Grades 6–8 Inquiry Equipment Kit. This economical option allows schools to buy equipment only if they need it and can be shared among teachers and across grade levels. For more information on the material kits or to order, contact your local Holt McDougal sales representative or call customer service at 800-462-6595.

Online Lab Resources

The *ScienceFusion* Lab Program offers many additional resources online through our web site thinkcentral.com. These resources include:

Teacher Notes, Transparencies, and **Copymasters** are found in the Online Toolkit. Student-friendly tutorial Transparencies are available to print as transparencies or handouts. Each set of Transparencies is supported by Teacher Notes that include background information, teaching tips, and techniques. Teacher Notes, Transparencies, and Copymatsters are available to teach a broad range of skills.

- **Modeling Experimental Design** Teacher Notes and Transparencies cover Scientific Methods skills, such as Making Qualitative Observations, Developing a Hypothesis, and Making Valid Inferences.

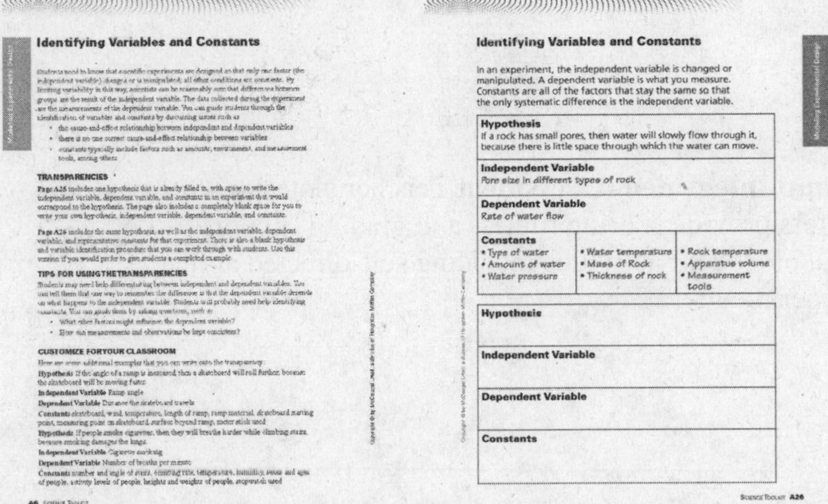

Identifying Variables and Constants

Students need to know that scientific experiments are designed so that only one factor (the independent variable) changes or is manipulated; all other conditions are constants. By limiting variability in this way, scientists can be reasonably sure that differences between groups are the result of the independent variable. The data collected during the experiment are the measurements of the dependent variable. You can guide students through the identification of variables and constants by discussing issues such as

- the cause-and-effect relationship between independent and dependent variables
- there is no one correct cause-and-effect relationship between variables
- constants typically include factors such as amounts, environment, and measurement tools, among others

TRANSPARENCIES

Page A25 includes one hypothesis that is already filled in, with space to write the independent variable, dependent variable, and constants in an experiment that would correspond to the hypothesis. The page also includes a completely blank space for you to write your own hypothesis, independent variable, dependent variable, and constants.

Page A26 includes the same hypothesis, as well as the independent variable, dependent variable, and representative constants for that experiment. There is also a blank hypothesis and variable identification procedure that you can work through with students. Use this version if you would prefer to give students a completed example.

TIPS FOR USING THE TRANSPARENCIES

Students may need help differentiating between independent and dependent variables. You can tell them that one way to remember the difference is that the dependent variable depends on what happens to the independent variable. Students will probably need help identifying constants. You can guide them by asking questions, such as

- What other factors might influence the dependent variable?
- How can measurements and observations be kept consistent?

CUSTOMIZE FOR YOUR CLASSROOM

Hypothesis If the angle of a ramp is increased, then a skateboard will roll farther, because the skateboard will be moving faster.

Independent Variable Ramp angle

Dependent Variable Distance the skateboard travels

Constants skateboard, wind, temperature, length of ramp, ramp material, skateboard starting point, measuring point on skateboard, surface beyond ramp, meter stick used

Hypothesis If people smoke cigarettes, then they will breathe harder while climbing stairs, because smoking damages the lungs.

Independent Variable Cigarette smoking

Dependent Variable Number of breaths per minute

A6 Science Toolkit

Identifying Variables and Constants

In an experiment, the independent variable is changed or manipulated. A dependent variable is what you measure. Constants are all of the factors that stay the same so that the only systematic difference is the independent variable.

Hypothesis If a rock has small pores, then water will slowly flow through it, because there is little space through which the water can move.		
Independent Variable *Pore size in different types of rock*		
Dependent Variable *Rate of water flow*		
Constants • *Type of water* • *Amount of water* • *Water pressure*	• *Water temperature* • *Mass of Rock* • *Thickness of rock*	• *Rock temperature* • *Apparatus volume* • *Measurement tools*

Hypothesis
Independent Variable
Dependent Variable
Constants

Science Toolkit A26

- **Writing in the Sciences** Teacher Notes and Transparencies teach written communication skills, such as Writing a Lab Report and Maintaining a Science Notebook. In addition, the Lab Report Template provides a structured format that students can use as the basis for their own lab reports.

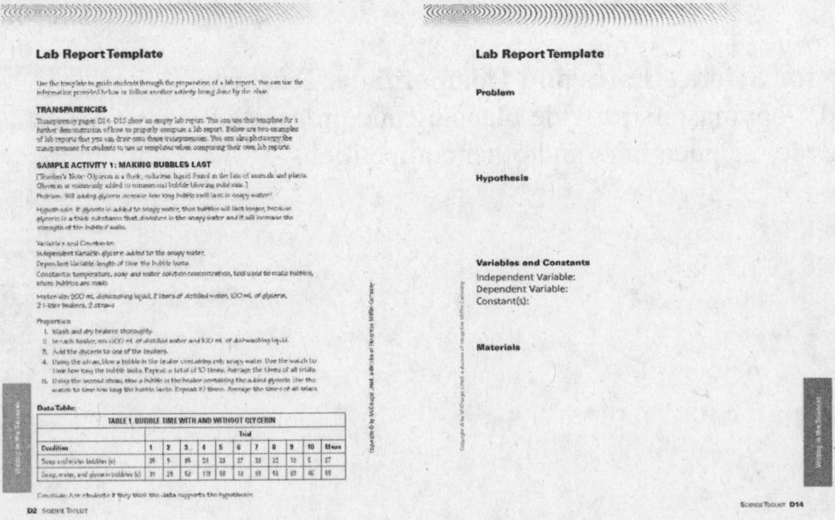

Lab Report Template

TRANSPARENCIES

SAMPLE ACTIVITY 1: MAKING BUBBLES LAST

Variables and Constants:

Data Table:

TABLE 1. BUBBLE TIME WITH AND WITHOUT GLYCERIN

D2 Science Toolkit

Lab Report Template

Problem

Hypothesis

Variables and Constants

Independent Variable:

Dependent Variable:

Constant(s):

Materials

Science Toolkit D14

- **Math in Science Tools** Teacher Notes and Transparencies teach the math skills that are needed for data analysis in labs. These Teacher Notes and Transparencies support the S.T.E.M. concepts found throughout the *ScienceFusion* program.

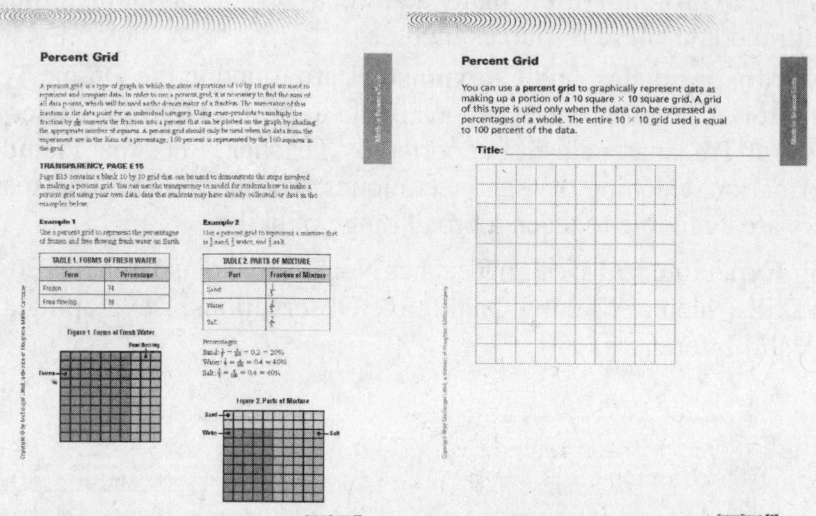

- **Rubrics and Integrated Assessment** Teacher Notes and Copymasters provide scoring rubrics and grading support for a range of student activities including self-directed and guided experiments.

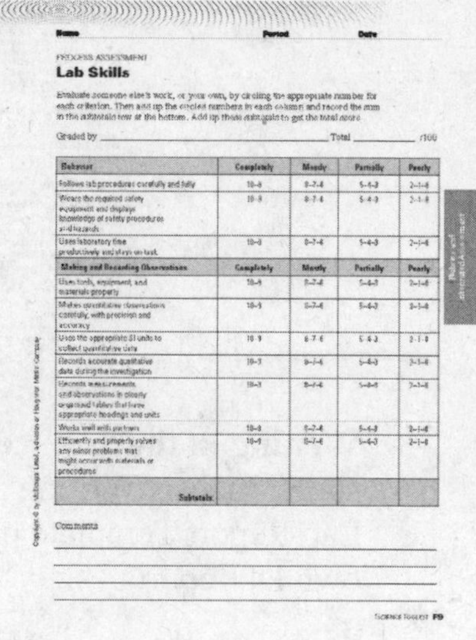

- **Planning for Science Fairs and Competitions** Teacher Notes and Copymasters provide planning and preparation techniques for science fairs and other competitions.

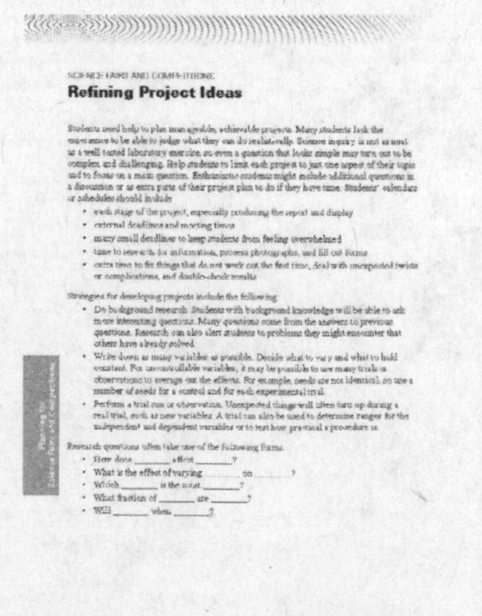

Making Your Laboratory a Safe Place

Concern for safety must begin before any activity in the classroom and before students enter the lab. A careful review of the facilities should be a basic part of preparation for each school term. You should investigate the physical environment, identify any safety risks, and inspect your work areas for compliance with safety regulations.

The review of the lab should be thorough, and all safety issues must be addressed immediately. Keep a file of your review, and add to the list each year. This will allow you to continue to raise the standard of safety in your lab and classroom.

Many classroom experiments, demonstrations, and other activities are classics that have been used for years. This familiarity may lead to a comfort that can obscure inherent safety concerns. Review all experiments, demonstrations, and activities for safety concerns before presenting them to the class. Identify and eliminate potential safety hazards.

1. **Identify the Risks** Before introducing any activity, demonstration, or experiment to the class, analyze it and consider what could possibly go wrong. Carefully review the list of materials to make sure they are safe. Inspect the equipment in your lab or classroom to make sure it is in good working order. Read the procedures to make sure they are safe. Record any hazards or concerns you identify.
2. **Evaluate the Risks** Minimize the risks you identified in the last step without sacrificing learning. Remember that no activity you perform in the lab or classroom is worth risking injury. Thus, extremely hazardous activities, or those that violate your school's policies, must be eliminated. For activities that present smaller risks, analyze each risk carefully to determine its likelihood. If the pedagogical value of the activity does not outweigh the risks, the activity must be eliminated.
3. **Select Controls to Address Risks** Even low-risk activities require controls to eliminate or minimize the risks. Make sure that in devising controls you do not substitute an equally or more hazardous alternative. Some control methods include the following:
   - Explicit verbal and written warnings may be added or posted.
   - Equipment may be rebuilt or relocated, parts may be replaced, or equipment be replaced entirely by safer alternatives.
   - Risky procedures may be eliminated.
   - Activities may be changed from student activities to teacher demonstrations.
4. **Implement and Review Selected Controls** Controls do not help if they are forgotten or not enforced. The implementation and review of controls should be as systematic and thorough as the initial analysis of safety concerns in the lab and laboratory activities.

Safety with Chemicals

Label student reagent containers with the substance's name and hazard class(es) (flammable, reactive, etc.). Dispose of hazardous waste chemicals according to federal, state, and local regulations. Refer to the MSDS for recommended disposal procedures. Remove all sources of flames, sparks, and heat from the laboratory when any flammable material is being used.

Material Safety Data Sheets

The purpose of a Material Safety Data Sheet (MSDS) is to provide readily accessible information on chemical substances commonly used in the science laboratory or in industry. The MSDS should be kept on file and referred to BEFORE handling ANY chemical. The MSDS can also be used to instruct students on chemical hazards, to evaluate spill and disposal procedures, and to warn of incompatibility with other chemicals or mixtures.

Storing Chemicals

Never store chemicals alphabetically, as this greatly increases the risk of promoting a violent reaction.

Storage Suggestions

1. Always lock the storeroom and all its cabinets when not in use.
2. Students should not be allowed in the storeroom and preparation area.
3. Avoid storing chemicals on the floor of the storeroom.
4. Do not store chemicals above eye level or on the top shelf in the storeroom.
5. Be sure shelf assemblies are firmly secured to the walls.
6. Provide anti-roll lips on all shelves.
7. Shelving should be constructed out of wood. Metal cabinets and shelves are easily corroded.
8. Avoid metal, adjustable shelf supports and clips. They can corrode, causing shelves to collapse.
9. Acids, flammables, poisons, and oxidizers should each be stored in their own locking storage cabinet.

Safety with Animals

It is recommended that teachers follow the NABT Position Statement "The Use of Animals in Biology Education" issued by the National Association of Biology Teachers (available at www.nabt.org).

Safety In Handling Preserved Materials

The following practices are recommended when handling preserved specimens:

1. NEVER dissect road-kills or nonpreserved slaughterhouse materials.
2. Wear protective gloves and splash-proof safety goggles at all times when handling preserving fluids and preserved specimens and during dissection.
3. Wear lab aprons. Use of an old shirt or smock under the lab apron is recommended.
4. Conduct dissection activities in a well-ventilated area.
5. Do not allow preservation or body-cavity fluids to contact skin. Fixatives do not distinguish between living or dead tissues. Biological supply firms may use formalin-based fixatives of varying concentrations to initially fix zoological and botanical specimens. Some provide specimens that are freezedried and rehydrated in a 10% isopropyl alcohol solution. Many suppliers provide fixed botanical materials in 50% glycerin.

Reduction Of Free Formaldehyde

Currently, federal regulations mandate a permissible exposure level of 0.75 ppm for formaldehyde. Contact your supplier for Material Data Safety Sheet (MSDS) that details the amount of formaldehyde present as well as gas-emitting characteristics for individual specimens. Prewash specimens (in a loosely covered container) in running tap water for 1–4 hours to dilute the fixative. Formaldehyde may also be chemically bound (thereby reducing danger) by immersing washed specimens in a 0.5–1.0% potassium bisulfate solution overnight or by placing them in 1% phenoxyethanol holding solutions.

Safety with Microbes

WHAT YOU CAN'T SEE CAN HURT YOU

Pathogenic (disease-causing) microorganisms are not appropriate investigation tools in the high school laboratory and should never be used.

Consult with the school nurse to screen students whose immune systems may be compromised by illness or who may be receiving immunosuppressive drug therapy. Such individuals are extraordinarily sensitive to potential infection from generally harmless microorganisms and should not participate in laboratory activities unless permitted to do so by a physician. Do not allow students who have any open cuts, abrasions, or open sores to work with microorganisms.

HOW TO USE ASEPTIC TECHNIQUE

- Demonstrate correct aseptic technique to students prior to conducting a lab activity. Never pipet liquid media by mouth. When possible, use sterile cotton applicator sticks instead of inoculating loops and Bunsen burner flames for culture inoculation. Remember to use appropriate precautions when disposing of cotton applicator sticks: they should be autoclaved or sterilized before disposal.
- Treat all microbes as pathogenic. Seal with tape all petri dishes containing bacterial cultures. Do not use blood agar plates, and never attempt to cultivate microbes from a human or animal source.
- Never dispose of microbe cultures without sterilizing them first. Autoclave or steam-sterilize at 120°C and 15 psi for 15 to 20 minutes all used cultures and any materials that have come in contact with them. If these devices are not available, flood or immerse these articles in full-strength household bleach for 30 minutes, and then discard. Use the autoclave or steam sterilizer yourself; do not allow students to use these devices.
- Wash all lab surfaces with a disinfectant solution before and after handling bacterial cultures.

HOW TO HANDLE BACTERIOLOGICAL SPILLS

- Never allow students to clean up bacteriological spills. Keep on hand a spill kit containing 500 mL of full-strength household bleach, biohazard bags (autoclavable), forceps, and paper towels.
- In the event of a bacterial spill, cover the area with a layer of paper towels. Wet the paper towels with bleach, and allow them to stand for 15 to 20 minutes. Wearing gloves and using forceps, place the residue in the biohazard bag. If broken glass is present, use a brush and dustpan to collect material, and place it in a suitably marked puncture-resistant container for disposal.

Personal Protective Equipment

Chemical goggles (Meeting ANSI Standard Z87.1) These should be worn with any chemical or chemical solution other than water, when heating substances, using any mechanical device, or observing physical processes that could eject an object.

Face shield (Meeting ANSI Standard Z87.1) Use in combination with eye goggles when working with corrosives.

Contact lenses The wearing of contact lenses for cosmetic reasons should be prohibited in the laboratory. If a student must wear contact lenses prescribed by a physician, that student should be instructed to wear eye-cup safety goggles, similar to swimmer's cup goggles, meeting ANSI Standard Z87.1.

Eye-wash station The device must be capable of delivering a copious, gentle flow of water to both eyes for at least 15 minutes. Portable liquid supply devices are not satisfactory and should not be used. A plumbed-in fixture or a perforated spray head on the end of a hose attached to a plumbed-in outlet is suitable if it is designed for use as an eye-wash fountain and meets ANSI Standard Z358.1. It must be within a 30-second walking distance from any spot in the room.

Safety shower (Meeting ANSI Standard Z358.1) Location should be within a 30-second walking distance from any spot in the room. Students should be instructed in the use of the safety shower in the event of a fire or chemical splash on their body that cannot simply be washed off.

Gloves Polyethylene, neoprene rubber, or disposable plastic may be used. Nitrile or butyl rubber gloves are recommended when handling corrosives.

Apron Rubber-coated cloth or vinyl (nylon-coated) halter is recommended.

Student Safety in the Laboratory

Systematic, careful lab work is an essential part of any science program. The equipment and apparatus students will use present various safety hazards. You must be aware of these hazards before students engage in any lab activity. The Teacher Resource Pages at the beginning of each lab in this Lab Manual will guide you in properly directing the equipment use during the experiments. Photocopy the information on the following pages for students. These safety rules always apply in the lab and in the field.

Name ______________________ Class ______________ Date ______________

Safety Symbols

The following safety symbols will appear in the instructions for labs and activities to emphasize important notes of caution. Learn what they represent so that you can take the appropriate precautions.

<table>
<tr><td></td><td>Eye Protection
• Wear approved safety goggles at all times in the lab as directed.
• If chemicals get into your eyes, flush your eyes immediately.
• Do not wear contact lenses in the lab.
• Do not look directly at the sun or any intense light source or laser.</td></tr>
<tr><td></td><td>Hand Safety
• Do not cut an object while holding the object in your hand.
• Wear appropriate protective gloves when working with an open flame, chemicals, solutions, or wild or unknown plants.
• Use a heat-resistant mitt to handle equipment that may be hot.</td></tr>
<tr><td></td><td>Clothing Protection
• Wear an apron or lab coat at all times in the lab.
• Tie back long hair, secure loose clothing, and remove loose jewelry so that they do not knock over equipment, get caught in moving parts, or come into contact with hazardous materials or electrical connections.
• Do not wear open-toed shoes, sandals, or canvas shoes in the lab.
• When outside for lab, wear long sleeves, long pants, socks, and closed shoes.</td></tr>
<tr><td></td><td>Glassware Safety
• Inspect glassware before use; do not use chipped or cracked glassware.
• Use heat-resistant glassware for heating materials or storing hot liquids.
• Notify your teacher immediately if a piece of glassware or a light bulb breaks.</td></tr>
<tr><td></td><td>Sharp-Object Safety
• Use extreme care when handling all sharp and pointed instruments.
• Cut objects on a suitable surface, always in a direction away from your body.
• Be aware of sharp objects or edges on equipment or apparatus.</td></tr>
<tr><td></td><td>Chemical Safety
• If a chemical gets on your skin, on your clothing, or in your eyes, rinse it immediately (shower, faucet or eyewash fountain) and alert your teacher.
• Do not clean up spilled chemicals yourself unless your teacher directs you to do so.
• Do not inhale any gas or vapor unless your teacher directs you to do so.
• Handle materials that emit vapors or gases in a well-ventilated area.</td></tr>
</table>

Name ______________________ Class ______________ Date ________________

Safety Symbols continued

	**Electrical Safety** • Do not use equipment with frayed electrical cords or loose plugs. • Fasten electrical cords to work surfaces by using tape. • Do not use electrical equipment near water or when clothing or hands are wet. • Hold the plug housing when you plug in or unplug equipment. • Be aware that wire coils in electrical circuits may heat up rapidly.
	**Heating Safety** • Be aware of any source of flames, sparks, or heat (such as open flames, heating coils, or hot plates) before working with any flammable substances. • Avoid using open flames. • Know the location of lab fire extinguishers and fire-safety blankets. • Know your school's fire-evacuation routes. • If your clothing catches on fire, walk to the lab shower to put out the fire. • Never leave a hot plate unattended while it is turned on or while it is cooling. • Use tongs or appropriate insulated holders when handling heated objects. • Allow all equipment to cool before storing it.
	**Plant Safety** • Do not eat any part of a plant or plant seed. • When outside, do not pick any wild plants unless your teacher instructs you to do so. • Wash your hands thoroughly after handling any part of a plant.
	**Animal Safety** • Handle animals only as your teacher directs. • Treat animals carefully and respectfully. • Wash your hands thoroughly after handling any animal.
	**Proper Waste Disposal** • Clean and sanitize all work surfaces and personal protective equipment after each lab period as directed by your teacher. • Dispose of hazardous materials only as directed by your teacher. • Dispose of sharp objects (such as broken glass) in the appropriate sharps or broken glass container as directed by your teacher.
	**Hygienic Care** • Keep your hands away from your face while you are working on any activity. • Wash your hands thoroughly before you leave the lab or after any activity. • Remove contaminated clothing immediately.

Name ____________________ Class ____________ Date ____________

Safety in the Laboratory

1. **Always wear a lab apron and safety goggles.** Wear these safety devices whenever you are in the lab, not just when you are working on an experiment.
2. **No contact lenses in the lab.** Contact lenses should not be worn during any investigations in which you are using chemicals (even if you are wearing goggles). In the event of an accident, chemicals can get behind contact lenses and cause serious damage before the lenses can be removed. If your doctor requires that you wear contact lenses instead of glasses, you should wear eye-cup safety goggles in the lab. Ask your doctor or your teacher how to use this very important and special eye protection.
3. **Personal apparel should be appropriate for laboratory work.** On lab days, avoid wearing long necklaces, dangling bracelets, bulky jewelry, and bulky or loose-fitting clothing. Long hair should be tied back. Loose, flopping, or dangling items may get caught in moving parts, accidentally contact electrical connections, or interfere with the investigation in some potentially hazardous manner. In addition, chemical fumes may react with some jewelry, such as pearls, and ruin them. Cotton clothing is preferable to wool, nylon, or polyesters. Wear shoes that will protect your feet from chemical spills and falling objects— no open-toed shoes or sandals and no shoes with woven leather straps.
4. **NEVER work alone in the laboratory.** Work in the lab only while supervised by your teacher. Do not leave equipment unattended while it is in operation.
5. **Only books and notebooks needed for the activity should be in the lab.** Only the lab notebook and perhaps the textbook should be used. Keep other books, backpacks, purses, and similar items in your desk, locker, or designated storage area.
6. **Read the entire activity before entering the lab.** Your teacher will review any applicable safety precautions before you begin the lab activity. If you are not sure of something, ask your teacher about it.
7. Always heed safety symbols and cautions in the instructions for the experiments, in handouts, and on posters in the room, and always heed cautions given verbally by your teacher. They are provided for your safety.
8. Know the proper fire drill procedures and the locations of fire exits and emergency equipment. Make sure you know the procedures to follow in case of a fire or other emergency.
9. **If your clothing catches on fire, do not run;** WALK to the safety shower, stand under the showerhead, and turn the water on. Call to your teacher while you do this.
10. **Report all accidents to the teacher** IMMEDIATELY, no matter how minor. In addition, if you get a headache or feel ill or dizzy, tell your teacher immediately.

11. **Report all spills to your teacher immediately.** Call your teacher, rather than cleaning a spill yourself. Your teacher will tell you if it is safe for you to clean up the spill. If it is not safe for you to clean up the spill, your teacher will know how the spill should be cleaned up safely.
12. If a lab directs you to design your own experiments, procedures must be approved by your teacher BEFORE you begin work.
13. DO NOT perform unauthorized experiments or use equipment or apparatus in a manner for which they were not intended. Use only materials and equipment listed in the activity equipment list or authorized by your teacher. Steps in a procedure should only be performed as described in the lab manual or as approved by your teacher.
14. **Stay alert while in the lab, and proceed with caution.** Be aware of others near you or your equipment when you are proceeding with the experiment. If you are not sure of how to proceed, ask your teacher for help.
15. **Horseplay in the lab is very dangerous.** Laboratory equipment and apparatus are not toys; never play in the lab or use lab time or equipment for anything other than their intended purpose.
16. Food, beverages, and chewing gum are NEVER permitted in the laboratory.
17. **NEVER taste chemicals.** Do not touch chemicals or allow them to contact areas of bare skin.
18. **Use extreme CAUTION when working with hot plates or other heating devices.** Keep your head, hands, hair, and clothing away from the flame or heating area, and turn the devices off when they are not in use. Remember that metal surfaces connected to the heated area will become hot by conduction. Gas burners should be lit only with a spark lighter. Make sure all heating devices and gas valves are turned off before leaving the laboratory. Never leave a hot plate or other heating device unattended when it is in use. Remember that many metal, ceramic, and glass items do not always look hot when they are heated. Allow all items to cool before storing them.
19. **Exercise caution when working with electrical equipment.** Do not use electrical equipment that has frayed or twisted wires. Be sure your hands are dry before you use electrical equipment. Do not let electrical cords dangle from work stations; dangling cords can cause tripping or electrical shocks.
20. **Keep work areas and apparatus clean and neat.** Always clean up any clutter made during the course of lab work, rearrange apparatus in an orderly manner, and report any damaged or missing items.
21. Always thoroughly wash your hands with soap and water at the conclusion of each investigation.

Name ______________________ Class ______________ Date ______________

Safety in the Field

Activities conducted outdoors require some advance planning to ensure a safe environment. The following general guidelines should be followed for fieldwork.

1. Know your mission. Your teacher will tell you the goal of the field trip in advance. Be sure to have your permission slip approved before the trip, and check to be sure that you have all necessary supplies for the day's activity.
2. Find out about on-site hazards before setting out. Determine whether poisonous plants or dangerous animals are likely to be present where you are going. Know how to identify these hazards. Find out about other hazards, such as steep or slippery terrain.
3. Wear protective clothing. Dress in a manner that will keep you warm, comfortable, and dry. Decide in advance whether you will need sunglasses, a hat, gloves, boots, or rain gear to suit the terrain and local weather conditions.
4. Do not approach or touch wild animals. If you see a threatening animal, call your teacher immediately. Avoid any living thing that may sting, bite, scratch, or otherwise cause injury.
5. Do not touch wild plants or pick wildflowers unless specifically instructed to do so by your teacher. Many wild plants can be irritating or toxic. Never taste any wild plant.
6. Do not wander away from others. Travel with a partner at all times. Stay within an area where you can be seen or heard in case you run into trouble.
7. Report all hazards or accidents to your teacher immediately. Even if the incident seems unimportant, let your teacher know what happened.
8. Maintain the safety of the environment. Do not remove anything from the field site without your teacher's permission. Stay on trails, when possible, to avoid trampling delicate vegetation. Never leave garbage behind at a field site. Leave natural areas as you found them.

Name ______________________ Class ______________ Date ______________

Laboratory Techniques

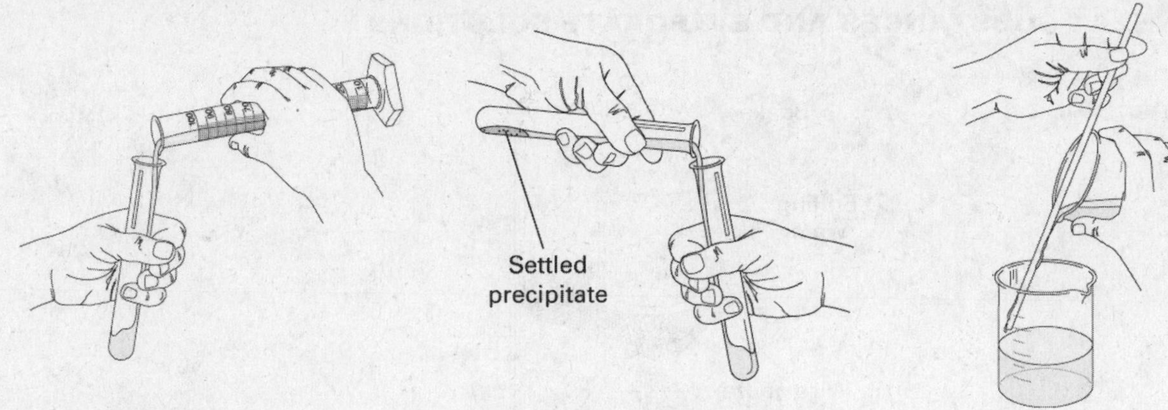

Figure A Figure B Figure C

HOW TO DECANT AND TRANSFER LIQUIDS

1. The safest way to transfer a liquid from a graduated cylinder to a test tube is shown in **Figure A**. The liquid is transferred at arm's length, with the elbows slightly bent. This position enables you to see what you are doing while maintaining steady control of the equipment.
2. Sometimes, liquids contain particles of insoluble solids that sink to the bottom of a test tube or beaker. Use one of the methods shown above to separate a supernatant (the clear fluid) from insoluble solids.

   a. **Figure B** shows the proper method of decanting a supernatant liquid from a test tube.

   b. **Figure C** shows the proper method of decanting a supernatant liquid from a beaker by using a stirring rod. The rod should touch the wall of the receiving container. Hold the stirring rod against the lip of the beaker containing the supernatant. As you pour, the liquid will run down the rod and fall into the beaker resting below. When you use this method, the liquid will not run down the side of the beaker from which you are pouring.

HOW TO HEAT SUBSTANCES AND EVAPORATE SOLUTIONS

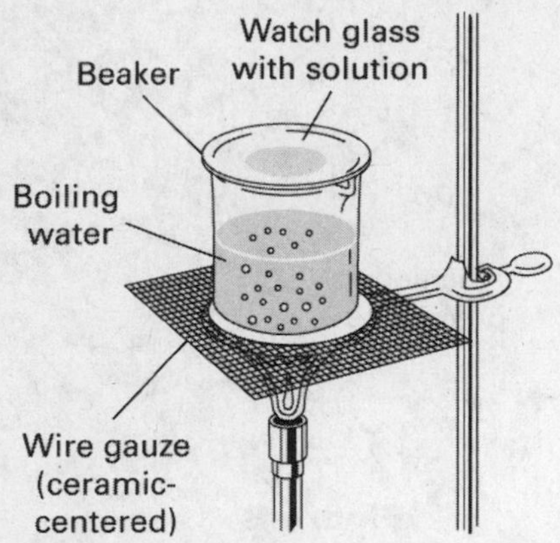

FIGURE D

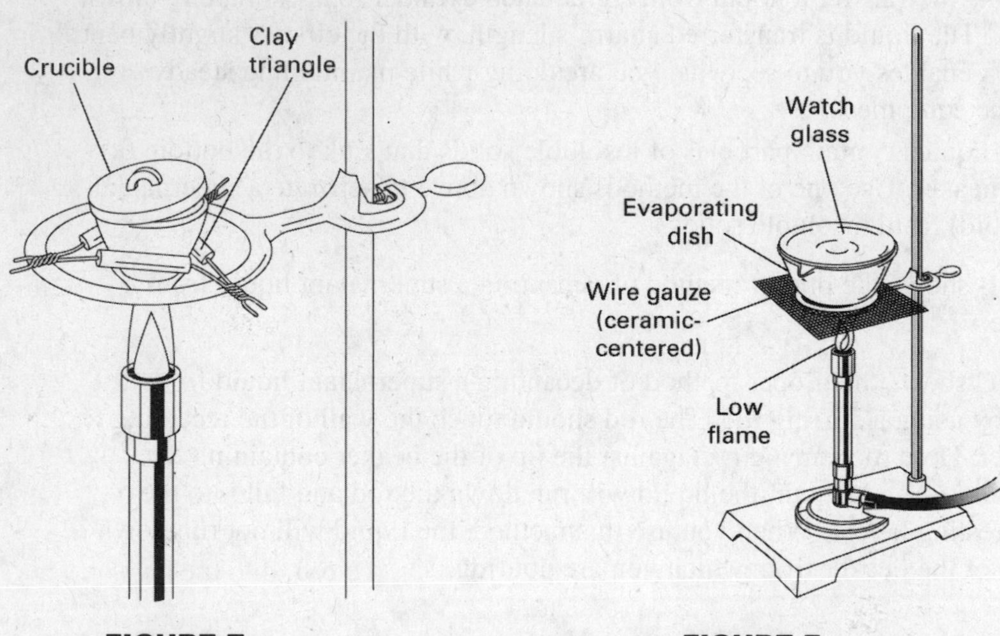

FIGURE E **FIGURE F**

1. Use care in selecting glassware for high-temperature heating. The glassware should be heat resistant.
2. When heating glassware by using a gas flame, use a ceramic-centered wire gauze to protect glassware from direct contact with the flame. Wire gauzes can withstand extremely high temperatures and will help prevent glassware from breaking. **Figure D** shows the proper setup for evaporating a solution over a water bath.
3. In some experiments, you are required to heat a substance to high temperatures in a porcelain crucible. Figure E shows the proper apparatus setup used to accomplish this task.
4. **Figure F** shows the proper setup for evaporating a solution in a porcelain evaporating dish with a watch glass cover that prevents spattering.

5. Glassware, porcelain, and iron rings that have been heated may look cool after they are removed from a heat source, but these items can still burn your skin even after several minutes of cooling. Use tongs, test-tube holders, or heat-resistant mitts and pads whenever you handle these pieces of apparatus.
6. You can test the temperature of beakers, ring stands, wire gauzes, or other pieces of apparatus that have been heated by holding the back of your hand close to their surfaces before grasping them. You will be able to feel any energy as heat generated from the hot surfaces. DO NOT TOUCH THE APPARATUS. Allow plenty of time for the apparatus to cool before handling.

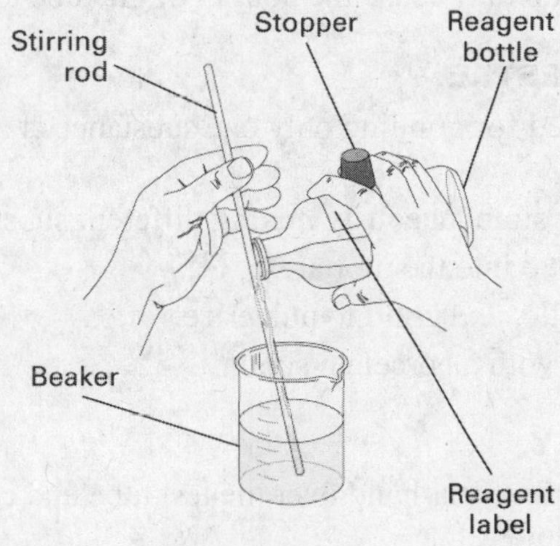

FIGURE G

HOW TO POUR LIQUID FROM A REAGENT BOTTLE

1. Read the label at least three times before using the contents of a reagent bottle.
2. Never lay the stopper of a reagent bottle on the lab table.
3. When pouring a caustic or corrosive liquid into a beaker, use a stirring rod to avoid drips and spills. Hold the stirring rod against the lip of the reagent bottle. Estimate the amount of liquid you need, and pour this amount along the rod, into the beaker. See **Figure G**.
4. Extra precaution should be taken when handling a bottle of acid. Remember the following important rules: Never add water to any concentrated acid, particularly sulfuric acid, because the mixture can splash and will generate a lot of energy as heat. To dilute any acid, add the acid to water in small quantities while stirring slowly. Remember the "triple A's"—*Always Add Acid* to water.
5. Examine the outside of the reagent bottle for any liquid that has dripped down the bottle or spilled on the counter top. Your teacher will show you the proper procedures for cleaning up a chemical spill.
6. Never pour reagents back into stock bottles. At the end of the experiment, your teacher will tell you how to dispose of any excess chemicals.

Laboratory Techniques continued

HOW TO HEAT MATERIAL IN A TEST TUBE

1. Check to see that the test tube is heat resistant.
2. Always use a test tube holder or clamp when heating a test tube.
3. Never point a heated test tube at anyone, because the liquid may splash out of the test tube.
4. Never look down into the test tube while heating it.
5. Heat the test tube from the upper portions of the tube downward, and continuously move the test tube, as shown in **Figure H**. Do not heat any one spot on the test tube. Otherwise, a pressure buildup may cause the bottom of the tube to blow out.

HOW TO USE A MORTAR AND PESTLE

1. A mortar and pestle should be used for grinding only one substance at a time. See **Figure I**.
2. Never use a mortar and pestle for simultaneously mixing different substances.
3. Place the substance to be broken up into the mortar.
4. Pound the substance with the pestle, and grind to pulverize.
5. Remove the powdered substance with a porcelain spoon.

HOW TO DETECT ODORS SAFELY

1. Test for the odor of gases by wafting your hand over the test tube and cautiously sniffing the fumes as shown in **Figure J**.
2. Do not inhale any fumes directly.
3. Use a fume hood whenever poisonous or irritating fumes are present. DO NOT waft and sniff poisonous or irritating fumes.

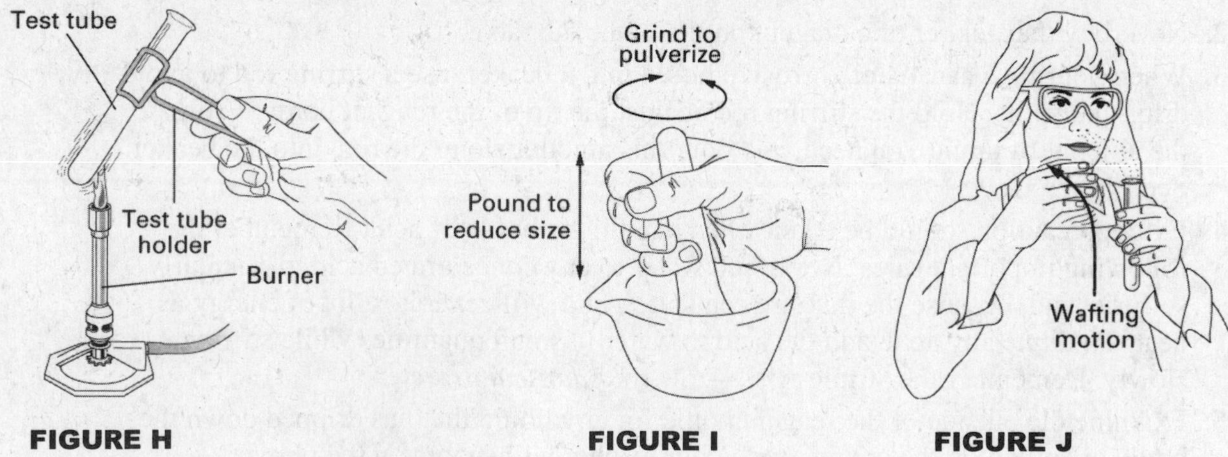

FIGURE H **FIGURE I** **FIGURE J**

Name ______________________________ Class ________________ Date ____________________

Student Safety Quiz

Circle the letter of the BEST answer.

1. Before starting an investigation or lab procedure, you should
   a. try an experiment of your own
   b. open all containers and packages
   c. read all directions and make sure you understand them
   d. handle all the equipment to become familiar with it

2. When pouring chemicals between containers, you should hold the containers over
   a. the floor or a waste basket
   b. a fire blanket or an oven mitt
   c. an eyewash station or a water fountain
   d. a sink or your work area

3. If you get hurt or injured in any way, you should
   a. tell your teacher immediately
   b. find bandages or a first aid kit
   c. go to the principal's office
   d. get help after you finish the lab

4. If your glassware is chipped or broken, you should
   a. use it only for solid materials
   b. give it to your teacher
   c. put it back into the storage cabinet
   d. increase the damage so that it is obvious

5. If you have unused chemicals after finishing a procedure, you should
   a. pour them down a sink or drain
   b. mix them all together in a bucket
   c. put them back into their original containers
   d. throw them away where your teacher tells you to

6. If electrical equipment has a frayed cord, you should

   a. unplug the equipment by pulling on the cord

   b. let the cord hang over the side of a counter or table

   c. tell your teacher about the problem immediately

   d. wrap tape around the cord to repair it

7. If you need to determine the odor of a chemical or a solution, you should

   a. use your hand to bring fumes from the container to your nose

   b. bring the container under your nose and inhale deeply

   c. tell your teacher immediately

   d. use odor-sensing equipment

8. When working with materials that might fly into the air and hurt someone's eye, you should wear

   a. goggles

   b. an apron

   c. gloves

   d. a hat

9. Before doing experiments involving a heat source, you should know the location of the

   a. door

   b. windows

   c. fire extinguisher

   d. overhead lights

10. If you get a chemical in your eye, you should

    a. wash your hands immediately

    b. put the lid back on the chemical container

    c. wait to see if your eye becomes irritated

    d. use the eyewash right away

11. When working with a flame or heat source, you should
    a. tie back long hair or hair that hangs in front of your eyes
    b. heat substances or objects inside a closed container
    c. touch an object with your bare hand to see how hot it is
    d. throw hot objects into the trash when you are done with them

12. As you cut with a knife or other sharp instrument, you should move the instrument
    a. toward you
    b. away from you
    c. vertically
    d. horizontally

Name ________________________________ Class ________________ Date ____________________

LAB SAFETY QUIZ

Answer Key

1. C	5. D	9. C
2. D	6. C	10. D
3. A	7. A	11. A
4. B	8. A	12. B

Name ________________________________ Class ________________ Date ____________________

Student Safety Contract

Read carefully the Student Safety Contract below. Then, fill in your name in the first blank, date the contract, and sign it.

Student Safety Contract

I will

- read the lab investigation before coming to class
- wear personal protective equipment as directed to protect my eyes, face, hands, and body while conducting class activities
- follow all instructions given by the teacher
- conduct myself in a responsible manner at all times in a laboratory situation

I, ________________________________, have read and agree to abide by the safety regulations as set forth above and any additional printed instructions provided by my teacher or the school district.

I agree to follow all other written and oral instructions given in class.

Signature: ________________________________

Date: ________________________________

QUICK LAB DIRECTED Inquiry

Mass and Weight GENERAL

Small groups
15 minutes

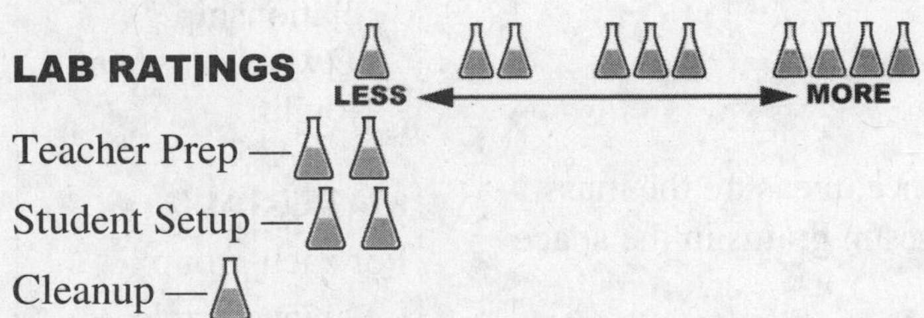

MATERIALS

For each group
- balance, triple beam or electronic
- graph paper
- small objects (5)
- spring scale

For each student
- lab apron
- safety goggles

My Notes

SAFETY INFORMATION

Remind students to review all safety cautions and icons before beginning this lab.

TEACHER NOTES

In this activity, students will identify forces acting on static objects and use a graph to explore the relationship between mass and weight. The objects students use should have a variety of masses. Examples of objects include toy cars, batteries, golf balls, small figurines, and metal washers. Students may need to use string or tape to attach the objects to the spring scale. If this is the case, make sure students include the string or tape when they find the mass of the object.

Skills Focus Practicing Lab Techniques, Constructing Graphs, Identifying Patterns

MODIFICATION FOR GUIDED Inquiry

Have students research the relationship between mass and weight. Students should develop a hypothesis about the relationship between these two quantities and design an experiment to test this hypothesis. Allow students to proceed with all reasonable experiments.

Answer Key

3. The graph is linear; as mass increases, so does weight.
Teacher Prompt What does a graph tell us about the two quantities involved? Sample answer: The shape of the graph shows how changes in one quantity affect the other quantity.

4. Sample answer: the force of the spring pulling upward

Name ______________________ Class ______________ Date ______________

QUICK LAB DIRECTED Inquiry

Mass and Weight

In this lab, you will compare the mass and weight of five different objects using a balance and a spring scale.

OBJECTIVE

- Describe the relationship between mass and weight.

MATERIALS

For each group
- balance, triple beam or electronic
- graph paper
- small objects (5)
- spring scale

For each student
- lab apron
- safety goggles

PROCEDURE

1. Using a triple-beam or electronic balance, measure the mass of five small objects. Record the masses in grams in the space below.

   ____
   ____
   ____
   ____
   ____

2. Using a spring scale, find the weight of the same five objects. Record the weights in consistent units.

   ____
   ____
   ____
   ____
   ____

3. On a piece of **graph paper**, make a graph of weight versus mass using your five objects. In the space below, write a sentence that describes the relationship between weight and mass.

   ____
   ____

4. The objects were not moving when you measured their weights. What was balancing the force of gravity pulling them downward?

   ____
   ____

QUICK LAB DIRECTED Inquiry

Finding Volume by Displacement BASIC

Small groups
15 minutes

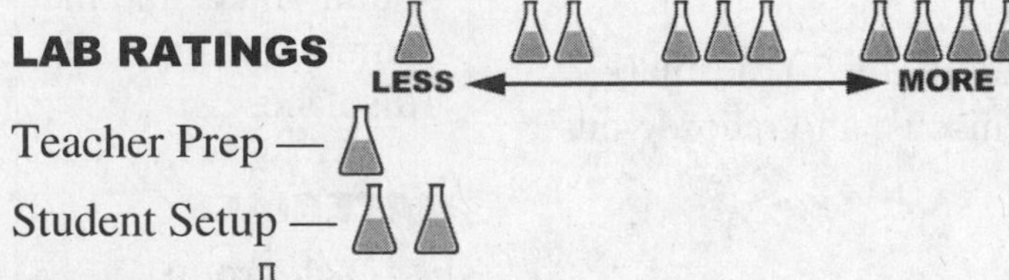

LAB RATINGS

Teacher Prep —
Student Setup —
Cleanup —

MATERIALS

For each group
- graduated cylinder, 100 mL
- object, solid metal
- water

For each student
- lab apron
- safety goggles

My Notes

SAFETY INFORMATION

Remind students to review all safety cautions and icons before beginning this lab.

TEACHER NOTES

In this activity, students will learn how to find the volume of irregularly shaped objects. Solid metal objects that could be used in this activity include large keys or bolts. A sufficiently large item should be used in order to accurately measure displacement. You may wish to use plastic graduated cylinders to avoid breakage. Coloring may be added to the water so that students can more easily read the volume of water in the cylinder.

Student Tip Be sure to lower the object into the graduated cylinder slowly to prevent splashing.

Skills Focus Practicing Lab Techniques, Performing Calculations

MODIFICATION FOR INDEPENDENT Inquiry

Give each group of students a solid metal object, and challenge them to determine the volume of the object. Students should brainstorm ways of making this measurement and write a list of materials and procedures necessary for conducting their investigations. Allow students to proceed with all reasonable investigations.

Answer Key

1. Sample answer: 50 mL
3. Sample answer: 55 mL
4. Sample answer: 55 mL – 50 mL = 5 mL of water displaced.
5. Sample answer: The volume of the object is 5 cm^3.

Name ______________________ Class ______________ Date ______________

QUICK LAB DIRECTED Inquiry

Finding Volume by Displacement

In this lab, you will determine the volume of an irregularly shaped object.

OBJECTIVE

- Describe the relationship between the volume of an object and the amount of liquid it displaces.

MATERIALS

For each group
- graduated cylinder, 100 mL
- object, solid metal
- water

For each student
- lab apron
- safety goggles

PROCEDURE

1. Fill a **100 mL graduated cylinder** to about the 50 mL mark with **water**. Read the volume at the meniscus, and record your reading.

   ____

2. Tip the graduated cylinder, and slide a **solid metal object** into the cylinder.

3. Carefully read the new level of water in the graduated cylinder, and record your results.

   ____

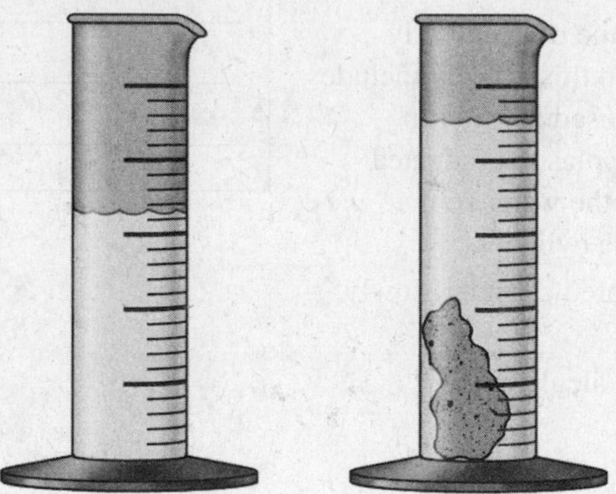

4. Calculate the volume of water displaced by the object.

   ____

   ____

   ____

5. Using your results, calculate the volume of the object. Express your result in cm^3. Hint: 1 mL = 1 cm^3.

   ____

   ____

   ____

QUICK LAB DIRECTED Inquiry

How Much Mass? GENERAL

Small groups
10 minutes

MATERIALS

For each group
- balloon, small
- golf ball
- handball
- marshmallow
- pumice stone
- rock
- other objects

For each student
- safety goggles

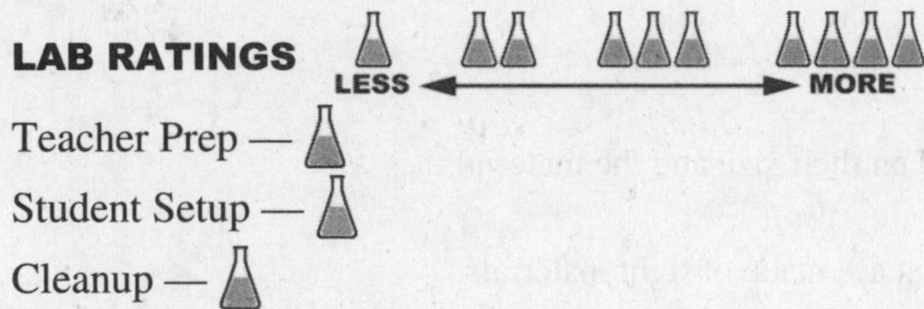

Teacher Prep —
Student Setup —
Cleanup —

SAFETY INFORMATION

Remind students to review all safety cautions and icons before beginning this lab.

TEACHER NOTES

In this activity, students will explore the relationship between mass, volume, and matter. The objects listed in the materials section are a suggestion and include pairs of objects similar in size and appearance, but with very different masses. A variety of objects with differences in mass, density, and type of material may be used.

Skills Focus Making Observations, Drawing Conclusions, Making Inferences

My Notes

MODIFICATION FOR GUIDED Inquiry

Have students brainstorm a list of objects and write procedures for comparing the volume, mass, and type of matter in each object. Allow students to work with all reasonable objects and procedures.

Quick Lab continued

Answer Key

1. Answers may vary.
2. Answers may vary.
3. Answers may vary.
4. Answers may vary.
5. Answers may vary.
6. Answers may vary.
7. Sample answer: I ordered the objects based on their size and the material they are made of.
8. Sample answer: Some objects look "big" but are made of light materials.
9. Answers may vary.
10. Answers may vary.
11. Sample answer: The object with less mass has more empty spaces among the particles that make up the object than the particles in the other object.

Name ______________________________ Class ________________ Date ______________________

QUICK LAB DIRECTED Inquiry

How Much Mass?

In this lab, you will compare the mass, volume, and type of matter in a variety of objects.

OBJECTIVES

- Differentiate between weight and mass.
- Recognize that weight is the amount of gravitational pull on an object and is distinct from, though proportional to, mass.

MATERIALS

For each group
- balloon, small
- golf ball
- handball
- marshmallow
- pumice stone
- rock
- other objects

For each student
- safety goggles

PROCEDURE

1. Do not touch the objects your teacher provides. Write your observations about each object in the space below.

____

____

____

____

____

____

____

____

2. Based on your observations, list the objects in order from least mass to greatest mass.

____

____

____

3. Pick each object up, one at a time. Write your observations about the mass of each object in the space below.

____

____

____

____

____

____

____

Quick Lab continued

4. Based on your observations from Step 3, create a new list of the objects in order from least mass to greatest mass.

5. Use the balance to measure and record the mass of each object to the nearest 0.1 gram. Record the mass of each object in the space below.

6. Based on your measurements from Step 5, create a new list of the objects in order from least mass to greatest mass.

7. What information did you use to decide what the order of the objects should be in Step 2?

Quick Lab continued

8. Why was it difficult to determine the object's mass based on visual observations alone?

9. In what way did your original list change after you were allowed to hold the objects?

10. How did your list change after you actually measured the mass of each object? Were you surprised by any of the results?

11. Consider the particles in two of your objects that are about the same size, but have different masses. Infer why one object has more mass than the other object.

EXPLORATION LAB DIRECTED *Inquiry* **AND** GUIDED *Inquiry*

Comparing Buoyancy GENERAL

Small groups
45 minutes

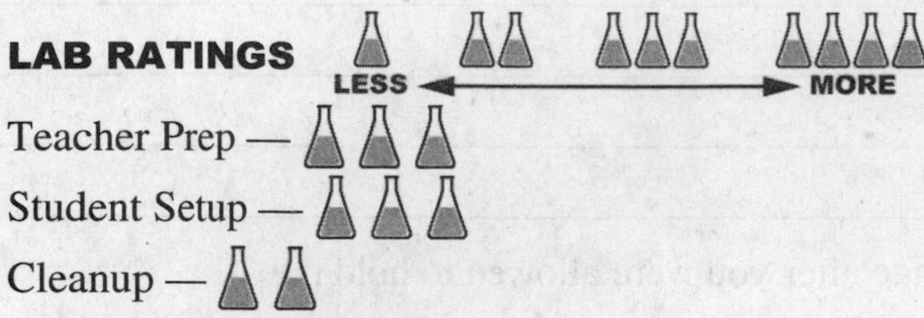

MATERIALS

For each group

- alcohol (30 mL)
- balance
- corn syrup (30 mL)
- glycerin (30 mL)
- graduated cylinder, (2)
- small objects made of rubber, cork, metal, plastic, coal, pumice, etc. (4)
- vegetable oil (30 mL)
- water, colored (30 mL)
- water, not colored (50 mL)

For each student

- gloves
- lab apron
- safety goggles

My Notes

SAFETY INFORMATION

Remind students to review all safety cautions and icons before beginning this lab. Students should wear gloves, goggles, and aprons at all times. Warn students to avoid breathing fumes from the alcohol. Any spills should be cleaned up immediately to prevent slipping. Students should not taste or ingest vegetable oil or any other liquid.

TEACHER NOTES

In this activity, students will make a density column of five liquids and use it to explore the buoyancy of four different objects. They will also calculate the densities of the liquids and solid objects and explore how density relates to buoyancy.

In order for students to clearly see the different levels of liquids within the density column, it is necessary to add dye to the corn syrup and water. Food coloring will create the necessary contrast between the glycerin, corn syrup, and water. For vegetable oil, use a darker oil such as corn or toasted sesame oil.

When selecting solid objects, try to choose different-size samples so that some of the smaller objects are heavy and some of the larger objects are light. Address any student misconceptions about density by providing less massive but highly dense items as well as more massive but less dense items.

To maximize lab time, students may record their data during the activity period and complete their calculations as a homework assignment.

Tip Use two different sized graduated cylinders during this lab. The larger graduated cylinder should be 200 to 250 mL. The smaller graduated cylinder should be 50 to 100 mL.

Skills Focus Making Predictions, Recording Observations

Exploration Lab continued

MODIFICATION FOR INDEPENDENT *Inquiry*

If you drop a penny into the ocean, it will sink, but enormous oil tankers and cargo barges float. What makes a giant ship more buoyant than a small coin? Ask students to think about what factors affect buoyancy. Have them design two different objects out of identical materials so that one object floats and one object sinks in water. Students should create a procedure for their investigation, including all materials they will need and descriptions and sketches of the objects they will construct. With teacher approval, they should carry out their experiment and present the results to the class in a demonstration. They should also provide a written description of the characteristics of each object that affect its buoyancy.

Answer Key for DIRECTED *Inquiry*

FORM A HYPOTHESIS

2. Answers will vary.

FORM A PREDICTION

3. Accept all reasonable answers.

MAKE OBSERVATIONS

4. Answers will vary, but should be nearly the same for all students (depending on calibration of balance).
5. Answers will vary, but should be nearly the same for all students (depending on calibration of balance)
6. Answers will vary, but should be nearly the same for all students (depending on calibration of balance).
9. Answers will vary, but should show liquids layered from the bottom up in order of densest to least dense.
10. Answers will vary.
12. Answers will vary.
13. Answers will vary.

TEST THE HYPOTHESIS

14. Answers will vary, but should accurately reflect the relationship between densities of the object and the liquid.
15. Answers will vary.

ANALYZE THE RESULTS

16. Answers will vary.
17. Sample answer: The densest liquids and objects sank to the bottom of the graduated cylinder.
18. Sample answer: The least dense liquids and solids floated at the top of the cylinder.

Exploration Lab continued

DRAW CONCLUSIONS

19. Answers will vary.

20. Sample answer: No, objects will be more buoyant in salt water than in freshwater because salt water is denser than freshwater. Salt water is denser because it contains salt, which adds mass.

Connect TO THE ESSENTIAL QUESTION

21. Sample answer: Density is the most important factor in determining the buoyancy of the object. It's the relationship between mass and volume that matters, not either characteristic by itself.

Answer Key for GUIDED Inquiry

FORM A HYPOTHESIS

2. Answers will vary.

FORM A PREDICTION

3. Answers will vary.

4. Answers will vary.

DEVELOP A PLAN

5. Answers will vary, but students should recognize that they will need to measure mass and volume in order to calculate density.

6. Sample answer: I can place each object in liquid and see whether it floats or sinks.

7. Sample answer: Since I need to measure the masses and volumes and calculate the densities of several different liquids and solids, a table would be the best way to record the data.
Teacher Prompt Ask students to consider the most effective way to organize lists of measurements and calculations.

8. Answers will vary.

MAKE OBSERVATIONS

9. Answers will vary.

ANALYZE THE RESULTS

10. Answers will vary.

11. Answers will vary.

Exploration Lab continued

DRAW CONCLUSIONS

12. Answers will vary.

13. Sample answer: No, objects will be more buoyant in salt water than in freshwater because salt water is denser than freshwater. Salt water is denser because it contains salt, which adds mass.

Connect TO THE ESSENTIAL QUESTION

14. Sample answer: Density is the most important factor in determining the buoyancy of the object. It's the relationship between mass and volume that matters, not either characteristic by itself.

Name ______________________ Class ______________ Date ______________

EXPLORATION LAB DIRECTED *Inquiry*

Comparing Buoyancy

In this lab, you will calculate the densities of five different liquids and then combine the liquids to form a density column. Then, you will calculate the densities of four small solid objects and observe the buoyancy of each object in the density column.

OBJECTIVES

- Calculate the densities of liquids and solids.
- Compare the buoyancies of different solids.
- Relate buoyancy to mass, volume, and density.

MATERIALS

For each group
- balance
- graduated cylinders, (2)
- liquids (30 mL each of alcohol, corn syrup, glycerin, vegetable oil, colored and uncolored water)
- small objects, assorted

For each student
- gloves
- lab apron
- safety goggles

PROCEDURE

ASK A QUESTION

1. Consider the size, shape, mass, and density of different objects that float and sink. Which factor determines how buoyant these objects are? Discuss your thoughts within your group.

FORM A HYPOTHESIS

2. Develop a hypothesis that states whether mass, volume, or density determines the buoyancy of an object. Record your hypothesis below.

____

____

____

FORM A PREDICTION

3. Examine the **four solid objects** that your teacher has provided. Rank them from the lowest to the highest buoyancy, or the relative levels at which they will float.

____

____

MAKE OBSERVATIONS

4. Select the smaller graduated cylinder. Use the **balance** to measure the mass of the empty **graduated cylinder**, and record it below.

____

Exploration Lab continued

5. Carefully pour **30 mL of water** into the graduated cylinder. Place it on the balance, and record the mass and volume in the table below. Then, subtract the mass of the empty graduated cylinder from the mass of the cylinder with water to find the mass of the water. Record the mass of the water in the table below.

6. Calculate the density of the water by dividing its mass by its volume (density = mass/volume). Record the density in the table below.

	Water	Corn Syrup	Glycerin	Vegetable Oil	Alcohol
Mass of Cylinder					
Mass of Liquid and Cylinder					
Mass of Liquid					
Volume					
Density					

7. Carefully pour the water into the **larger graduated cylinder**.

8. Repeat Steps 5, 6, and 7 with the **corn syrup, glycerin, vegetable oil**, and **alcohol**. Slightly tilt the larger cylinder, and pour each liquid slowly so that it runs down the inside of the cylinder. This will prevent the liquids from splashing and mixing.

9. Observe the five liquids in the graduated cylinder. Make a sketch of what you see, and label each layer.

Exploration Lab continued

10. Use the balance to determine the mass of each solid object. Record the masses in the table below.

	Object 1	Object 2	Object 3	Object 4
Mass				
Volume of Water and Object				
Volume of Object				
Density				

11. Pour **30 mL of water** into the smaller graduated cylinder. Place each solid object in the water, and record the total volume in the graduated cylinder. Carefully remove and dry off each object before measuring the volume of the next object. Make sure that the graduated cylinder contains 30 mL of water before measuring each object. You may have to add water between each measurement.

12. To find the volume of the object, subtract 30 mL from the total volume of the object and water. Record each object's volume in the table above.

13. To calculate an object's density, divide its mass by its volume. Record the density of each object in the table above.

TEST THE HYPOTHESIS

14. Gently place the object you predicted would float at the lowest level into the graduated cylinder. Observe and record where it floats. What liquid is above and/or below it?

____

____

15. Repeat Step 14 for each of the other three solid objects in the order in which you ranked them.

____

____

____

____

Exploration Lab continued

ANALYZE THE RESULTS

16 **Analyze Results** Did the objects float at the levels you predicted?

17 **Comparing Data** Compare the densities of the liquids toward the bottom of the graduated cylinder to the objects that sank to the bottom of the graduated cylinder. What trends do you notice?

18 **Comparing Data** Compare the densities of the liquids toward the top of the graduated cylinder to objects that floated in the graduated cylinder. What trends do you notice?

19 **Evaluating Hypotheses** Was your hypothesis supported by your data?

20 **Applying Concepts** Will solid objects have the same buoyancy in salt water as they do in freshwater? Explain.

____

____

____

____

____

____

Connect TO THE ESSENTIAL QUESTION

21 **Describing Concepts** What is the most significant factor in determining the buoyancy of an object: mass, volume, or density? Explain.

____

____

____

____

____

____

Name ______________________ Class ______________ Date ______________________

EXPLORATION LAB GUIDED Inquiry

Comparing Buoyancy

In this lab, you will calculate the densities of five different liquids and then combine the liquids to form a density column. Then you will calculate the densities of four small solid objects and observe the buoyancy of each object in the density column.

OBJECTIVES

- Calculate the densities of liquids and solids.
- Compare the buoyancies of different solids.
- Relate buoyancy to mass, volume, and density.

MATERIALS

For each group

- balance
- graduated cylinders, (2)
- liquids (30 mL each of alcohol, corn syrup, glycerin, vegetable oil, colored and uncolored water)
- small objects, assorted

For each student

- gloves
- lab apron
- safety goggles

PROCEDURE

ASK A QUESTION

1. Consider the size, shape, mass, and density of different objects that float and sink. Which factor determines how buoyant these objects are? Discuss your thoughts within your group.

FORM A HYPOTHESIS

2. Develop a hypothesis that states whether mass, volume, or density determines the buoyancy of an object. Record your hypothesis below.

____

____

____

____

____

FORM A PREDICTION

3. Examine the **four solid objects** that your teacher has provided. Rank them from the lowest to the highest buoyancy, or the relative levels at which they will float.

____

____

____

____

Exploration Lab continued

4. Examine the **water**, **corn syrup**, **glycerin**, **vegetable oil**, and **water** your teacher has provided. Do liquids have buoyancy? Form a prediction about how these liquids will behave when carefully combined.

____

____

____

____

____

DEVELOP A PLAN

5. Look at the materials your teacher has provided. Consider the objectives of this activity, and develop a procedure to carry out the investigation. What data will you need to collect to determine the densities of the liquids and solid objects?

____

____

____

____

____

6. What type of experimental setup will allow you to observe the buoyancies of the solid objects?

____

____

____

____

____

7. What is the best way to record your data?

____

____

____

____

____

Exploration Lab continued

8 In the space below, describe an experimental setup and procedure that will allow you to complete an investigation that addresses the objectives of this activity. Make sure to include all materials you will use, the steps in your procedure, and a method for recording data.

____

____

____

____

____

____

____

____

MAKE OBSERVATIONS

9 Show your proposed procedure to your teacher. With teacher approval, carry out your investigation. Record your observations and data below. Use additional paper if necessary.

____

____

____

____

____

____

____

____

ANALYZE THE RESULTS

10 **Describing Results** Did the solid objects have the buoyancies you predicted? Did they float at the levels you expected?

____

____

____

Exploration Lab continued

11 **Evaluating Methods** Evaluate your experimental setup and procedure. Did it allow you to make the observations and collect the data you needed to answer the questions? How could you modify your procedure to get the data you needed? Explain any changes you would make to your experimental design and procedure, including any changes to data collection techniques.

DRAW CONCLUSIONS

12 **Evaluating Hypotheses** Was your hypothesis supported by your data?

13 **Applying Concepts** Will solid objects have the same buoyancy in salt water as they do in freshwater? Explain.

Connect TO THE ESSENTIAL QUESTION

14 **Describing Concepts** What is the most significant factor in determining the buoyancy of an object: mass, volume, or density? Explain.

QUICK LAB DIRECTED Inquiry

Comparing Two Elements BASIC

Small groups
15 minutes

LAB RATINGS LESS ⟵⟶ MORE

Teacher Prep —
Student Setup —
Cleanup —

MATERIALS

For each group
- magnet, bar
- nails, aluminum
- nails, iron

For each student
- safety goggles

My Notes

SAFETY INFORMATION

Remind students to review all safety cautions and icons before beginning this lab. Caution students that nails are sharp and can cause puncture wounds.

TEACHER NOTES

In this activity, students will learn that elements have properties that are not always visually apparent. Students will also learn that a mixture can be separated by physical means. When obtaining nails, try to find aluminum and iron nails that are similar in appearance.

Tip This lab may help students understand that different elements have different properties.

Skills Focus Making Observations, Applying Concepts

MODIFICATION FOR INDEPENDENT Inquiry

Provide students with the mixture of nails, and tell them that the mixture contains nails made of different elements. Break students into groups, and ask them to think of what elements would commonly be found in nails. Once students have written down their ideas, challenge them to devise a way to separate nails of different elements. Allow them to follow all reasonable plans.

Answer Key

2. Sample answer: Some of the nails were attracted to the magnet, and some were not.
4. Sample answer: They look alike but are not the same. The iron nails were attracted to the magnet, but the aluminum nails were not.
5. Sample answer: A magnet can be used to separate materials that are magnetic from those that are not magnetic. In a recycling plant, a magnet could be used to separate cans containing iron from cans made entirely of aluminum.

Name ______________________________ Class ________________ Date ______________________

QUICK LAB DIRECTED Inquiry

Comparing Two Elements

In this lab, you will use a magnet to separate a mixture of nails made from two different elements.

OBJECTIVE

- Use properties of elements to separate them from a mixture.

MATERIALS

For each group
- magnet, bar
- nails, aluminum
- nails, iron

For each student
- safety goggles

PROCEDURE

1. Examine a sample of **nails** provided by your teacher.
2. Pass a **bar magnet** over the pile of nails. Record your results.

   ____

   ____

   ____

3. Carefully separate the nails into two piles based on the observations you made in Step 2.
4. Your sample contains aluminum nails and iron nails. Based on your observations, how are aluminum and iron similar? How are they different?

   ____

   ____

5. Explain how the properties of aluminum and iron could be used to separate cans in a recycling plant.

   ____

   ____

   ____

   ____

   ____

   ____

   ____

6. All matter is composed of elements. Which elements would you expect to find in each of your nails?

   ____

QUICK LAB INDEPENDENT Inquiry

Observe Physical Properties BASIC

Individual student
25 minutes

LAB RATINGS LESS ⟷ MORE

Teacher Prep —
Student Setup —
Cleanup —

MATERIALS

For each student

- balance
- beaker
- graduated cylinder
- magnet
- magnifying lens
- objects, assorted (5)
- stirring rod
- water

SAFETY INFORMATION

Remind students to review all safety cautions before beginning this lab. If any objects selected for this investigation are sharp or potentially hazardous to students, be sure to warn them to use caution when handling those objects.

My Notes

TEACHER NOTES

In this activity, students will observe physical properties of objects and then classify the objects according to their physical properties. Before beginning this activity, gather various materials for students to observe and classify. Some suggestions are: rocks, plastic spoons, wooden craft sticks, iron nails, coins, paperclips, sugar, salt, erasers, and drinking straws. Choose objects that share properties with others so that students will be able to group them in obvious ways. Also provide tools such as balances, graduated cylinders, magnets, and water that students can use to make their observations and classifications.

Skills Focus Making Observations, Classifying Objects

MODIFICATION FOR DIRECTED Inquiry

Provide students with a specific set of objects to examine and a particular list of properties to observe. For example, students may be provided with a rock, coin, plastic spoon, iron nail, and paper clip, and they may be challenged to observe the magnetic properties, texture, color, and shape of each object. Have students record their observations and group the objects based on their physical properties.

Quick Lab continued

Answer Key

1. Sample answer: I will observe the following objects: iron nail, paper clip, eraser, salt, and sugar.
2. Sample answer: I will observe the following properties: magnetism, color, texture, and solubility.
3. Sample answer: I will use the following materials to make my observations: magnet, cup with water, stirring rod, and magnifying lens. To determine the magnetic properties of the objects, I will hold a magnet close to each object and observe whether the object is attracted to the magnet. To determine the color and texture of objects, I will observe each object with a magnifying lens and record my observations. To determine the solubility of each object, I will drop each object in water and stir the water to observe if the object dissolves in the water.
4. Accept all reasonable tables.
5. Sample answer: The iron nail and paper clip can be grouped as "magnetic." The salt and sugar can be grouped as "soluble in water" and "white in color." The iron nail, paper clip, and eraser can be grouped as "smooth in texture."
   Teacher Prompt What physical properties do the objects share with one another?

QUICK LAB INDEPENDENT *Inquiry*

Observe Physical Properties

In this activity, you will observe the physical properties of various objects. You will then use these physical properties to classify the objects. Recall that density, mass, magnetism, color, texture, odor, and solubility are all physical properties of objects.

OBJECTIVES

- Observe physical properties of objects.
- Classify objects based on their physical properties.

MATERIALS

For each student

- objects (5) to be determined by the student

PROCEDURE

1. Observe the objects that are available for you to examine and choose five objects that you will examine.

   ____

   ____

   ____

2. Create a list of four physical properties that you observe.

   ____

   ____

3. Brainstorm a list of materials that you will need in order to observe the physical properties of these objects. Write out a list of procedures that you will follow to observe these properties.

   ____

   ____

   ____

   ____

   ____

   ____

Quick Lab continued

4 Obtain the materials you need and carry out your investigation. Record your observations in a table below. Make the table to include a column for each object and a row for each physical property.

5 Organize the objects into groups based on their physical properties. List the groups below.

____

____

____

____

EXPLORATION LAB GUIDED *Inquiry* **AND** INDEPENDENT *Inquiry*

Identifying an Unknown Substance GENERAL

Small groups
45 minutes

LAB RATINGS

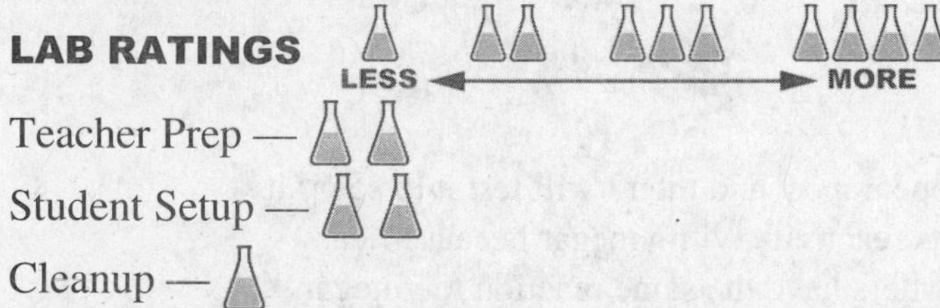

Teacher Prep —
Student Setup —
Cleanup —

SAFETY INFORMATION

Remind students to review all safety cautions and icons before beginning this lab. Liquids and powders on the floor are a slipping hazard, and students should immediately report and clean up all spills. Tell students not to touch broken glass but to report it so that it can be cleaned up. Warn students never to inhale or ingest unknown substances and to wash their hands if their skin comes in contact with any substances.

TEACHER NOTES

In this activity, students will perform a variety of tests to determine the identity of an unknown sample. The unknown substances are A) sugar, B) table salt, C) fine white sand, D) baking soda, and E) crushed calcium carbonate chalk. Ideally, each group should receive a different unknown substance. Provide students with a list of the unknown substances but do not reveal the identify of any particular substances until the end of the investigation. Keep a record of which substance you give to each group.

Tip This activity may help students understand that substances that appear similar may have very different physical and chemical properties.

Skills Focus Making Observations, Practicing Lab Techniques, Analyzing Results

MATERIALS

For each group
- balance
- beakers (2)
- graduated cylinder
- paper, filter
- spoon
- stirring rod
- unknown substance (5 g or more)
- vinegar, white
- water, room temperature

For each student
- gloves
- lab apron
- safety goggles

My Notes

MODIFICATION FOR DIRECTED *Inquiry*

Guide students as they observe the physical characteristics of their substance. Ask them if it is made up of white powder or white crystals. Then, help them test their substance's solubility in water and its reaction with vinegar. Guide students as they use the table from the student datasheet to determine which substance they have.

Exploration Lab continued

Answer Key for GUIDED Inquiry

MAKE OBSERVATIONS

1. Accept all reasonable answers.

FORM A PREDICTION

2. Sample answer: I will be able to identify my sample because it is powder, and only one of the two powders listed dissolves in water.

DEVELOP A PLAN

3. Sample answer: I will closely observe its appearance, and then I will test it to see if it dissolves in water. I will probably not test its reactivity with vinegar because I can already tell that it is a powder, and both powders have the same reaction to vinegar. Therefore, performing that test would not give me any new information.

4. Sample answer: To test its appearance, I will examine it closely in a well-lit area, noting its color and consistency. To test its solubility in water, I will pour my sample into a beaker and add 200 milliliters (mL) of room-temperature water. I will stir the sample and see if the substance dissolves.

EVALUATE THE PLAN

5. Sample answer: My substance is white and powdery like substances D and E. It did not dissolve in water like substances C and E.

ANALYZE THE RESULTS

6. Sample answer: Yes, it is substance E.

7. Sample answer: Yes, I was able to identify my sample.

DRAW CONCLUSIONS

8. Sample answer: Other tests that might distinguish between these substances are melting point, flammability, and pH.

9. Sample answer: appearance: physical property; solubility: physical property; reactivity with vinegar: chemical property.

Connect TO THE ESSENTIAL QUESTION

10. Knowing the physical and chemical properties of various substances makes it easier to identify unknown substances.

Exploration Lab continued

Answer Key for INDEPENDENT Inquiry

ASK A QUESTION

1. Sample answer: I can use its physical and chemical properties to identify my substance.

MAKE OBSERVATIONS

2. Accept all reasonable answers.
3. Sample answer: I will closely observe its appearance, and then I will test to see if it dissolves in water. I can use a stirring rod to speed up the process. I will probably not test its reactivity with vinegar because I can already tell that it is a powder, and both powders have the same reaction to vinegar. Therefore, performing that test would not give me any new information.

MAKE A PLAN

4. Accept all reasonable answers.

EVALUATE THE PLAN

5. Sample answer: My substance is white and powdery like substances D and E. It did not dissolve in water like substances C and E.

ANALYZE THE RESULTS

6. Sample answer: Yes, it is substance E.
7. Sample answer: Yes, I was able to identify my sample.

DRAW CONCLUSIONS

8. Sample answer: Other tests that might distinguish between these substances are melting point, flammability, and pH.
9. Sample answer: appearance: physical property; solubility: physical property; reactivity with vinegar: chemical property.

Connect TO THE ESSENTIAL QUESTION

10. Knowing the physical and chemical properties of various substances makes it easier to identify unknown substances.

Name ________________ Class ________________ Date ________________

EXPLORATION LAB GUIDED *Inquiry*

Identifying an Unknown Substance

In this activity, you will perform several tests to identify an unknown substance.

OBJECTIVE

- Identify an unknown substance by testing its properties.

MATERIALS

For each group
- balance
- beakers (2)
- graduated cylinder
- paper, filter
- spoon
- stirring rod
- unknown substance (5 g or more)
- vinegar, white
- water, room temperature

For each student
- gloves
- lab apron
- safety goggles

PROCEDURE

MAKE OBSERVATIONS

1 Without touching it, observe your sample. Record your observations.

____

____

____

____

____

____

FORM A PREDICTION

2 Review the table below. Your sample is one of the substances listed in the table. Based on the information in the table, will you be able to identify your unknown substance? Explain your answer.

____

____

____

____

____

Substance	Appearance	Soluble in water at room temperature	Reactivity with vinegar
A	White crystals	Yes	None
B	White crystals	Yes	None
C	White crystals	No	None
D	White powder	Yes	Bubbles form
E	White powder	No	Bubbles form

DEVELOP A PLAN

❸ Which of your substance's properties will you test? Will you test all of the properties listed in the table? Explain your reasoning.

____

____

____

____

❹ How will you test each property? What materials will you use? Describe your plan.

____

____

____

____

EVALUATE THE PLAN

❺ Once your teacher has approved your plan, perform the tests you described in Step 4. Record your observations and compare them to the information in the table.

____

____

____

____

ANALYZE THE RESULTS

❻ **Analyzing Data** Based on the results of your tests, can you identify your unknown sample? If yes, which substance is it? If not, why are you unable to identify it?

____

____

____

____

____

❼ **Evaluating Predictions** Review your prediction. Was your prediction correct?

____

____

____

____

Exploration Lab continued

DRAW CONCLUSIONS

8 **Applying Concepts** According to the table, Substance A and Substance B have similar appearances, solubility, and reactivity with vinegar. What further tests could you conduct to distinguish between these two substances?

____

____

____

____

____

9 **Classifying Observations** List each property of the unknown substance that you observed during this experiment. Then, list whether the property is a physical property or a chemical property.

____

____

____

____

____

____

____

____

____

____

____

____

____

____

Connect TO THE ESSENTIAL QUESTION

10 **Synthesize Information** Why would it be useful to know the different physical and chemical properties of substances?

____

____

____

____

____

Name ______________________ Class ______________ Date ______________

EXPLORATION LAB INDEPENDENT *Inquiry*

Identifying an Unknown Substance

In this activity, you will perform several tests to identify an unknown substance.

OBJECTIVE

- Identify an unknown substance by testing its properties.

MATERIALS

For each group

- balance, metric
- beakers (2)
- graduated cylinder
- paper, filter
- spoon
- stirring rod
- unknown substance (5 g or more)
- vinegar, white
- water, room temperature

For each student

- gloves
- lab apron
- safety goggles

PROCEDURE

ASK A QUESTION

1. In this activity, you will identify an unknown substance. How do you think you can do this?

____

____

____

____

MAKE OBSERVATIONS

2. Without touching it, observe your sample. Record your observations.

____

____

____

____

____

____

3. Review the table shown on the next page. Your sample is one of the substances listed in the table. Based on the information in the table, will you be able to identify your unknown substance? Explain your answer.

____

____

____

____

____

Exploration Lab continued

Substance	Appearance	Soluble in water at room temperature	Reactivity with vinegar
A	White crystals	Yes	None
B	White crystals	Yes	None
C	White crystals	No	None
D	White powder	Yes	Bubbles form
E	White powder	No	Bubbles form

MAKE A PLAN

4. Write a plan to identify the substance. Include tests you plan to perform and any variables you need to consider.

____

____

____

____

____

____

____

EVALUATE THE PLAN

5. Once your teacher has approved your plan, perform the tests you described in Step 4. Record your observations and compare them to the information in the table.

____

____

____

ANALYZE THE RESULTS

6. **Analyzing Data** Based on the results of your tests, can you identify your unknown sample? If yes, which substance is it? If not, why are you unable to identify it?

____

____

____

7. **Evaluating Predictions** Review your prediction. Was your prediction correct? Explain your answer.

____

____

DRAW CONCLUSIONS

8. **Applying Concepts** According to the table, Substance A and Substance B have similar appearances, solubility, and reactivity with vinegar. What further tests could you conduct to distinguish between these two substances?

____

____

____

____

9. **Classifying Observations** List each property of the unknown substance that you observed during this experiment. Then, list whether the property is a physical property or a chemical property.

____

____

____

____

Exploration Lab continued

Connect TO THE ESSENTIAL QUESTION

⑩ **Synthesize Information** Why would it be useful to know the different physical and chemical properties of substances?

____

____

____

____

____

QUICK LAB DIRECTED *Inquiry*

Physical or Chemical Change? GENERAL

Small groups
20 minutes

LAB RATINGS

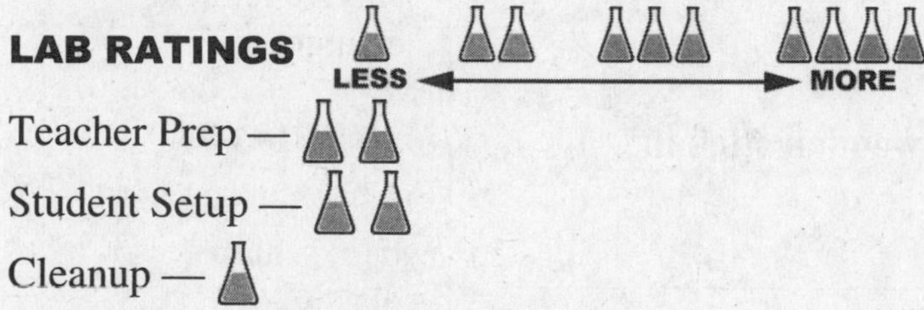

Teacher Prep —
Student Setup —
Cleanup —

SAFETY INFORMATION

Remind students to review all safety cautions and icons before beginning this lab. Smoke can cause respiratory irritations. If possible, conduct the first experiment in a fume hood. Caution students to avoid bringing multiple magnets and other metal objects together, as strong magnets can be a pinching hazard. Explain to students that the effervescent tablets should not be ingested.

TEACHER NOTES

In this activity, students distinguish between chemical and physical changes. Be sure students do not open the bag of iron filings and sand when using the magnet.

Skills Focus Making Observations, Drawing Conclusions

MODIFICATION FOR GUIDED *Inquiry*

Have students identify an everyday change and develop a hypothesis about the nature of this change. Students should write up a list of procedures to determine the nature of the change they identified. Allow students to proceed with all reasonable procedures.

MATERIALS

For each group

- bag, sealable plastic
- beaker
- effervescent tablet
- iron filings
- magnet, bar
- sand
- stick, wooden
- test tube
- water

For each student

- gloves
- lab apron
- safety goggles

My Notes

Answer Key

1. Sample answer: The burning stick is extinguished.
2. Sample answer: The magnet attracts the iron filings and can be used to separate them from the sand.
3. Sample answer: The tablet dissolves and the solution bubbles.
4. Sample answer: Burning the stick and putting the tablet in water are chemical changes because new substances form. Separating iron filings from sand is a physical change because no new substances form.

Name ______________________ Class ______________ Date ______________

QUICK LAB DIRECTED Inquiry

Physical or Chemical Change?

In this lab, you will observe a series of changes and use your observations to determine if they are physical changes or chemical changes.

OBJECTIVE

- Describe the difference between a physical change and a chemical change.

MATERIALS

For each group

- bag, sealable plastic
- beaker
- effervescent tablet
- iron filings
- magnet, bar
- sand
- stick, wooden
- test tube
- water

For each student

- gloves
- lab apron
- safety goggles

PROCEDURE

1. Watch as your teacher places a burning **wooden stick** into a **test tube**. Record your observations.

____

____

____

____

____

____

____

2. Place a mixture of **sand** and **iron filings** into a **sealable plastic bag**, and seal the bag. Place a **bar magnet** on top of the bag, and try to separate the iron filings from the sand. Write your observations in the space below.

____

____

____

____

____

____

____

____

____

Quick Lab continued

3. Drop an **effervescent tablet** into a **beaker** of **water**. Record your observations.

4. For each step, identify which kind of change happens: a physical change or a chemical change. Explain your answers.

QUICK LAB DIRECTED Inquiry

Properties of Combined Substances GENERAL

Small groups
20 minutes

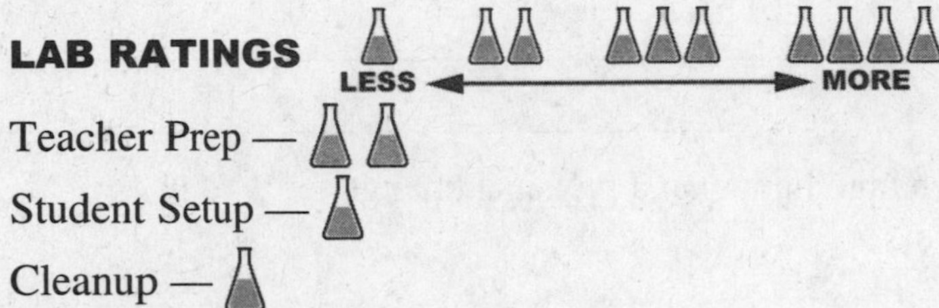

MATERIALS

For each group
- balance
- borax solution, 40g/L (100 mL)
- glue solution (1:1 solution of glue and water)
- plastic spoon
- small paper cup (2)

For each student
- gloves
- lab apron
- safety goggles

SAFETY INFORMATION

Remind students to review all safety cautions and icons before beginning this lab. Caution students to always wear goggles, aprons, and gloves during this entire activity. Caution students to keep their hands away from their eyes and mouths during this lab activity. Make sure students thoroughly wash their hands and work area after completing this activity.

TEACHER NOTES

In this activity, students will investigate the results of combining common substances to form a new substance that has very different properties. They will combine a borax solution with a glue solution and observe whether any of the properties of the original substances are still evident in the new substance.

Tip This activity may help students understand that mass is conserved during a chemical change.

Skills Focus Making Observations, Making Predictions, Drawing Conclusions

My Notes

____

____

____

____

____

MODIFICATION FOR GUIDED Inquiry

Instead of giving students the instructions for how to perform the activity, have them think about different ways of combining substances and observing properties. Provide them with the materials, and ask them to write a procedure that will investigate what happens when the glue and borax solutions are mixed together. They should define an experimental setup and procedure, including all materials and methods for making observations and recording data. With teacher approval, they should carry out their procedures and present their conclusions in a lab report.

Quick Lab continued

MODIFICATION FOR INDEPENDENT *Inquiry*

Have students design their own experiments to determine what happens to the properties of common substances when they are mixed together. They should decide which substances they will test and how they will be combined. They might mix substances in a lab environment, or they might consider combinations such as the reactions between foods when they are cooked. Students should create an experimental setup and procedure, including all necessary materials. With teacher approval, they should carry out their experiments and present their conclusions in a lab report.

Answer Key

4. Sample answer: It is a thin, white liquid that pours easily.
5. Sample answer: It is a clear fluid.
6. Sample answer: I predict that a combination of these two substances will produce a thin, whitish fluid.
8. Sample answer: No, the substance became thicker and whiter, not thinner and clearer.
9. Sample answer: The white color of the original glue solution is still visible, but none of the other original properties are still evident.
10. Sample answer: The new substance is white and gooey, like putty.
11. Sample answer: The change is a chemical change because a new substance has been formed.
12. Sample answer: The combined masses of the glue and borax solution equals the mass of the new product. Mass is conserved in this chemical reaction.

Name ______________________ Class ______________ Date ______________

QUICK LAB DIRECTED Inquiry

Properties of Combined Substances

In this lab, you will combine two common substances to create a new substance and then see if you can still identify properties of the original substances. You will combine a glue solution with a borax solution and determine whether it results in a physical or a chemical change in the original substances. Glue contains particles that bond with, or "grab" onto, particles of other substances. This is how glue holds objects together. Borax is a common household cleanser in the form of a white powdery crystal that dissolves easily in water.

OBJECTIVES

- Differentiate between physical and chemical changes.
- Describe the changes when two substances are combined.

MATERIALS

For each group
- balance
- borax solution, 40g/L (100 mL)
- glue solution (1:1 solution of glue and water)
- plastic spoon
- small paper cup (2)

For each student
- gloves
- lab apron
- safety goggles

PROCEDURE

1. Obtain two **small paper cups** and a **plastic spoon** from your teacher. Use a balance to measure the mass of each empty cup.

2. Fill your first paper cup about ¼ full of the **glue solution** provided by your teacher. Measure the mass of the cup and glue. Subtract to find the mass of the glue. Record the mass.

   ____

   ____

3. Fill your second paper cup about ¼ full of the **borax solution** provided by your teacher. Measure the mass of the cup and borax solution. Subtract to find the mass of the borax solution. Record the mass.

   ____

   ____

4. What are some of the physical properties of the glue solution?

   ____

   ____

   ____

5. What are some of the physical properties of the borax solution?

   ____

   ____

   ____

Quick Lab continued

6 Make a prediction about what will happen when these two substances are mixed together. Record your prediction below.

7 Slowly pour the borax solution into the glue solution while stirring with the plastic spoon. The mixture will stiffen as it thickens. When it becomes too thick to stir with the spoon, remove it from the cup and knead it with your fingers.

8 Was your prediction about the properties of the new substance correct?

9 Are any of the original properties of the glue or borax solution still observable? If so, list them. If not, explain why not.

10 What are some of the physical properties of the new substance?

11 Is the change that occurred a physical change or a chemical change? How do you know?

12 Find the mass of the new substance. Compare this mass to the combined masses of the glue and the borax solution. What do you observe?

QUICK LAB GUIDED Inquiry

Observing Mixtures BASIC

Individual student
30 minutes

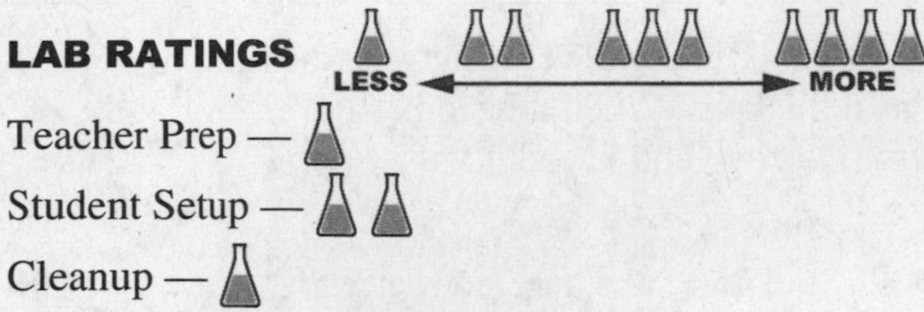

Teacher Prep —
Student Setup —
Cleanup —

MATERIALS

For each student

- beaker
- gloves
- ground coffee
- hot water
- lab apron
- other materials for your experiment
- safety goggles
- stirring rod
- sugar

SAFETY INFORMATION

Remind students to review all safety cautions and icons before beginning this lab. Students should exercise extreme caution when handling hot water and wear heat-resistant gloves when touching the glass beakers filled with hot water. Lab aprons should be worn to protect clothing. Remind students never to ingest any substances in a lab.

My Notes

TEACHER NOTES

In this activity, students will make mixtures of coffee and water and sugar and water and determine if they are homogeneous or heterogeneous. Do not use instant coffee for this activity. Then students will determine if common foods are solutions, colloids, or suspensions. You may wish to have each of the items listed in the chart in the classroom for students to observe. Review all vocabulary before beginning this activity.

Tip Use this activity to discuss the difference between physical and chemical changes. Mixtures undergo physical changes; each part of the mixture remains the same molecularly.

Skills Focus Making Observations, Developing Procedures, Comparing Results

MODIFICATION FOR INDEPENDENT Inquiry

Have students ask a question about mixtures and write a hypothesis to answer the question. Students should then design an experiment to prove their hypothesis. Allow students to carry out any reasonable and safe procedures. Have students share their results with the class.

Quick Lab continued

Answer Key

1. Accept all reasonable answers. Most students will observe that the coffee starts to seep into the water.
2. Accept all reasonable plans.
3. Accept all reasonable answers.
4. The water should be brown. It is a homogeneous mixture. The students have already separated the coffee from the water; what is left cannot be separated.
5. Accept all reasonable answers. Most students will observe that sugar starts to dissolve in the water and is not easy to separate.
6. Sample answer: The sugar cannot be separated from the water, while the coffee can.
7.

Mixture	Solution	Colloid	Suspension
sugar water	X		
homogenized milk		X	
coffee	X		
salad dressing			X
whipped cream		X	
food coloring			X
butter		X	
lemonade	X		

Name ______________________ Class ______________ Date ______________

QUICK LAB GUIDED Inquiry

Observing Mixtures

Mixtures are combinations of different substances. Sometimes a mixture can be two solids, a solid and a liquid, or two liquids. In this lab, you will observe different mixtures and try to separate them.

OBJECTIVES

- Create and separate mixtures.
- Classify mixtures.

MATERIALS

For each student

- beaker
- gloves
- ground coffee
- hot water
- lab apron
- other materials for your experiment
- safety goggles
- stirring rod
- sugar

PROCEDURE

1. Mix hot water and ground coffee in a beaker. Stir for a few minutes. Record what happens.

____

____

____

2. How can you separate the coffee from the water?

____

____

____

3. Carry out your procedure. Record what happens.

____

____

____

____

4. Observe the water. How has it changed? Is it a homogeneous or heterogeneous mixture? Explain.

____

____

____

____

____

____

Quick Lab continued

5 Repeat the experiment, this time adding hot water to sugar and stirring. Record your observations.

6 How is the mixture with sugar different than the mixture with coffee?

7 Mixtures can be classified as a solution, a colloid, or a suspension. Look at the chart below. It lists different types of mixtures. Determine if the mixture is a solution, a colloid, or a suspension.

Mixture	Solution	Colloid	Suspension
sugar water			
homogenized milk			
coffee			
salad dressing			
whipped cream			
food coloring			
butter			
lemonade			

QUICK LAB DIRECTED Inquiry

Identifying Elements and Compounds GENERAL

Small groups
20 minutes

LAB RATINGS LESS ⟷ MORE

Teacher Prep — 3
Student Setup — 1
Cleanup — 1

MATERIALS
For each group
- periodic table
- prepared cards

My Notes

TEACHER NOTES

In this activity, students will classify common substances as elements or compounds. For the substances they identify as compounds, students will also determine the elements that make up each compound. Hand out periodic tables to the groups and give a short review of the way the periodic table is organized before starting the lab. Students will identify all elements as either metals or non-metals. Prior to class, prepare a set of cards for each group, each labeled with one of the following: salt ($NaCl$), gold (Au), sugar ($C_{12}H_{22}O_{11}$), aluminum (Al), iron (Fe), ammonia (NH_3), carbon (C), water (H_2O).

Skills Focus Classifying Substances

MODIFICATION FOR GUIDED Inquiry

Have students identify common substances in the classroom and classify these substances as elements, compounds, metals, and non-metals in the table provided.

Quick Lab continued

Answer Key

1. Sample answers in table below.

CLASSIFYING SUBSTANCES

Substance	Compound	Element	Metal	Non-metal
salt	NaCl		Na	Cl
gold		Au	Au	
sugar	$C_{12}H_{22}O_{11}$			C, H, O
aluminum		Al	Al	
iron		Fe	Fe	
ammonia	NH_3			N, H
carbon		C		C
water	H_2O			H, O

3. Sample answer: An element is made up of only one type of atom while compounds are made of atoms representing two or more different elements.

4. Sample answer: The characteristics of the compound differ from the characteristics of the elements that make up the compound. Water is made of hydrogen and oxygen. Both elements are gases at room temperature, but water is a liquid at room temperature. **Teacher Prompt** What are the properties of hydrogen and oxygen? How do these properties compare with the properties of water?

Name ______________________ Class ______________ Date ______________

QUICK LAB DIRECTED *Inquiry*

Identifying Elements and Compounds

In this activity, you will classify common substances as either elements or compounds. You will also identify the elements that make up the compounds and categorize all of the elements as metals or non-metals.

OBJECTIVES

- Classify common substances as compounds or elements.
- Identify the elements in a compound.
- Classify elements as metals or non-metals.

MATERIALS

For each group

- periodic table
- prepared cards

PROCEDURE

1. Read each card provided. Write the name of each substance in the first column of the table below. Sort the cards into two categories, compounds and elements. Identify each substance as either a compound or an element by writing the chemical formula for the substance in the appropriate column in the table.

CLASSIFYING SUBSTANCES

Substance	Compound	Element	Metal	Non-metal

2. Use the periodic table to determine whether the elements in each substance are metals or non-metals. Fill in the table by writing the elements for each substance in the appropriate column.

Name ______________________________ Class ________________ Date ______________________

Quick Lab continued

3 What is the difference between an element and a compound?

____

____

____

4 Do the characteristics of a compound share the characteristics of the elements that make up that compound? Use water as an example in your explanation.

____

____

____

____

____

EXPLORATION LAB DIRECTED *Inquiry* **AND** GUIDED *Inquiry*

Investigating Separating Mixtures GENERAL

Small groups

Three 45-minute class periods

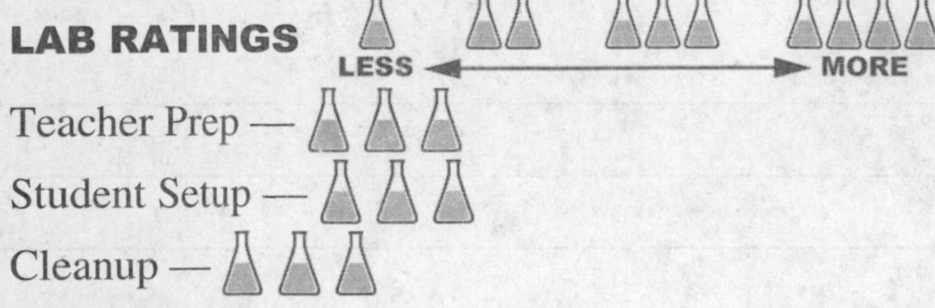

SAFETY INFORMATION

Remind students to review all safety cautions and icons before beginning this lab. Students should wear goggles during this lab to protect their eyes from the small particles. Remind students to be cautious when using water to separate mixtures as spilled water can create a slip hazard.

TEACHER NOTES

Students will be given three different task cards to complete. Students will have items such as coffee filters, funnels, cups, pie tins, magnets, water, and large storage bags. Each card will ask students to perform a separation of a mixture. The cards can be completed in any order. The students will be presented with three challenges: separating a mixture of sand and salt; separating a mixture of beads, marbles, and BBs or ball bearings; and performing a chromatographic separation of ink from colored markers. To prepare the salt/sand mixture, combine equal volumes of salt and sand to make a total volume of about 200 mL for each class (about 30 mL for each group). To prepare the bead mixture, combine equal volumes of beads, marbles, and BBs to make a total volume of about 1 L for each class (about 150 mL for each group). Use marbles and beads that are similar in size.

For the Directed Inquiry, the teacher will provide the materials and procedure. Students will practice different separation techniques for different mixtures. In the case of the sand and salt mixture, students will use differences in water solubility for the separation. In the case of the mixture of beads, marbles, and BBs, students will use magnetic properties and differences in density for the separation. In the case of the marker inks, students will use paper chromatography for the separation.

MATERIALS

For each group
- beaker
- bucket or tub
- cup, plastic, large
- cup, plastic, small
- filter, coffee
- filter paper (2 cm × 8 cm)
- funnel
- index cards with task descriptions
- magnet
- markers, water-based (4 different colors)
- mixture of beads, BBs, and marbles
- mixture of sand and salt
- pencil
- pie tin
- ruler, metric
- spoons, metal
- water

For each student
- lab apron
- safety goggles

My Notes

Exploration Lab continued

Test all materials prior to the activity to make sure the mixtures can be separated. If these BBs are steel but brass or copper plated, they will be attracted by a magnet, but they will not be attracted if they are solid brass. BBs currently on the market, such as those for AirSoft guns, are not necessarily metallic but may be made of plastic, ceramics, or biodegradeable materials such as rock dust or wheat products; these would not be attracted by a magnet. Plastic beads may or may not float because some plastics are denser than water.

In the Guided Inquiry, the teacher will provide the materials and the problem for the students to investigate, but students will develop their own procedures for the separations. Review all procedures before allowing students to begin.

Tip This activity will allow students to look at several different separation techniques. All techniques are based on the properties of the substances in the mixtures being separated.

Tip This activity will take about 3 class periods of 45 minutes each. If only 1 or 2 class periods are available, groups can be assigned only one separation challenge. Each group can then share its results with the class.

Student Tip Be sure to consider how the properties of substances differ. This will help you think about how each separation is accomplished.

Skills Focus Making Observations, Practicing Lab Techniques

MODIFICATION FOR INDEPENDENT Inquiry

Ask students, "How can mixtures be separated into their components?" and provide the three different mixtures. Have the students devise a procedure to separate each mixture.

Answer Key for DIRECTED Inquiry

MAKE OBSERVATIONS

2. a. Sample answer: The sand appears as larger brown crystals. The salt appears as white and clear crystals.

c. Sample answer: The sand remains in the filter, but the salt does not. The salt dissolved in the water and passed through the filter. The liquid passing through the filter is clear and colorless.

d. Most of the liquid has evaporated. A white, crusty solid remains where the water completely evaporated.

3. a. Sample answer: The marbles are clear and colorless and present in two different sizes. The BBs are shiny and silver in color. The beads are white in color and appear to be made of plastic.

b. The magnet picks up the BBs but not the marbles or the beads.

c. The beads float on the water and the marbles sink to the bottom.

d. We scooped the beads out of the water with the spoon.

4. a. Answers will vary depending on the markers used. Students should record each color ink they observe.

c. Answers will vary depending on the markers used. Students should observe that the inks separate into a number of colors indicating that each ink is a mixture of pigments.

ANALYZE THE RESULTS

5. Sample answer: We used differences in water solubility to separate sand from salt. We dissolved the salt in the water to separate it from the sand.

Exploration Lab continued

6. Sample answer: We used the metallic nature of the BBs to separate them from the mixture using the magnet. We used differences in density to separate the plastic beads from the marbles.
7. Sample answer: Each of the pigments in the various inks moves at a different rate during chromatography. Each moves at a different rate as the water moves up the filter paper because of differences in their affinities for the coffee filter fibers.

DRAW CONCLUSIONS

8. Accept all reasonable answers. Students should explain that differences in properties can be used to effectively separate substances from one another. They should provide at least one specific example of this that came from the observations they made during their experiments.

Connect TO THE ESSENTIAL QUESTION

9. Sample answer: Elements and compounds are pure substances. Elements are made of only one kind of atom, so separation is not necessary. Compounds are made of two or more elements chemically combined. In order to separate compounds, chemical changes need to occur. Mixtures are made by physically combining two or more substances. Mixtures can be separated by physical means by taking advantage of the differences in physical properties of the substances in the mixture.

Answer Key for GUIDED Inquiry

DEVELOP A PLAN

2. a. Sample answer: The sand appears as larger brown crystals. The salt appears as white and clear crystals.
   b. Sample answer: Sand is insoluble in water, and salt is soluble in water.
   c. Accept all reasonable plans.
3. a. Sample answer: The marbles are clear and colorless and present in two different sizes. The BBs are shiny and silver in color. The beads are white in color and appear to be made of plastic.
   b. Sample answer: The marbles are denser than the beads. The BBs are metal so they will be attracted to magnets.
   c. Accept all reasonable plans.
4. a. Answers will vary depending on the markers used. Students should record each color ink they observe.
   b. Answers will vary depending on the markers used. Students should suggest that chromatography be used to see if the inks can be separated into different pigments.
   c. Accept all reasonable plans.

Exploration Lab continued

MAKE OBSERVATIONS

5. Accept all reasonable observations.

ANALYZE THE RESULTS

6. Sample answer: We used the insolubility of the sand and the solubility of the salt to separate the two substances. We dissolved the salt in the water to separate it from the sand and pepper.
7. Sample answer: The BBs are attracted to magnets. We used the magnet to separate the BBs from the mixture. The plastic beads are less dense than water, and the glass marbles are denser than water. By using a spoon to scoop up the beads, we separated those two items. We cut openings in a piece of cardboard just big enough to let the small marbles through while keeping the larger marbles out, and separated the marbles by pouring them through.
8. Sample answer: The ink in the marker is a mixture of several ink pigments that are soluble in water. When the ink spot dissolve in water, the individual pigments are separated from the mixture on the coffee filter.

DRAW CONCLUSIONS

9. Accept all reasonable answers.
10. Accept all reasonable answers.
11. Accept all reasonable answers.
12. Sample answer: Writing down the physical properties of the components of the mixture helped us design a separation scheme. We were able to separate components in mixtures by taking advantage of the different properties that they have. For example, differences in density caused some substances to float on water while others sank, allowing us to easily scoop up the floating items.

Connect TO THE ESSENTIAL QUESTION

13. Sample answer: Elements and compounds are pure substances. Elements are made of only one kind of atom, so separation is not necessary. Compounds are made of two or more elements chemically combined. In order to separate compounds, chemical changes need to occur. Mixtures are made by physically combining two or more substances. Mixtures can be separated by physical means by taking advantage of the differences in physical properties of the substances in the mixture.

EXPLORATION LAB DIRECTED Inquiry

Investigating Separating Mixtures

In this lab, you will be given three task cards. Each card will list a procedure for you to follow in order to separate three different mixtures. The cards can be completed in any order. You will be practicing several different separation techniques during this activity. Each technique takes advantage of a different property of one of the substances to separate it from the mixture.

OBJECTIVE

- Use differences in properties to separate substances in a mixture.

MATERIALS

For each group

- beaker
- bucket or tub
- cup, plastic, large
- cup, plastic, small
- filter, coffee
- filter paper, 2 cm × 8 cm
- funnel
- index cards with task descriptions
- magnet
- markers, water-based (4 different colors)
- mixture of beads, BBs, and marbles
- mixture of sand and salt
- pencil
- pie tin
- ruler, metric
- spoons, metal
- water

For each student

- lab apron
- goggles

PROCEDURE

ASK A QUESTION

1 In this lab, you will be investigating the question, "How can a mixture be separated?"

MAKE OBSERVATIONS

2 Task Card 1

a. Observe the mixture of sand and salt. Write your observations below.

____

____

____

Place the remaining mixture in a cup. Add water to the mixture until it is completely covered. Stir the mixture thoroughly to allow any substances to completely dissolve in the water.

c. Build a filtering apparatus by adding a coffee filter to a funnel. Place the funnel over a cup. Pour the mixture into the filter and observe the filtration process. What do you observe remaining in the filter? What do you observe about the liquid that passed through the filter?

____

____

____

d. Pour the filtered liquid into a pie tin and place it in a sunny spot or near a radiator or other heat source. Allow it to sit overnight. Record your observations the next day.

____

____

3 Task Card 2

a. Observe the mixture of marbles, BBs, and plastic beads. Write your observations below.

____

____

____

b. Pass a magnet over the mixture. Record your observations. Did you need to pass the magnet over the mixture more than one time?

____

____

c. Set aside any substance that the magnet picks up. Then pour the remaining mixture into a bucket or tub and add water. Record your observations.

____

____

d. Use a spoon to separate the beads from the marbles. Explain how you carried out this step.

____

____

4 Task Card 3

a. Observe the four markers. Write your observations below.

____

____

____

b. Draw a light pencil line 2 centimeters (cm) from the bottom of the filter paper and parallel to the bottom edge. Use each marker to place a separate dot on the pencil line at various points along the line. Spread out the dots so that they are about equally distant from one another on the pencil line.

Exploration Lab continued

c. Add water to a beaker until the water depth is about 1 cm. Carefully lower the filter paper marked with the ink spots into the water in the beaker so that only the bottom edge of the filter paper makes contact with the water. If the filter paper will not stand by itself, tape it to the beaker to hold it in this position. Record your observations.

____

____

____

ANALYZE THE RESULTS

5 **Analyzing Data** What property of salt did you use to separate it from sand?

____

____

____

____

____

Exploration Lab continued

6 **Analyzing Data** What property of the BBs did you use to separate them from the marbles and the beads? What property of the plastic beads did you use to separate them from the marbles?

____

____

____

____

____

7 **Analyzing Data** What property of ink did you use to separate it into its components?

____

____

____

____

____

Exploration Lab continued

DRAW CONCLUSIONS

8 **Explaining Results** How were you able to use the properties of matter to separate substances in the mixtures you encountered? In your explanation include information about one or more of the mixtures you worked with in this experiment.

____

____

____

____

____

Connect TO THE ESSENTIAL QUESTION

9 **Applying Concepts** Explain how pure substances and mixtures differ.

____

____

____

____

EXPLORATION LAB GUIDED *Inquiry*

Investigating Separating Mixtures

In this lab, you will be given three task cards. Each card will list a procedure for you to follow in order to separate three different mixtures. The cards can be completed in any order. You will be practicing several different separation techniques during this activity. All of the techniques take advantage of differences in properties of the substances in each mixture.

OBJECTIVE

- Use differences in properties to separate substances in a mixture.

MATERIALS

For each group

- beaker
- bucket or tub
- cup, plastic, large
- cup, plastic, small
- filter, coffee
- filter paper, 2 cm × 8 cm
- funnel
- index cards with task descriptions
- magnet
- markers, water-based (4 different colors)
- mixture of beads, BBs, and marbles
- mixture of sand and salt
- pencil
- pie tin
- ruler, metric
- spoons, metal
- water

For each student

- lab apron
- goggles

PROCEDURE

ASK A QUESTION

1 In this lab, you will be investigating the question, "How can a mixture can be separated?"

DEVELOP A PLAN

2 Task Card 1

a. Observe the mixture of sand and salt. Write your observations below.

____

____

____

b. List the properties of each of the substances that might be used to separate them.

____

____

____

____

c. Develop a plan for separating the mixture of sand and salt. Record your plan on a separate piece of paper. Look at your list detailing the properties of each substance and review the materials available to you to help guide your separation plan. Once you have developed a plan, ask for your teacher's approval before continuing.

Exploration Lab continued

3 Task Card 2

a. Observe the mixture of marbles, BBs, and beads. Write your observations below.

____

____

____

b. List the properties of each of the substances that might be used to separate them from the others.

____

____

____

____

c. Develop a plan for separating the mixture of marbles, BBs, and beads. Record your plan on a separate piece of paper. Look at your list detailing the properties of each substance and review the materials available to you to help guide your separation plan. Once you have developed a plan, ask for your teacher's approval before continuing.

4 Task Card 3

a. Use each of the four markers to draw on a separate sheet of paper. Write your observations of the ink below.

____

____

____

b. List the properties of the ink that you are aware of.

____

____

c. Develop a plan for separating the inks in the markers. Record your plan on a separate piece of paper. Look at your list detailing the properties of the inks and review the materials available to you to help guide your separation plan. Once you have developed a plan, ask for your teacher's approval before continuing.

Exploration Lab continued

MAKE OBSERVATIONS

5. Carry out your plans for each separation. Record your observations at each step of each separation on a separate sheet of paper.

ANALYZE THE RESULTS

6. **Analyzing Data** What property of salt did you use to separate it from the sand?

____

____

7. **Analyzing Data** What property of the marbles did you use to separate them from the beads and BBs? What property of the BBs did you use to separate them from the marbles and the beads? What property of the beads did you use to separate them from the marbles and the BBs?

____

____

8. **Analyzing Data** What property of the ink did you use to separate it into its components?

____

____

DRAW CONCLUSIONS

9. **Evaluating Methods** Evaluate the separation procedure you used for Task Card 1. Was your procedure successful? How would you modify your procedure if you were to perform this separation again?

____

____

____

____

____

Exploration Lab continued

10 **Evaluating Methods** Evaluate the separation procedure you used for Task Card 2. Was your procedure successful? How would you modify your procedure if you were to perform this separation again?

____

____

____

____

____

11 **Evaluating Methods** Evaluate the separation procedure you used for Task Card 3. Was your procedure successful? How would you modify your procedure if you were to perform this separation again?

____

____

____

____

____

12 **Explaining Results** How were you able to use the properties of matter to separate substances in the mixtures you encountered? In your explanation include information about one or more of the mixtures you worked with in this experiment.

____

____

____

____

____

Connect TO THE ESSENTIAL QUESTION

13 **Applying Concepts** Explain how pure substances and mixtures differ.

____

____

____

____

QUICK LAB DIRECTED Inquiry

Changing Volumes BASIC

Small groups
15 minutes

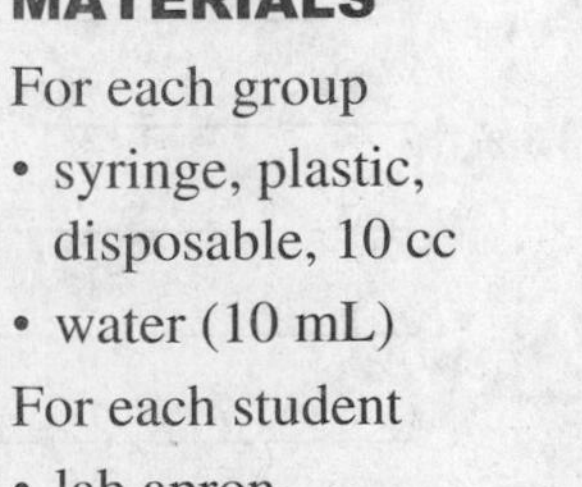

MATERIALS

For each group
- syringe, plastic, disposable, 10 cc
- water (10 mL)

For each student
- lab apron
- safety goggles

LAB RATINGS

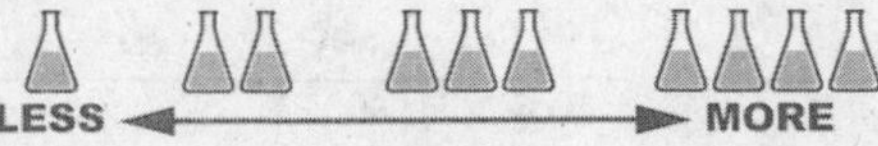

Teacher Prep —
Student Setup —
Cleanup —

SAFETY INFORMATION

Remind students to review all safety cautions and icons before beginning this lab. Water can be a slipping hazard if spilled on the floor. All spills should be cleaned up immediately.

My Notes

TEACHER NOTES

In this activity, students will investigate the relationship between the pressure and volume of liquids and gases. Students will fill a syringe with a fluid, cap the tip of the syringe, and then compress the plunger to determine how the fluid behaves under compression. The students will investigate both air and water.

Tip If the syringe does not come with a cap, students may use their palms to cover the tip of the syringe.

Student Tip Be careful not to push on the plunger before the cap is applied to the syringe.

Skills Focus Making Observations, Explaining Results, Making Predictions

MODIFICATION FOR INDEPENDENT Inquiry

Have students brainstorm ways to observe and model how the volume of liquids and gases changes in response to pressure. Have students think of the materials they would need to model this. It is helpful for students to consider what kinds of containers wouldn't work. Also, have students consider what things they will need to keep constant in order to test the effect of pressure on volume. Once students have determined a set of materials and procedures, allow them to perform their investigations. Encourage students to think about the relationship between the particle spacing of different materials and how much the materials compress. Have students design controlled experiments to test their models. Allow students to carry out all reasonable procedures.

Quick Lab continued

Answer Key

2. Sample answer: The plunger moved 7 mL.
4. Sample answer: The plunger did not move at all.
5. Sample answer: The gas could be compressed because there is space between the particles of a gas. The liquid could not be compressed because the liquid's particles are already very close together.
   Teacher Prompt Did any of the air or gas escape out of the syringe when you pushed the plunger? Sample answer: No. If the plunger moved, what happened to the particles inside the liquid or gas? Sample answer: They had to get closer together.
6. Sample answer: It would be very difficult to compress a solid because its particles are already very close together, like those in a liquid.

Name ______________________ Class ______________ Date ____________________

QUICK LAB DIRECTED Inquiry

Changing Volumes

In this lab, you will observe how the volumes of liquids and gases change in response to pressure. To model this, you will fill a syringe with the liquid or gas and then compress the plunger to observe how the volume of the material changes.

OBJECTIVE

- Demonstrate how the volumes of air and water change in response to pressure.

MATERIALS

For each group

- syringe, plastic, disposable, 10 cc
- water (10 mL)

For each student

- lab apron
- safety goggles

PROCEDURE

1. Draw 10 mL of air into a **syringe**. Tighten the cap.
2. Push in the plunger. Record your observations.

   ____

   ____

   ____

3. Draw 10 mL of **water** into the syringe. Tighten the cap.
4. Push in the plunger. Record your observations.

   ____

   ____

   ____

5. Explain any difference in your results in terms of how close or far apart the particles are in each material.

   ____

   ____

   ____

   ____

6. How easy would it be to compress a solid? Explain, in terms of the particles in the solid.

   ____

   ____

   ____

   ____

QUICK LAB DIRECTED Inquiry

Can Crusher GENERAL

Large groups
20 minutes

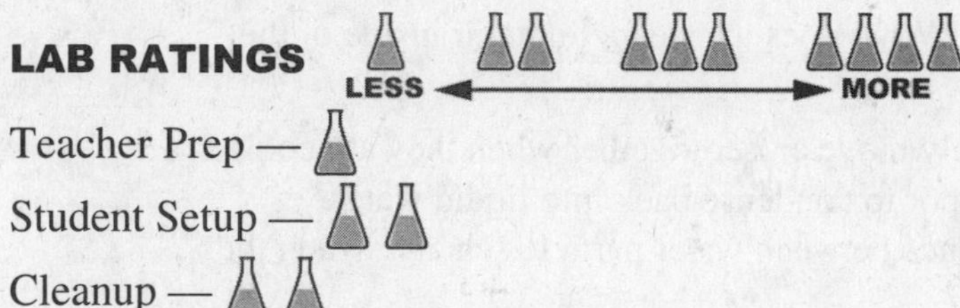

MATERIALS

For the teacher

- beaker, large
- can, aluminum
- lab apron
- gloves, heat-resistant
- hot plate
- ice
- safety goggles
- tongs
- water, cold

My Notes

SAFETY INFORMATION

Remind students to review all safety cautions and icons before beginning this lab. Caution students to remain a safe distance from the site where you will perform this activity as a demonstration.

TEACHER NOTES

In this activity, you will conduct a demonstration that will allow students to explore how particles in water and water vapor change in response to heating and cooling. Set up an area where you can conduct the demonstration so that students can clearly observe every step without being too close. It is advisable to practice this demonstration a couple of times on your own to be sure that you can carry it out successfully.

The demonstration begins with heating a small amount of water in an aluminum can until the can fills with water vapor. As the water vaporizes, it pushes air out of the can. Then, when you invert the vapor-filled can and submerge it top down into a beaker of cold water, the water vapor inside condenses rapidly, forming a partial vacuum inside of the can. Briefly explain vacuums, pressure, and net force due to pressure differences to students before beginning the lab. Because the pressure inside of the can decreases, the can collapses inward from the greater atmospheric pressure outside. Because the collapse occurs so rapidly, it is usually accompanied by a loud noise that can be startling to observers. Prepare students before the demonstration by explaining that they may hear a noise such as a sharp crack when the can is placed in the water.

Skills Focus Making Observations, Applying Concepts

MODIFICATION FOR INDEPENDENT Inquiry

Perform this experiment for students as a demonstration. Then, ask students to identify a variable that might change the outcome of the investigation. Have students design an investigation that explores the effect of a particular variable on the degree to which the can crushes inward. Once procedures are approved, have students carry out their investigations under your supervision. Have students share their procedures and results with the class.

Quick Lab continued

Answer Key

7. Sample answer: The can collapses inward very rapidly and with a loud noise.

8. Sample answer: The water molecules spread out when they are heated and liquid water changes into water vapor when the water boils. The water vapor pushes air out of the aluminum can.
Teacher Prompt How does steam form? What does the steam do to air inside of the aluminum can?

9. Sample answer: The water molecules quickly move closer together when they are cooled by the cold water. This causes the water vapor to condense back into liquid water.
Teacher Prompt Does the average distance between water particles change when the can is plunged into the cold water?

10. Sample answer: The water vapor pushed the air out of the can in Step 4. When submerged, that water vapor quickly condensed back to liquid water, which takes up much less space since the molecules are much closer together. This creates a vacuum in the can, so the pressure inside of the can is less than the pressure outside of the can. The outside pressure pushes inward on the can and causes the can to collapse.
Teacher Prompt What happens when the pressure outside of an object becomes greater than the pressure inside of an object?

Name ______________________ Class ______________ Date ______________

QUICK LAB DIRECTED Inquiry

Can Crusher

In this activity, you will observe a demonstration that will allow you to think about how water changes in response to heating and cooling. Heating liquid water causes the water molecules to move more quickly and spread apart, eventually forming water vapor. Cooling water vapor causes the water molecules to get closer together and move more slowly. This changes water vapor back to liquid water. If cooling continues, water molecules pack together even more tightly and move more slowly. This eventually changes liquid water to the solid phase of water, ice.

OBJECTIVES

- Describe the motion of particles in a gas.
- Observe how the movement of particles in a gas can change the properties of the gas.

MATERIALS

For the teacher

- beaker, large
- can, aluminum
- lab apron
- gloves, heat-resistant
- hot plate
- ice
- safety goggles
- tongs
- water, cold

PROCEDURE

1. Your teacher will carry out the following procedure.
2. Add enough water to fill a large beaker to about ¾ of its volume. Then add ice to fill it the rest of the way.
3. Pour enough water in an aluminum can to slightly cover the bottom of the can, to a depth of about 1 cm.
4. Put on heat-resistant gloves. Place the aluminum can on a hot plate and turn the hot plate to the highest temperature setting.
5. Heat the can until the water is boiling. Allow the water in the can to boil for 30 seconds. You should observe steam moving up through the top of the can. Turn off the hot plate.
6. Use tongs to lift the can from the hot plate. Quickly turn the can upside down and plunge it top down into the ice cold water.
7. Record your observations.

    ____

    ____

8. What happens to the water molecules in the aluminum can during Step 5 when the water is heated? What happens to air in the aluminum can during that step?

    ____

    ____

    ____

    ____

Quick Lab continued

9. What happens to the water molecules in the aluminum can when the can is turned upside down and quickly submerged in the cold water?

____

____

____

10. How can your answer to the question in Step 9 explain your observations in Step 7?

____

____

____

____

____

QUICK LAB INDEPENDENT Inquiry

Investigating Conservation of Mass GENERAL

MATERIALS

For each student
- glass jar with lid
- lab apron
- safety goggles
- scale
- ice cubes

My Notes

Individual student
30 minutes

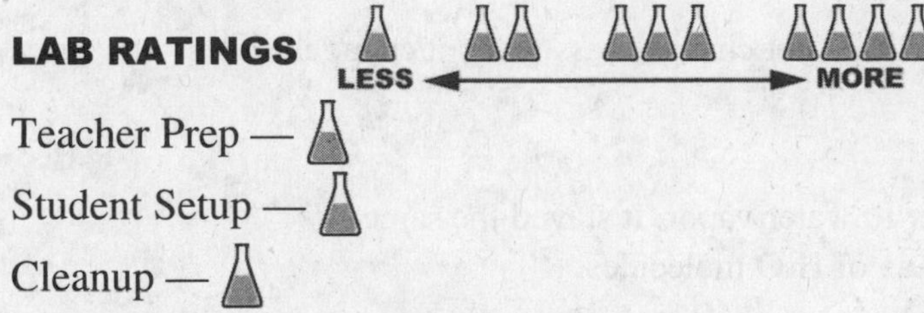

Teacher Prep —
Student Setup —
Cleanup —

SAFETY INFORMATION

Remind students to review all safety cautions and icons before beginning this lab. If students wish to use a hot plate to melt the ice, review proper safety procedures.

TEACHER NOTES

In this activity, students will design a procedure that will test the law of conservation of matter. Ideal designs will involve students replacing the lid on the jar so that water vapor cannot escape. Some students may wish to leave the glass in the sun to melt the ice, while others may wish to use a heat source. If you do not have enough glass jars for every student, this experiment can be done with disposable pie plates and plastic wrap. Make sure students tightly secure one piece of plastic wrap over the dish tightly so nothing can escape.

Student Tip Remember how molecules in each state move. How can you prevent gas molecules from escaping into the room?

Skills Focus Developing Procedures, Making Predictions, Drawing Conclusions

MODIFICATION FOR DIRECTED Inquiry

Provide students with setup directions that include weighing the jar filled with ice, weighing it once the ice has melted, and once again when some condensation has begun to form. Make sure each student knows to keep the lid tightly on the jar to make sure no water vapor escapes. You may want to have half of the class perform the experiment with the lid on and the other half perform the experiment with the lid off. When the experiment is over, have the two groups compare their results.

Quick Lab continued

Answer Key

1. Accept all procedures that will prove the law of conservation of mass.
2. Sample answer: I intend to do the experiment with both the lid on and the lid off; I intend to refreeze the contents of the jar and see if the new ice weighs the same as the original ice.
3. Sample answer: The data I am going to collect is the mass of the jar with ice, when the ice melts, and when the water starts to evaporate.
4. Sample answer: I intend to prove that matter does not change mass when it changes state.
5. Accept all reasonable responses.
6. Sample answer: It changed from ice to water to water vapor. It stayed the same because it retained its mass and was still made of H_2O molecules.
7. Sample answer: The mass of the jar with the water and condensation was the same as the mass of the jar with the ice, meaning that although the ice underwent a change of state, its mass remained the same.
8. Sample answer: One variable that could affect the procedure is leaving the lid off of the jar, thus allowing water vapor to escape and changing the mass.
9. Sample answer: Changes in states are physical changes; the object remains the same and can be returned to its original state. Physical changes do not change the identity of an object, and mass is part of the identity of an object.

Name ______________________ Class ______________ Date ______________

QUICK LAB INDEPENDENT *Inquiry*

Investigating Conservation of Mass

When an object undergoes a change of state, does the mass of the object stay the same, or does it change? In this lab, you will design an investigation to find out.

OBJECTIVES

- Recognize that substances do not change identity when they change state.
- Investigate conservation of mass during changes of state.

MATERIALS

For each student

- glass jar with lid
- lab apron
- safety goggles
- scale
- ice cubes

PROCEDURE

1. Design a procedure to test conservation of mass.

____

____

____

____

____

____

____

2. What variables do you need to include in your procedure?

____

____

____

____

3. What data will you collect during your experiment? How will you use the data?

____

____

____

____

4. What results are you expecting from your experiment?

____

____

____

Quick Lab continued

5. Have your procedure approved by your teacher and then carry out your procedure. Record your observations.

____

____

____

____

____

____

6. How did the ice change during your experiment? How did it remain the same?

____

____

____

____

7. What did your experiment show about the conversation of mass?

____

____

____

____

8. What variables could you change in your experiment that might change the outcome? Explain.

____

____

____

____

9. Why doesn't the mass of an object change when the object undergoes a change of state?

____

____

____

____

QUICK LAB GUIDED *Inquiry*

Modeling Particle Motion GENERAL

Student pairs

15 minutes on Day 1, 10 minutes on Day 2

LAB RATINGS LESS ⟷ MORE

Teacher Prep — 1

Student Setup — 2

Cleanup — 1

MATERIALS

For each pair
- beakers
- hot plate
- ice cube

For each student
- gloves
- lab apron
- pencil
- safety goggles

SAFETY INFORMATION

Remind students to review all safety cautions and icons before beginning this lab. If necessary, review how to use a hot plate safely. Remind students not to get too close to the flame.

TEACHER NOTES

In this activity, students will write a procedure in which they facilitate the change of state in an ice cube. Once you have approved pairs' procedures, allow them to carry out their plans. With each change of state, students will draw a model depicting the movement of particles within the ice cube. Melted ice cubes can be left out overnight to evaporate.

If hot plates are unavailable, students may use Bunsen burners instead.

Skills Focus Developing Procedures, Making Models

My Notes

MODIFICATION FOR DIRECTED *Inquiry*

Give each student pair the materials and walk them through the experiment. First, students will use the hot plate to melt the ice cube. Then, they will set the water aside to evaporate or continue heating the water with the hot plate to vaporize the water. With each change of state, have students draw a model depicting how the ice cube's particles are moving.

Quick Lab continued

Answer Key

1. Sample answer: We can use the materials to change the ice into water and water vapor.
2. Sample answer: We can use the hot plate to melt the ice. We can then leave the water out overnight to evaporate. We also can continue heating the water with the hot plate. When the water boils, the water forms water vapor or a gas.
3. Student drawings should show that gas particles move quickly and have large amounts of space between them. In the liquid the particles move past each other but are not neatly arranged, and in solids the particles move very little and are neatly arranged.
4. Sample answer: Particles in solids don't move a lot and they are tightly arranged. Particles in gases move freely and have large spaces between them. Liquid particles move like gas particles but are arranged more like solid particles.
   Teacher Prompt For an extension, have students design an experiment in which they show changes in state between liquids and gases and solids and gases.

QUICK LAB GUIDED *Inquiry*

Modeling Particle Motion

In this lab, you will observe water as it changes state. With each change of state, you will draw a model of the particles in the water and how their motion is also changing.

OBJECTIVES

- Observe matter as it changes state.
- Draw a model of particle motion in changes of state.

MATERIALS

For each pair
- beakers
- hot plate
- ice cube

For each student
- gloves
- lab apron
- pencil
- safety goggles

PROCEDURE

1. With a partner, describe how you can use the materials listed to facilitate changes in state.

   ____

   ____

   ____

   ____

2. Plan a procedure that will show how you will change ice from a solid to a liquid, and then to a gas. Describe your plan.

   ____

   ____

   ____

   ____

   ____

3. After your teacher approves your procedure, perform your experiment. Use the space below to draw models of how the particles in the ice move during each state.

Quick Lab continued

4. Describe how the movement of the particles changes with each change of state.

QUICK LAB DIRECTED Inquiry

Boiling Water Without Heating It GENERAL

Small groups
15 minutes

LAB RATINGS LESS ⟷ MORE

Teacher Prep — 2
Student Setup — 2
Cleanup — 1

MATERIALS

For each group
- syringe, 10 mL or larger
- water, warm

For each student
- lab apron
- safety goggles

My Notes

SAFETY INFORMATION

Remind students to review all safety cautions and icons before beginning this lab. Wet floors pose a slipping hazard. Spills should be cleaned up and reported immediately.

TEACHER NOTES

In this activity, students will investigate the connection between pressure and boiling point. As they draw the plunger out of a capped syringe, the water inside the syringe will boil due to the decreased air pressure inside the syringe. If necessary, have students use syringe locks to hold the caps on the syringes.

Skills Focus Making Observations, Explaining Results, Applying Concepts

MODIFICATION FOR GUIDED Inquiry

Instead of telling students what procedure to follow, simply present them with the problem and provide them with the syringes. Explain that boiling points decrease with decreased atmospheric pressure, and allow them to brainstorm ways to use the syringes to decrease atmospheric pressure. Check students' ideas before allowing them to proceed with the activity.

MODIFICATION FOR INDEPENDENT Inquiry

Present students with a challenge: boil water without heating it. Ask students to design a solution to this problem. Students can research what factors other than temperature affect boiling point and develop a plan to boil water by manipulating a condition other than heat. If their solutions are correct and plausible based on available materials, allow them to proceed. You may wish to have students present their solutions and results to the rest of the class.

Quick Lab continued

Answer Key

5. Sample answer: The pressure must decrease.
6. Sample answer: The air pressure inside the syringe decreased when the plunger was pulled out.
7. Sample answer: The air pressure became low enough for the water to boil at this temperature.
8. Sample answer: Normally, I see water boil because of heating rather than a change in pressure.
   Teacher Prompt What do you do at home to make water boil? Sample answer: I put it in a pot on the stove and turn on the burner.
9. Student drawings should show particles representing gas molecules escaping from the particles representing liquid and collecting above the liquid in the syringe.

Name _______________ Class _______________ Date _______________

QUICK LAB DIRECTED Inquiry

Boiling Water Without Heating It

In this lab, you will boil water without adding heat. By pulling on the plunger of a syringe, you will be able to decrease the atmospheric pressure within the syringe. As a result, the warm water within the syringe will boil.

OBJECTIVE

- Determine how atmospheric pressure affects the boiling point of water.

MATERIALS

For each group
- syringe, 10 mL or larger
- water, warm

For each student
- lab apron
- safety goggles

PROCEDURE

1. Remove the cap from the **syringe**.
2. Place the tip of the syringe in the **warm water**. Pull the plunger out until you have 5 mL of water in the syringe.
3. Place the cap tightly on the syringe. Hold the syringe, and slowly pull the plunger out.
4. Record any changes you see in the water.

____

____

____

5. If the temperature stays the same, what must happen to the atmospheric pressure in order to cause the liquid to boil?

____

____

____

6. What happened to the air inside the syringe above the water as you pulled the plunger out of the syringe?

____

____

____

____

____

____

Quick Lab continued

7 How did this cause the water to boil?

8 What is different about the conditions under which water normally boils, compared to what you just saw?

9 In the space below, draw a model that shows the motion of the particles in the syringe.

EXPLORATION LAB DIRECTED Inquiry **AND** GUIDED Inquiry

Changes of State GENERAL

Small groups
45 minutes

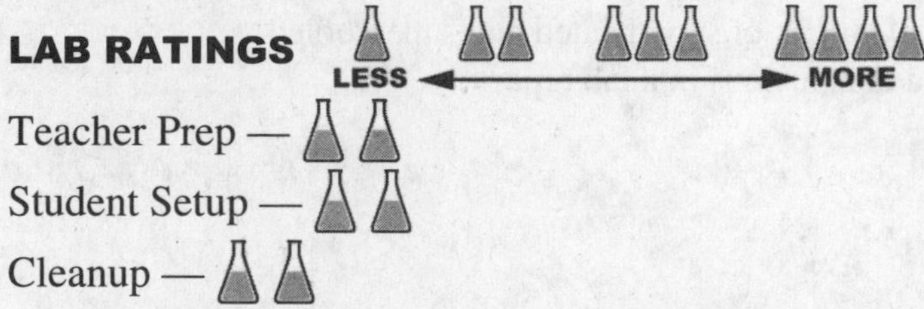

Teacher Prep —
Student Setup —
Cleanup —

MATERIALS

For each group
- beaker
- coffee can, large
- copper wire, 25 cm
- crushed ice
- graduated cylinder
- graph paper
- hot plate
- rock salt
- stopwatch
- thermometer, alcohol
- water

For each student
- heat resistant gloves
- lab apron
- safety goggles

SAFETY INFORMATION

Remind students to review all safety cautions and icons before beginning this lab. Students should wear gloves, goggles, and aprons at all times during this activity. Students should use extreme caution around the hot plate and wear protective gloves when handling any hot items. Students should also be extremely cautious of steam generated by boiling water.

TEACHER NOTES

In this activity, students will investigate the relationship between temperature and the change of state of water. When you add energy to a substance through heating, does the substance's temperature always go up? When you remove energy from a substance through cooling, does the substance's temperature always go down? In this lab, students will investigate these questions using water. Recommended beaker size is 250 mL; recommended graduated cylinder size is 100 mL.

Students will have to be very efficient and productive to complete both parts of this activity in the allotted time. In order to save time, you may wish to divide the class in half and have some groups perform Part I while other groups work on Part II. When students are done, they can simply switch workstations rather than make a new experimental setup. You may also wish to have students record data during class and then complete graphs and questions for homework. Alternatively, you might want to do Part I and Part II in two separate class periods.

Tip This activity may help students better understand how energy levels relate to the physical states of matter.

Student Tip Make sure the thermometer does not rest on the bottom of the beaker while it is on the hot plate.

Skills Focus Recording Data, Making Graphs

My Notes

Exploration Lab continued

MODIFICATION FOR INDEPENDENT Inquiry

Scientists have developed ways of superheating and supercooling water so that it remains in a liquid state above its boiling point and below its freezing temperature. Ask students to research methods of superheating and supercooling to explain how these phenomena are possible. How are conditions modified so that water is not susceptible to changes of state at the normal temperature? Is the energy in the system the same as under normal conditions? Is the temperature? What are the commercial applications of superheated and supercooled water? Students should present their research and conclusions in a lab report.

Answer Key for DIRECTED Inquiry

MAKE OBSERVATIONS

6. Answers will vary, but graph should show a steady increase in temperature, leveling off at about 100 °C and then remaining constant.

13. Answers will vary, but graph should show a steady decrease in temperature, leveling off at about 0 °C and then remaining constant.

ANALYZE THE RESULTS

13. Sample answer: The slope of each graph represents the temperature change.

15. Sample answer: The temperature remains constant.

16. Sample answer: As the water reaches freezing, the temperature levels off and remains constant.

DRAW CONCLUSIONS

17. Sample answer: When the particles speed up enough, water can become gas (steam), which has more energy at the same temperature. Even though energy is being added the whole time, the temperature stops rising when the liquid starts changing into a gas. When the particles slow down enough, the water can become solid ice, which has less energy at the same temperature. Even though energy is being removed the whole time, the temperature stops falling when the liquid starts changing to a solid. The fact that the temperature stops rising or falling explains the parts of the graphs that level off. **Teacher Prompt** If boiling point and freezing point are both constant temperatures, what happens to the energy in a system beyond those temperatures? Sample answer: It goes toward a change of state.

Connect TO THE ESSENTIAL QUESTION

18. Sample answer: Pressure can affect the state of matter. If enough pressure is applied to matter, the molecules are forced closer together. Pressure can be used to change a gas a liquid and a liquid to a solid.

Exploration Lab continued

Answer Key for GUIDED Inquiry

DEVELOP A PLAN

2. Sample answer: Water can change to ice (solid) and steam (gas).
3. Sample answer: I can control the temperature of the water by heating and cooling it.
4. Sample answer: I will record the temperature of the water as it heats and cools, especially the temperature at which it changes state.
5. Accept all reasonable answers.
   Teacher Prompt Remind students that a table is an efficient method for recording lots of measurements, and a graph is a useful tool for plotting data and observing trends.

MAKE OBSERVATIONS

6. Answers will vary.

ANALYZE THE RESULTS

7. Answers will vary.
8. Answers will vary, but students should recognize that water must be heated and cooled to critical temperatures to change state into steam or ice.
9. Answers will vary.

DRAW CONCLUSIONS

10. Sample answer: The temperature will remain constant once water reaches the boiling or freezing point. The energy added by heating boiling water turns into steam, which has more energy than water at the same temperature. The energy removed by cooling frozen water allows ice crystals to form and turn liquid water into solid ice, which has less energy than water at the same temperature.

Connect TO THE ESSENTIAL QUESTION

11. Sample answer: Pressure can affect the state of matter. If enough pressure is applied to matter, the molecules are forced closer together. Pressure can be used to change a gas a liquid and a liquid to a solid.

Name ______________________ Class ______________ Date ______________

EXPLORATION LAB DIRECTED Inquiry

Changes of State

In this lab, you will investigate the relationship between temperature and change of state in water.

PROCEDURE

ASK A QUESTION

1. In this activity, you will investigate the following question: How does the temperature of a substance affect its state?

MAKE OBSERVATIONS

PART I

2. Construct a **thermometer** harness with the **copper wire**. Make a small loop about the size of the thermometer at one end of the wire. Angle the loop so that it is perpendicular to the rest of the wire. Make a handle at the other end of the wire that extends in the opposite direction of the loop. Place the loop around the thermometer, and use the handle to gently place it in the beaker. Use the harness to put the thermometer in a position where it is NOT touching the bottom of the beaker.

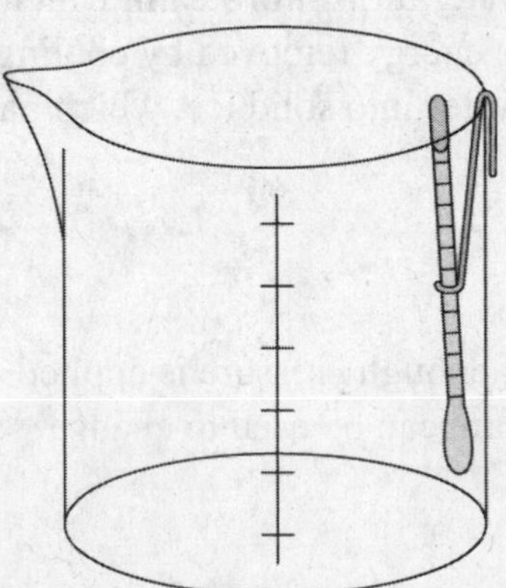

3. Fill the **beaker** about one-third to one-half full with **water**.
4. Turn on the **hot plate**, and put the beaker on it.

OBJECTIVE

- Measure the temperature of water as it changes state.

MATERIALS

For each group

- beaker
- coffee can, large
- copper wire, 25 cm
- crushed ice
- graduated cylinder
- graph paper
- hot plate
- rock salt
- stopwatch
- thermometer, alcohol
- water

For each student

- heat resistant gloves
- lab apron
- safety goggles

Exploration Lab continued

5. Observe the heating water, and use your **stopwatch** to record the temperature of the water every 30 seconds. Continue doing this until about one-fourth of the water boils away. Make a special note of the temperature at which the water is steadily boiling. Record your data in the table below. When you run out of space in the table, draw a new table on a piece of paper or in your lab notebook and continue to record data.

Time (seconds)	30	60	90	120	150	180	210	240	270	300	330	360
Temperature (°C)												

6. Turn off the hot plate, but do not move the beaker or thermometer. While the beaker is cooling, use your **graph paper** to make a graph of temperature (y-axis) versus time (x-axis). Draw an arrow pointing to the first temperature at which the water was steadily boiling.

7. After you finish the graph, use heat-resistant gloves to pick up the beaker. Pour the warm water out, and rinse the warm beaker with cool water. Caution: Even after cooling, the beaker is still too warm to handle without gloves.

PART II

8. Put approximately 30–35 mL of water in the **graduated cylinder**.

9. Use the wire harness to place the thermometer in the graduated cylinder.

10. Put the graduated cylinder in the **coffee can**, and fill in the space around the graduated cylinder with **crushed ice**. Pour **rock salt** on top of the ice around the graduated cylinder.

11. Gently stir the water with the **stirring rod**. As the ice melts, the level of ice will decrease. Add ice and rock salt to the can as needed to maintain the level of ice and salt, and keep the water consistently cool.

Exploration Lab continued

12 Use your stopwatch to record the temperature of the water in the graduated cylinder every 30 seconds. Note the temperature when you first notice ice crystals forming in the water. Once the water begins to freeze, stop stirring. Continue taking readings until the water in the graduated cylinder is completely frozen. Do NOT try to pull the thermometer out of the solid ice in the cylinder. Record your data in the table below. When you run out of space in the table, draw a new table on a piece of paper or in your lab notebook and continue to record data.

Time (seconds)	30	60	90	120	150	180	210	240	270	300	330	360
Temperature (°C)												

13 Use your graph paper to make a graph of temperature (y-axis) versus time (x-axis). Draw an arrow to the temperature reading at which the first ice crystals formed in the water in the graduated cylinder.

ANALYZE THE RESULTS

14 **Analyzing Data** What does the slope of each graph represent?

____

____

____

____

15 **Evaluating Data** After the water reaches a boil, what happens to the temperature of the water when you continue to add energy through heating?

____

____

____

____

16 **Evaluating Data** What happens to the temperature of freezing water when you continue to remove energy through cooling?

____

____

____

____

Exploration Lab continued

DRAW CONCLUSIONS

17 **Applying Concepts** The particles that make up solids, liquids, and gases are in constant motion. Adding or removing energy causes changes in the movement of these particles. Using this idea, explain why the temperature graphs of the two experiments level off after the water has reached the boiling or freezing temperature.

____

____

____

____

____

____

____

____

____

____

Connect TO THE ESSENTIAL QUESTION

18 **Applying Concepts** Temperature is one quality that helps determine the state of matter. What do you think another could be? Explain your answer.

____

____

____

____

Name ______________________ Class ______________ Date ______________

EXPLORATION LAB GUIDED *Inquiry*

Changes of State

In this lab, you will investigate the relationship between temperature and change of state in water.

OBJECTIVE

- Measure the temperature of water as it changes state.

MATERIALS

For each group

- beaker
- coffee can, large
- copper wire, 25 cm
- crushed ice
- graduated cylinder
- graph paper
- hot plate
- rock salt
- stopwatch
- thermometer, alcohol
- water

For each student

- heat resistant gloves
- lab apron
- safety goggles

PROCEDURE

ASK A QUESTION

1. In this activity, you will investigate the following question: How does the temperature of water relate to its physical state?

DEVELOP A PLAN

2. The state of a substance—solid, liquid, or gas—depends on the movement of the particles that make up the substance. Adding or removing energy changes the movement of particles. In this activity, you will investigate the relationship between temperature and changes of state in water. What state changes can water undergo?

   ____

   ____

   ____

   ____

   ____

3. What variable can you control in this experiment? How can you control it?

   ____

   ____

   ____

   ____

4. What data will you collect?

   ____

   ____

   ____

   ____

5. In the space below, describe an experimental setup that will allow you to observe how a change in temperature relates to a change of state in water. Make sure you include the materials you will use, the observations you will make, and the methods you will use to record and analyze your data.

____

____

____

____

____

____

____

____

MAKE OBSERVATIONS

6. Show your procedure to your teacher. Make any changes your teacher requires. When you get approval, carry out your procedure. Record your data in the space below. You may create tables and graphs if appropriate. Use additional **paper** or **graph paper** if necessary.

____

____

____

____

____

____

____

____

ANALYZE THE RESULTS

7. **Describing Observations** What state changes did you observe in your experiment?

____

____

____

____

Name ______________________ Class ______________ Date ________________

Exploration Lab continued

8 **Analyzing Data** How did temperature relate to changes of state?

9 **Evaluating Methods** Evaluate your experimental setup and procedure. Did it allow you to collect the data you needed to answer your question? Did your method of data recording and analysis allow you to reach conclusions? Explain any problems you experienced and modifications you would make to your procedure.

Exploration Lab continued

DRAW CONCLUSIONS

10. **Applying Concepts** The boiling point and freezing point of water are constant temperatures. If you continue to add energy by heating boiling water or to remove energy by cooling freezing water, what happens to the temperature? What happens to the energy?

Connect TO THE ESSENTIAL QUESTION

11. **Applying Concepts** Temperature is one quality that helps determine the state of matter. What do you think another could be? Explain your answer.

QUICK LAB INDEPENDENT *Inquiry*

Setting Objects in Motion GENERAL

Student pairs

20 minutes

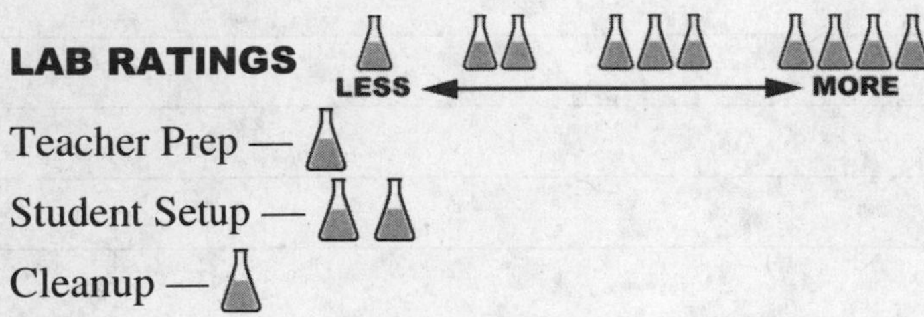

LAB RATINGS LESS ⟷ MORE

Teacher Prep — 1

Student Setup — 2

Cleanup — 1

MATERIALS

For each pair

- bouncing ball
- jack-in-the-box
- matches
- rubber band
- windup cars

For each student

- safety goggles

SAFETY INFORMATION

Remind students to review all safety cautions and icons before beginning this lab. If necessary, review the proper way to light and extinguish matches.

My Notes

TEACHER NOTES

In this activity, students will write a procedure in which they will use objects to transform potential energy into kinetic energy. Once you have approved pairs' procedures, allow them to carry out their plans. With each change of energy, they will record their observations and determine which type of potential energy each object has.

Tip If you can't find any jack-in-the-box toys, any wind up toys may be successfully substituted.

Skills Focus Developing Procedures, Applying Concepts

MODIFICATION FOR DIRECTED *Inquiry*

Before beginning this experiment, remind students that potential energy is the energy that an object has because of the position, shape, or condition of the object, and kinetic energy is the energy of an object that is due to the object's motion. Explain that there are different types of potential energy. Give each student pair the materials and walk them through the experiment. Demonstrate how to set each object in motion. Before students determine which type of potential energy each object has, give them a list to choose from: gravitational, chemical, elastic, mechanical. If necessary, review each type of potential energy to help students make their decisions.

Quick Lab continued

Answer Key

1. Accept all reasonable answers.
2. Sample answer:

Object	How Did We Set It in Motion?	How Did It Move?	What Type of Potential Energy Does It Have?
Bouncing Ball	We dropped it.	It bounced several times.	Gravitational
Jack-in-the-Box	We turned the crank.	It sprung up.	Mechanical or Elastic
Match	We struck the match to light it.	It turned into a flame.	Chemical
Rubber Band	We snapped it.	It sprung back.	Elastic
Windup Car	We turned the key.	It moved forward.	Mechanical or Elastic

3. Accept all reasonable answers.

Name ______________________ Class ______________ Date ______________________

QUICK LAB INDEPENDENT *Inquiry*

Setting Objects in Motion

In this lab, you will observe how potential energy changes into kinetic energy by setting several objects into motion. You will then determine which type of potential energy each of the objects has.

OBJECTIVES

- Observe how potential energy transforms into kinetic energy.
- Determine which type of potential energy objects have.

MATERIALS

For each pair

- bouncing ball
- jack-in-the-box
- matches
- rubber band
- windup cars

For each student

- safety goggles

PROCEDURE

1. Look at the items your teacher has given you. With a partner, create a procedure to help you determine how to set each object into motion and verify which type of potential energy each of the items has. Record your procedure below.

Name ______________________________ Class __________________ Date ________________________

Quick Lab continued

2. After your teacher approves your procedure, perform your experiment. Use the chart below to record your data.

Object	How Did We Set It in Motion?	How Did It Move?	What Type of Potential Energy Does It Have?
Bouncing Ball			
Jack-in-the-Box			
Match			
Rubber Band			
Windup Car			

3. Choose one of the items above. How can you change its potential energy into kinetic energy? Explain.

____

____

____

____

____

____

QUICK LAB DIRECTED *Inquiry*

Conservation of Energy GENERAL

Student pairs
20 minutes

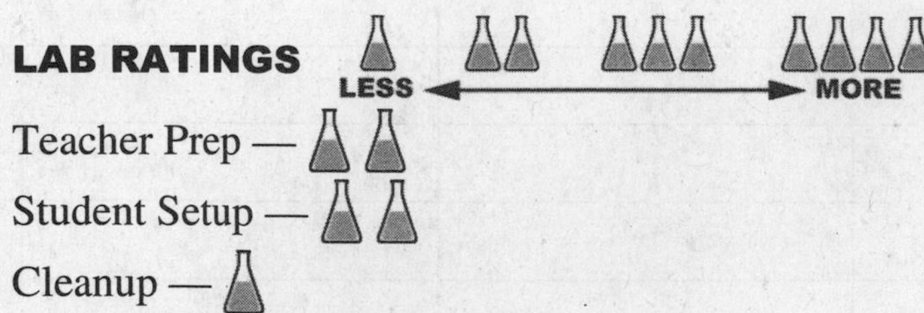

MATERIALS

For each pair
- balance
- calculator
- small ball of clay
- stopwatch
- tape measure

For each student
- gloves
- safety goggles

My Notes

SAFETY INFORMATION

Remind students to review all safety cautions and icons before beginning this lab. Find a place from which to drop the object where the dropper will not be in danger of falling and the timer will not be in danger of being hit by the object. Remind students to use caution when walking through the lab area.

Skills Focus Practicing Lab Techniques, Performing Calculations, Comparing Results

TEACHER NOTES

In this lab, students will demonstrate the law of conservation of energy by examining how the potential energy of a small falling object changes as the kinetic energy changes.

MODIFICATION FOR INDEPENDENT *Inquiry*

Have students identify questions they have about conservation of energy and design investigations to answer their questions. Allow students to carry out all reasonable procedures. They should share their results with the class.

Answer Key

1. Sample answer: 50 g, or 0.050 kg
2. Sample answer: 10 m
3. Sample answer: 1.4 s
4. Sample answer: 1.4 s
5. Sample answer: 4.9 J
6. Sample answer: 13.7 m/s
7. Sample answer: 4.7 J
8. Sample answer: Potential energy was slightly greater than kinetic energy.
9. Sample answer: Energy was conserved, but small errors made it look as if it was not. Air resistance is a source of error.
10. Sample answer: rubbing your hands together

Name ______________________________ Class ________________ Date ______________________

QUICK LAB DIRECTED *Inquiry*

Conservation of Energy

In this lab, you will demonstrate the law of conservation of energy by examining how potential energy changes as kinetic energy changes.

OBJECTIVES

- Measure kinetic and potential energy.
- Show that when energy is transferred from one system to another, the total quantity of energy does not change.

MATERIALS

For each pair
- balance
- calculator
- small ball of clay
- stopwatch
- tape measure

For each student
- gloves
- safety goggles

PROCEDURE

1. Measure the mass of a **small ball of clay** in kilograms, and record it below.

   ____

2. Find a place from which the clay can be safely dropped to the ground. Measure the distance in meters the clay will fall when dropped to the ground. Record it below.

   ____

3. One student should hold the clay. The other student should stand near where the clay will land with the **stopwatch**. The first student should drop the clay at the same time that the second student starts the stopwatch. The second student should stop the stopwatch as soon as the clay hits the ground. Record the time required for the clay to fall in the table below.

Trial	Time of Fall
1	
2	
3	
4	
Average	

Quick Lab continued

4. Repeat the time measurement three times, and find the average time for the four trials. Record the average in the table.

5. Calculate the potential energy (PE) of the clay before it is dropped. To calculate potential energy, multiply the mass of the clay (in kilograms) by the height it fell (in meters). Then, multiply that number by 9.8. The result is the potential energy in joules. Record the potential energy below.

____

6. Calculate the velocity of the clay just before it strikes the ground. To calculate the velocity, multiply the clay average fall time (in seconds) by 9.8. The result is the average velocity in meters per second. Record the average velocity below.

____

7. Calculate the kinetic energy (KE) of the clay just before it strikes the ground. To calculate kinetic energy, first square the velocity (that is, calculate *velocity* × *velocity*). Then, multiply that number by the mass of the clay (in kilograms). Finally, divide by 2. The result is the kinetic energy in joules. Record the kinetic energy below.

____

8. Compare *PE* to *KE*.

____

____

9. Was energy conserved? What are some possible sources of error?

____

____

____

10. Although you could not observe it, the kinetic energy of the clay was converted to heat energy when it struck the ground. In the space below, describe an example of kinetic energy being converted to heat energy that you *can* observe easily.

____

____

____

QUICK LAB DIRECTED Inquiry

Bungee Jumping GENERAL

Small groups
15 minutes

LAB RATINGS

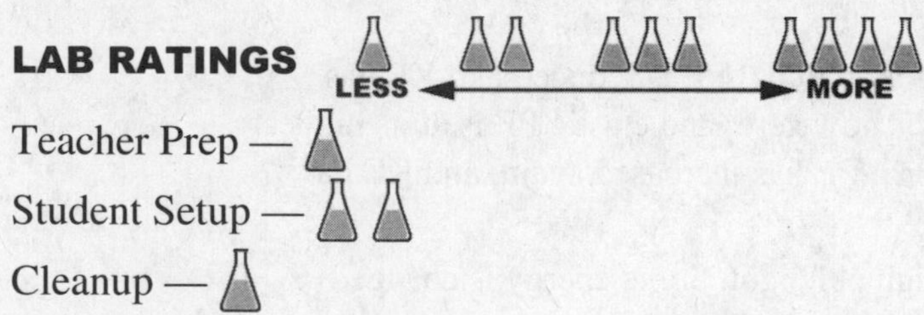

Teacher Prep —
Student Setup —
Cleanup —

MATERIALS

For each group
- elastic cord, 45.75 cm
- mass, 100 g
- ring stand and ring
- tape

For each student
- paper, blank
- safety goggles

My Notes

SAFETY INFORMATION

Remind students to review all safety cautions and icons before beginning this lab. Students should stand clear of the rebounding mass to avoid injury.

TEACHER NOTES

In this activity, students will observe changes between gravitational potential energy, elastic potential energy, and kinetic energy. The type of elastic cord and height of the fall will determine the appropriate mass. More mass may be needed.

Tip This activity may help students better understand the relationship between kinetic and potential energy.

Skills Focus Making Observations, Applying Concepts, Explaining Results

MODIFICATION FOR INDEPENDENT Inquiry

Ask students to design models that will illustrate the relationship between potential energy and kinetic energy. Once you have approved their designs, have them proceed with their demonstration, being sure to record their observations and account for changes to energy.

Quick Lab continued

Answer Key

4. Accept all reasonable drawings. Drawings should show the following for each point: (A) slack elastic cord and mass held level with the ring; (B) released mass falling and elastic cord slack; (C) mass at farthest point in its path from the ring, elastic cord fully stretched; and (D) released mass in same position as in (B) with elastic cord contracting.
5. Sample answer: (A) gravitational PE; (B) gravitational PE is reduced and KE has increased; (C) gravitational PE is zero, KE is now zero, and elastic PE is at its highest level; (D) elastic PE is now zero, gravitational PE has increased again, and KE has increased again.
6. Sample answer: It does not return to the original height. Some energy is changed into heat as the cord stretches.
   Teacher Prompt Remind students that energy cannot be destroyed, but can change form.

QUICK LAB DIRECTED Inquiry

Bungee Jumping

In this lab, you will drop a mass attached to an elastic cord in order to observe and describe how energy changes form. You will describe the state of kinetic energy as well as different kinds of potential energy as the mass bounces up and down.

OBJECTIVE

- Observe the energy changes as your bungee jumper falls and bounces back.

MATERIALS

For each group
- elastic cord, 45.75 cm
- mass, 100 g
- ring stand and ring
- tape

For each student
- safety goggles

PROCEDURE

1. Set your **ring stand** at the edge of your lab table. Tie the **elastic cord** to the **ring** on your ring stand so it hangs over the edge of your lab table.
2. Wrap the elastic cord around the **mass** and tie it. Then **tape** the cord and mass to further secure them.
3. Hold the mass near the ring. Release it and watch it carefully as it falls and rebounds upward. Repeat several times, paying attention to the speed of the mass and the behavior of the cord.
4. In the space below, sketch the cord and mass as it appears at the following times: (A) when first released; (B) just before the cord begins to stretch; (C) at the bottom of the fall; and (D) when it reaches (B) again on the way back up.

Quick Lab continued

5. State the type of energy the mass has at each of these four positions and how the energy is changing at each point.

____

____

____

____

6. Does the mass return to its original height? Why or why not?

____

____

____

____

____

S.T.E.M. LAB DIRECTED *Inquiry* **AND** INDEPENDENT *Inquiry*

Designing a Simple Device GENERAL

Individual student
40 minutes

LAB RATINGS LESS ⟵⟶ MORE

Teacher Prep — 1
Student Setup — 3
Cleanup — 1

MATERIALS

For each student

- empty spool of thread
- pencil
- rubber band
- ruler
- safety goggles
- tape
- toothpick
- washers, (3)

SAFETY INFORMATION

Remind students to review all safety cautions and icons before beginning this lab. Racers can cause personal injury if they fly out of control. Have students wear safety goggles as a precaution. For the independent inquiry, make sure students are aware of lab safety rules and safety measures they need to take.

My Notes

PREPARATION

In this activity, students will make and design simple devices that use potential and kinetic energies. Students completing the designed inquiry will make racers out of an empty spool of thread while students completing the independent inquiry will choose their own simple devices and the materials to make them. Make sure you have different types of materials available for students to use, such as blocks, strings, pulley mechanics, building toys, etc. The spools of thread do not need to be empty; new spools of thread are often less expensive than empty spools.

Tip This activity may help students better understand the different types of simple machines and the relationship between potential energy and kinetic energy.

Skills Focus Identifying Patterns, Describing Events

MODIFICATION FOR GUIDED *Inquiry*

Give students the materials to make a spool racer and ask them to use those materials to design a simple device that uses potential and kinetic energy. After you have approved their procedures, allow students to carry them out. Have students share their devices with the class and explain how they use potential energy and kinetic energy. Display finished products in the class.

S.T.E.M. Lab continued

Answer Key for DIRECTED Inquiry

ASK A QUESTION

1. Accept all reasonable answers.

BUILD A MODEL

5. Sample answer: The racer spins, and the spinning action causes it to move across the room.

6. Answers will vary.

ANALYZE THE RESULTS

7. Answers will vary.

8. Answers will vary.

9. Sample answer: The more I wound the racer, the farther it traveled.

DRAW CONCLUSIONS

10. Sample answer: The potential energy was greatest when it was wound in the trial it went the farthest. It had the greatest kinetic energy when it moved in that trial.

11. Students will recognize that the least potential energy was in the trial when the racer moved the least.

12. Accept all reasonable answers.

13. Accept all reasonable answers and drawings.

Connect TO THE ESSENTIAL QUESTION

14. Sample answer: The greater the potential energy is, the greater the kinetic energy is.

S.T.E.M. Lab continued

Answer Key for INDEPENDENT Inquiry

ASK A QUESTION

1. Accept all reasonable answers.

DEVELOP A PLAN

2. Accept all reasonable answers.
3. Accept all reasonable answers.
4. Accept all reasonable answers.
5. Accept all reasonable answers.
6. Accept all reasonable drawings.

BUILD A MODEL

7. Accept all reasonable answers.
8. Answers will vary.

ANALYZE THE RESULTS

9. Accept all reasonable answers.
10. Accept all reasonable answers.

DRAW CONCLUSIONS

11. Answers will vary.
12. Answers will vary.
13. Accept all reasonable answers.
14. Accept all reasonable answers and drawings.

Connect TO THE ESSENTIAL QUESTION

15. Sample answer: The greater the potential energy is, the greater the kinetic energy is.

Name ______________________ Class ______________ Date ______________

S.T.E.M. LAB DIRECTED Inquiry

Designing a Simple Device

Think of some of the devices you use every day. What is the source of energy for these devices? In this lab, you will make a simple device from an empty thread spool that runs on potential and kinetic energy.

OBJECTIVES

- Construct a simple device that uses potential and kinetic energy to work.
- Describe factors that affect how your device works.

MATERIALS

For each student

- empty spool of thread
- pencil
- rubber band
- ruler
- safety goggles
- tape
- toothpick
- washers, (3)

PROCEDURE

ASK A QUESTION

1. In this lab, you will investigate the following question: How does a simple device use only potential and kinetic energy to work? Write any thoughts you have about the question below.

____

____

____

____

BUILD A MODEL

2. Lay a **rubber band** flat on the table. Place a **toothpick** on top of the rubber band so that the toothpick and the rubber band intersect. Lift one end of the rubber band over the toothpick and thread it through the loop on the other side of the toothpick. Pull tightly to create a knot.

3. Thread the rubber band through the **empty spool of thread**. Break off the ends of the toothpick so that the toothpick does not extend beyond the diameter of the spool. **Tape** the toothpick into place.

4. Thread the other end of the rubber band through a **washer**. Slip the rubber-band loop around the **pencil**. Use more than one washer if needed.

5. Hold the spool firmly with one hand while twisting the pencil. Place the spool on the floor and let go. Observe what happens.

____

____

____

____

S.T.E.M. Lab continued

6 Repeat Step 5 five times. Vary how tightly you wind up the racer, counting how many times you wind the pencil. Measure how far the racer moves. Record your data in the chart below.

Trial	How Many Times Wound	Distance Traveled
1		
2		
3		
4		
5		

ANALYZE THE RESULTS

7 **Evaluating Results** What was the shortest distance the racer traveled? How many times did you wind it up?

8 **Evaluating Results** What was the farthest distance the racer traveled? How many times did you wind it up?

9 **Explaining Models** What is the relationship between the number of times you wound the pencil and how far the racer traveled?

DRAW CONCLUSIONS

10 **Describing Models** When did your racer have the greatest potential energy? When did it have the greatest kinetic energy?

Name ______________________ Class ______________ Date ______________

S.T.E.M. Lab continued

11 **Interpreting Results** Which trial had the least potential energy? Explain.

12 **Explaining Costs and Benefits** For which types of jobs could your simple device be used?

13 **Constructing Models** Think of another device you could build that uses potential and kinetic energies to do work. Write about your device. Draw a picture.

Connect TO THE ESSENTIAL QUESTION

14 **Explaining Conclusions** What is the relationship between the amount of potential energy and the amount of kinetic energy?

Name ______________________________ Class ________________ Date ______________________

S.T.E.M. LAB INDEPENDENT Inquiry

Designing a Simple Device

Think of some of the devices you use every day. What is the source of energy for these devices? In this lab, you will make a simple device from an empty thread spool that runs on potential and kinetic energy.

OBJECTIVES

- Construct a simple device that uses potential and kinetic energy to work.
- Describe factors that affect how your device works.

MATERIALS

For each student

- materials to build your device
- washers, (3)
- safety goggles

PROCEDURE

ASK A QUESTION

1. In this lab, you will investigate the following question: How does a simple device use only potential and kinetic energy to work? Write any thoughts you have about the question below.

____

____

____

____

____

____

____

DEVELOP A PLAN

2. What materials could you use to build a simple device?

____

____

____

____

____

S.T.E.M. Lab continued

3. Describe how you plan to build your device.

____

____

____

____

____

____

____

____

4. What are the variables in your experiment? How will you control them?

____

____

____

5. What data will you collect during your experiment?

____

____

____

6. Draw a sketch of what you think your device will look like.

BUILD A MODEL

7. Show your proposed procedure and sketch to your teacher. When your teacher tells you, carry out your procedure. Record your observations.

___

___

___

___

___

8. Make a table to show the data collected during your experiment.

ANALYZE THE RESULTS

9. **Evaluating Results** Did your device work as you expected? Explain.

___

___

___

___

10. **Identifying Constraints** How could you improve your design?

___

___

___

___

DRAW CONCLUSIONS

11 **Describing Models** When did your device have the greatest potential energy? When did it have the greatest kinetic energy?

12 **Interpreting Results** Which trial had the least potential energy? Explain.

13 **Explaining Costs and Benefits** For what types of jobs could your simple device be used?

14 **Constructing Models** Think of another device you could build that uses a different type of potential and kinetic energies to do work. Write about your device. Draw a picture.

Connect TO THE ESSENTIAL QUESTION

15 **Explaining Conclusions** What is the relationship between the amount of potential energy and the amount of kinetic energy?

QUICK LAB DIRECTED Inquiry

Exploring Temperature GENERAL

Small groups
20 minutes

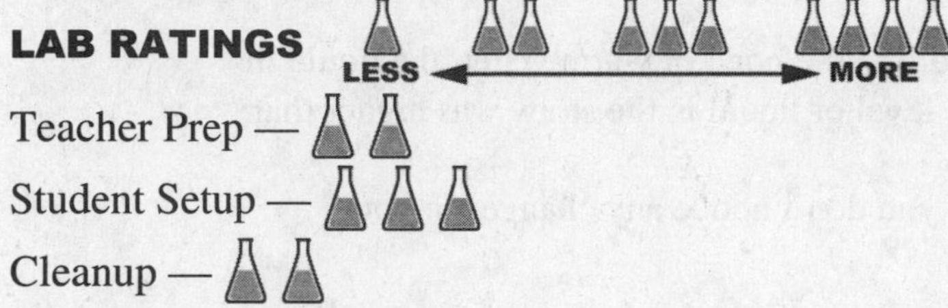

MATERIALS

For each group

- bottle, 16 oz
- bowls (2) at least one heatproof
- clay, modeling
- food coloring
- funnel
- hot plate
- ice
- kettle, tea
- straw, colorless
- water

For each student

- lab apron
- safety goggles

My Notes

SAFETY INFORMATION

Remind students to review all safety cautions and icons before beginning this lab. Students should use caution when working with hot water and avoid touching the water to prevent burning themselves.

TEACHER NOTES

In this activity, students will build a simple model thermometer that reacts to increases and decreases in temperature. The thermometer is not calibrated, so it does not show actual temperatures but does show qualitative changes.
A tight seal on the lid of the bottle is imperative for this model thermometer to work properly. Circulate as students carry out the activity, checking student thermometers to make sure that air cannot escape through cracks in the clay surrounding the straw placed in the bottle; if you wish, you may use an alternate method to seal off the mouths of the bottles. Instead of using clay, you can pre-drill holes in the lids of the bottle, just big enough for the straw to fit through. Once the straw is inserted in the bottle, a small amount of glue can be added around the straw to prevent any air from escaping around the straw. Once the glue dries, the bottle will be airtight, except for the desired opening of the straw itself. One of the bowls that your students use should be able to hold water at a near-boiling temperature. Let students know that the hot water may cause the plastic bottles to warp, but they are unlikely to melt. You may choose to use heat-resistant plastic bottles or glass bottles instead.

Tip Students should monitor the kettle closely as the water is heated; it is important to be sure that it does not become too hot. This will cause water to rise up through the top of the drinking straw. The water should be just warm to the touch.

Student Tip You may experience difficulties if any air can escape around your straw. Be very thorough when you complete Step 3.

Skills Focus Creating Models, Making Observations, Applying Concepts

Quick Lab continued

MODIFICATION FOR GUIDED *Inquiry*

Students should build the model thermometer as instructed in the student datasheet. Then, challenge them to devise their own procedures for changing the kinetic energy (temperature) of the solution in the bottle.

Answer Key

7. Sample answer: When the bottle was placed into the bowl of warm water, the liquid in the bottle moved up through the straw. The level of liquid in the straw was higher than the level of liquid in the rest of the bottle.
Teacher Prompt What should you do if you don't notice any changes in your model when it is placed in hot water?

8. Accept all reasonable answers. Some students may also observe that the level of liquid in the straw temporarily drops below the level of liquid in the rest of the bottle.

9. Sample answer: When the bottle is in warm water, the kinetic energy of the liquid increases. When the bottle is in cold water, the kinetic energy of the liquid decreases.

10. Accept all reasonable answers. Students should understand that the increased kinetic energy of the liquid in the plastic bottle caused the liquid to move up into the straw. When the seal around the straw is tight, the only place liquid can escape is through the straw. If there were any gaps in the clay, the increased pressure in the bottle (caused by the increased kinetic energy) would escape through these holes rather than move up through the straw.

Name ______________________ Class ______________ Date ______________

QUICK LAB DIRECTED *Inquiry*

Exploring Temperature

In this lab, you will work with your group to build a simple model thermometer. You will apply your observations about your model thermometer to help you understand that temperature is a way to measure kinetic energy of particles.

OBJECTIVES

- Build a model thermometer.
- Understand that objects with higher temperatures have higher kinetic energy.

MATERIALS

For each group
- bottle, 16 oz
- bowl (2), at least one heatproof
- clay, modeling
- food coloring
- funnel
- hot plate
- ice
- kettle, tea
- straw, colorless
- water

For each student
- lab apron
- safety goggles

PROCEDURE

1. Place the funnel in the empty plastic bottle. Fill half the bottle with tap water.
2. Add 8 to 10 drops of food coloring to the water in the bottle. Swirl the bottle so the water and food coloring are mixed well. Fill the bottle to the top with tap water.
3. Place the straw in the bottle. Hold it so that about 8 cm of the straw sticks out of the bottle. Seal off the top of the bottle with modeling clay. Make sure that no liquid from inside the bottle can escape from your clay lid. See the image below; your bottle should look like this when you finish this step.

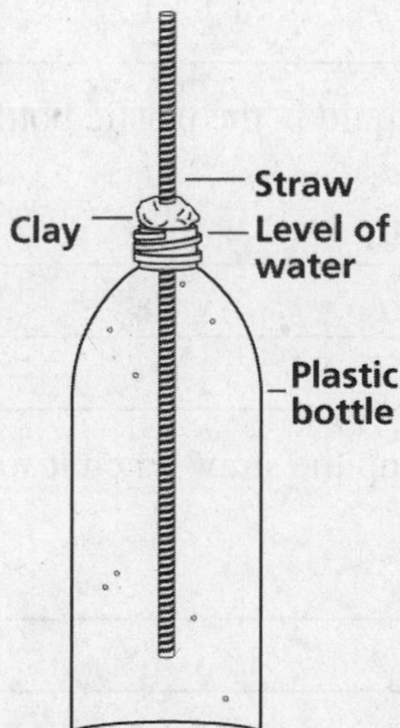

4. Place the kettle containing water on the hot plate. Turn on the hot plate and allow the temperature of the water in the kettle to increase until it is warm; do not allow the kettle to boil.

Quick Lab continued

5. While you are waiting for the water in the kettle to become warm, prepare a bowl of ice water by placing several ice cubes in one of the bowls. Then, add enough tap water so that the level of the water in the bowl is 1/3 to 1/2 the height of the bottle. Set this ice water bowl aside.

6. When the water becomes warm, carefully pour the warm water into the second bowl. Again, the level of the water in this bowl should be 1/3 to 1/2 the height of the bottle.

7. Place the plastic bottle into the bowl with warm water and observe what happens. If liquid does not rise in the straw, air may be escaping somewhere around your straw. Add more clay if necessary to make sure that the only place air can escape from the plastic bottle is through the straw. Write down your observations below.

____

____

____

8. Place the plastic bottle in the bowl of ice water and observe what happens. Write down your observations.

____

____

____

9. What happens to the kinetic energy of the liquid in the plastic bottle when it is placed in hot water and cold water?

____

____

____

10. Explain why the liquid in the bottle moved up the straw when it was placed in hot water.

____

____

____

QUICK LAB DIRECTED Inquiry

Understanding Temperature Scales BASIC

Small groups
20 minutes

LAB RATINGS LESS ⟷ MORE

Teacher Prep — 2
Student Setup — 2
Cleanup — 2

MATERIALS

For each group
- beaker
- containers, plastic (2)
- hot plate
- ice
- thermometer, Celsius scale
- thermometer, Fahrenheit scale
- water

For each student
- lab apron
- safety goggles

SAFETY INFORMATION

Remind students to review all safety cautions and icons before beginning this lab. Students should always use caution when handling hot water and when working with appliances that have heating elements. Students should use caution when inserting the thermometer into the water so that the thermometer does not break.

TEACHER NOTES

In this activity, students will use thermometers to record the temperatures of three containers of water: room temperature water, boiling water, and ice water. They'll record their results in both Fahrenheit and Celsius to help them understand the differences between the two scales. Students will also learn about the kinetic energy of the different liquids, and consider how one might use the third temperature scale, Kelvin.

Tip Some students may know the freezing or boiling temperatures of water; before students measure temperatures, tell them to only use the measurements they take in the lab (and, if they already know the temperatures, to keep that information to themselves). In this way, all students will discover the temperatures of boiling and (near) freezing water on their own.

Skills Focus Practicing Lab Techniques, Recording Data, Making Measurements

My Notes

MODIFICATION FOR GUIDED Inquiry

For a Guided Inquiry option, many of the methods of the lab can remain the same, but students should develop their own methods for presenting their data that could include creating a graph or table.

Quick Lab continued

Answer Key

3. Sample answer:

	Degrees in Fahrenheit	Degrees in Celsius
Room temperature water	65	18
Boiling water	210	98
Ice water	35	2

Note that students' answers may be slightly different from the actual boiling and freezing temperatures of water. This is acceptable, but at this point you should tell students the actual answer (boiling water: 212 °Fahrenheit, 100 °Celsius; frozen water: 32 °Fahrenheit, 0 °Celsius).

Teacher Prompt What might cause your measured temperatures to be slightly different from the actual freezing and boiling temperatures of water?

4. Sample answer: The actual boiling temperature of water is 212 °Fahrenheit and 100 °Celsius. The actual freezing temperature of water is 32 °Fahrenheit and 0 °Celsius.

5. Accept all reasonable answers. Students should understand that as the temperature of the water increases, so does the kinetic energy of the water molecules. Temperature is a measure of kinetic energy.

6. Sample answer: The kinetic energy of the ice water is much less than the kinetic energy of the boiling water. The less kinetic energy the molecules that make up an object have, the colder the object feels.

7. Accept all reasonable answers. Students should note similarities such as the 100-degree difference between freezing and boiling in the Celsius and Kelvin scales. They should also note numerical differences in the three scales; each scale registers a different temperature to indicate boiling, freezing, and room temperature water.

8. Sample answer: The lower numbers on the Kelvin scale represent temperatures that are below freezing (or below the temperature of frozen water). As the temperatures drop lower on the Kelvin scale, so does the kinetic energy of the object. The temperature could theoretically drop so low that the object would have no kinetic energy.

Teacher Prompt What is absolute zero? How does absolute zero relate to the Kelvin scale?

QUICK LAB DIRECTED Inquiry

Understanding Temperature Scales

In this lab, you will work with your group to determine the temperatures of three different liquids. You will take your measurements in both Fahrenheit and Celsius, and record your measurements in a table.

OBJECTIVES

- Understand that temperatures can be measured using three different scales.
- Relate the temperature of an object to its kinetic energy.

MATERIALS

For each group
- beaker
- containers, plastic (2)
- hot plate
- ice
- thermometer, Celsius scale
- thermometer, Fahrenheit scale
- water

For each student
- lab apron
- safety goggles

PROCEDURE

1. Fill one container with room temperature tap water. Insert the two thermometers into the water and watch until the liquid sensors inside of the thermometers stop moving. Record the temperatures, in both Celsius and Fahrenheit, in the table below.

	Degrees in Fahrenheit	Degrees in Celsius
Room temperature water		
Boiling water		
Ice water		

2. Place enough water in the beaker to fill it halfway. Place it on the hot plate. Turn on the hot plate until the water starts to boil. Turn off the hot plate. Insert the two thermometers into the water and watch until the liquid sensors inside the thermometers stop moving. Record the temperatures, in both Celsius and Fahrenheit, in the table.

3. Fill a plastic container with ice. Add just a bit of water so that there is some liquid in the bowl. Wait about one minute so that the water becomes very cold. Insert the two thermometers into the ice water and watch until the liquid sensors inside of the thermometers stop moving. Record the temperatures, in both Celsius and Fahrenheit, in the table.

4. What are the actual temperatures of boiling water and ice, in both Fahrenheit and Celsius? Your teacher will tell you the answer; write it below.

____

____

Quick Lab continued

5 What is happening to the kinetic energy of the water molecules in the boiling water?

____

____

6 What is happening to the kinetic energy of the water molecules in the ice water?

____

____

7 On the Kelvin scale, water boils at 373 K and freezes at 273 K. What are some similarities and differences between the Kelvin, Celsius, and Fahrenheit scales?

____

____

____

8 What do you think the lower numbers on the Kelvin scale (0–273 K) represent? What would be the kinetic energy of an object with a temperature of 0 K?

____

____

____

____

QUICK LAB DIRECTED Inquiry

Simple Heat Engine GENERAL

Small groups
30 minutes

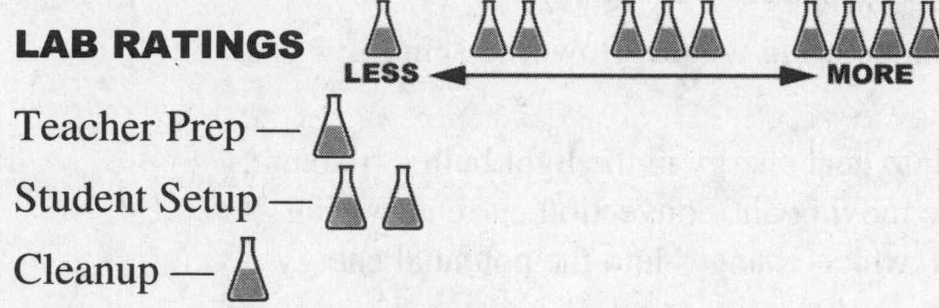

LAB RATINGS

Teacher Prep —
Student Setup —
Cleanup —

SAFETY INFORMATION

Remind students to review all safety cautions and icons before beginning this lab. The hot light bulb should remain near the center of the table, and students should exercise caution around the heat source. The spiral should be mounted at least 6" above the light bulb.

TEACHER NOTES

In this activity, students will observe a simple heat engine and learn about energy conversions from chemical potential energy to kinetic energy. The string must be flexible and easy to twist or else the resistance will prevent the motion.

Skills Focus Drawing Conclusions, Applying Concepts, Making Predictions

MODIFICATION FOR GUIDED Inquiry

Show students an example of the heat engine described in the directed inquiry lab. Have students develop a hypothesis about the relationship between spiral shape and spiral motion. Students should develop a list of procedures to test their hypothesis. Allow students to proceed with all reasonable investigations.

MATERIALS

For each group
- electric lamp with 60 W incandescent bulb
- paper circle, 6 inches in diameter
- ring stand
- ring
- scissors
- string, cotton, 18 inches long

For each student
- lab apron
- safety goggles

My Notes

Quick Lab continued

Answer Key

4. Sample answer: The spiral spins and then eventually slows and stops.
5. Sample answer: The string winds up and becomes harder to twist.
   Teacher Prompt Ask students what happens to the spiral after the light is turned off. Sample answer: The string unwinds in the opposite direction.
6. Sample answer: Let the string unwind. A longer string would allow it to spin for a longer period of time.
7. Sample answer: Electrical energy changes into heat energy in the light bulb's filament, which changes into the kinetic energy of the moving air (convection current), which changes into the kinetic energy of the spiral, which changes into the potential energy stored in the wound-up string.
8. Sample answer: yes, with a bulb with greater wattage or more flexible string
9. Sample answer: Automobile engines, lawn mower engines, and power plants all use heat to produce motion. Automobile engines use heat from the combustion of fuel.

Name ______________________ Class ______________ Date ______________

QUICK LAB DIRECTED *Inquiry*

Simple Heat Engine

In this lab, you will observe a series of energy transfers by creating a simple heat engine from paper and a wax candle.

OBJECTIVES

- Describe the direction of heat flow from a candle.
- Explain how thermal energy can transform into other kinds of energy.

MATERIALS

For each group
- electric lamp with 60 W incandescent bulb
- paper circle, 6 inches in diameter
- ring stand
- ring
- scissors
- string, cotton, 18 inches long

For each student
- lab apron
- safety goggles

PROCEDURE

1. Cut a **6-inch paper circle** into a ¾-inch-wide spiral. Tie the **string** through a hole in the end of the spiral. Tie the string to a **ring stand** so the spiral is suspended about 12 inches above the table.
2. Place the **lamp** on the lab table away from the spiral, and turn it on.
3. With the spiral at least 6 inches above the light bulb, slide the lamp so it is directly under the center of the spiral. Observe for about 1 minute. Turn off the lamp.
4. What happens to the spiral during this time? Does the motion of the spiral change during the time you observed?

____

____

____

____

____

____

____

5. Why do you think the motion changes?

____

____

____

____

____

____

____

Quick Lab continued

6. After the motion stopped, how could you get it to start spinning again?

7. Consider the energy transformations that have occurred in your simple heat engine. Beginning with the electricity through the light bulb, briefly describe the energy changes that occur until the spiral finally stops spinning.

8. Could you make your heat engine spin faster? Explain.

9. What other devices can you think of that produce motion from heat? Explain.

QUICK LAB DIRECTED *Inquiry*

Observing the Transfer of Energy BASIC

Individual student
30 minutes

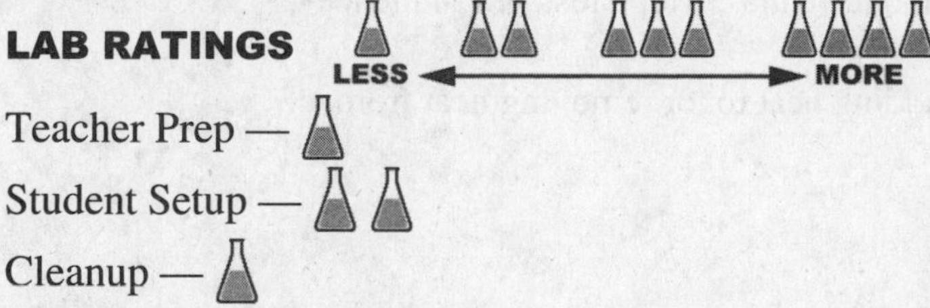

MATERIALS

For each student
- glass beaker
- hot plate
- ice cubes
- safety goggles
- thermometer

My Notes

____

____

____

____

____

SAFETY INFORMATION

Remind students to review all safety cautions and icons before beginning this lab. Tell students that hot plates can become extremely hot, so it is important to be extra cautious. Instruct students that they are not allowed to touch the setup once the ice cube is melting. Review the proper first aid for burn injuries as a precaution.

TEACHER NOTES

In this activity, students will force a change of state in ice to observe the transfer of heat energy. During the experiment, they will record the temperature of the ice. It is important to remind students that temperature is not the same as heat. Heat is the energy transferred between objects that are at different temperatures. You may also want to review the terms radiation, convection, and conduction before beginning this experiment.

Tip This activity can be used to discuss the difference between insulators and conductors. Ask students if they think the glass is a conductor or an insulator.

Skills Focus Making Observations, Drawing Conclusions, Explaining Results

MODIFICATION FOR INDEPENDENT *Inquiry*

Ask each student to think of a question about the transfer of heat energy. Have them develop a hypothesis to answer their question and design a procedure to prove their hypothesis. Allow students to carry out all reasonable procedures and share their findings with the class.

Quick Lab continued

Answer Key

2. Accept all reasonable answers.
3. Sample answer: The ice cube melted and the water started to evaporate, showing that heat moved through the system.
   Teacher Prompt Remind students that adding heat to, or removing heat from, a system may result in a change of state.
4. Sample answer: Energy was transferred to the ice cubes, which resulted in the ice cubes melting and then boiling.
   Teacher Prompt Remind students that adding heat to, or removing heat from, a system may result in a change of state.

Name ______________________ Class ______________ Date ________________

QUICK LAB DIRECTED Inquiry

Observing the Transfer of Energy

In this lab, you will observe how heat energy is transferred through a system. You will determine how the energy moved: through radiation, convection, or conduction. Finally, you will explain the difference between heat and temperature.

OBJECTIVES

- Describe how energy is transferred between objects.
- Explain the difference between heat and temperature.

MATERIALS

For each student

- glass beaker
- heating plate
- ice cubes
- safety goggles
- stopwatch
- thermometer

PROCEDURE

1. Add one or more **ice cubes** to the **beaker**. Record the temperature of the ice cube with the **thermometer**. Place the beaker on the **heating plate** and turn it on.

2. After 30 seconds, record the temperature of the ice cubes. Draw what the ice cubes look like. Repeat at 60 seconds. When the ice is completely melted, record the temperature and the elapsed time, and draw a picture of what you see. Repeat when the melted ice is boiling.

Trial 1	Elapsed Time	Description of Ice Cubes	Temperature	Sketch of Ice Cubes
1	30 seconds			
2	60 seconds			
3		Ice is completely melted.		
4		Melted ice is boiling.		

Quick Lab continued

3 Review your drawings. How do you know that heat was transferred from the hot plate?

____

____

____

____

____

____

____

____

____

4 Review the data that you collected. How would you explain the difference between heat and temperature in this activity?

____

____

____

____

____

____

____

____

QUICK LAB DIRECTED Inquiry

Exploring Thermal Conductivity BASIC

MATERIALS

For each pair
- cup, plastic foam
- graphite lead
- water, very warm
- wire, copper

For each student
- safety goggles

Student pairs
10 minutes

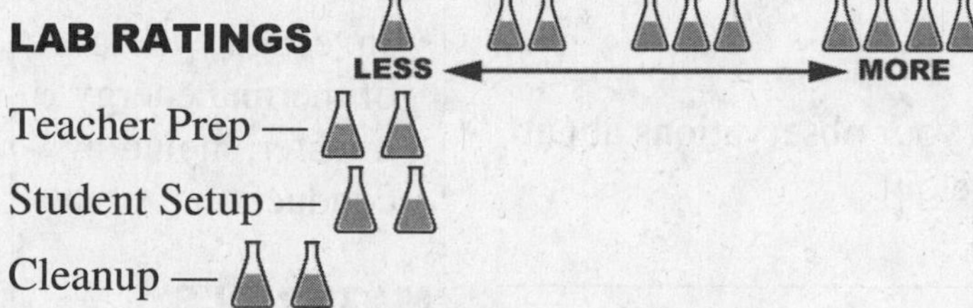

My Notes

SAFETY INFORMATION

Remind students to review all safety cautions and icons before beginning this lab.

TEACHER NOTES

In this activity, students will explore the relationship between material type and thermal conductivity. They will experiment with the thermal conductivity of a metal (copper wire) and a nonmetal (carbon graphite). For best results, the wire and pencil lead should be the same length and diameter.

Skills Focus Making Observations, Drawing Conclusions, Evaluating Procedures

MODIFICATION FOR GUIDED Inquiry

Give students the list of materials for the lab, and encourage them to brainstorm ways of determining the thermal conductivity of the materials provided. Students should write a list of procedures for any experiments they would like to conduct. Allow students to proceed with all reasonable experiments.

Answer Key

1. Sample answer: The wire is at room temperature.
2. Sample answer: The graphite is at room temperature.
5. Sample answer: The copper wire feels warmer.
6. Sample answer: The graphite lead feels the same as it did before.
7. Sample answer: Thermal energy flowed from the hot water to the room temperature copper and graphite. The copper wire got warmer, so it conducted thermal energy better.
8. Sample answer: No, graphite lead is probably not a metal because it does not conduct thermal energy well.
9. Sample answer: It was necessary to touch the objects before placing them in hot water so that I could compare the temperatures of the objects before and after the experiment.

Name ______________________ Class ______________ Date ______________

QUICK LAB DIRECTED Inquiry

Exploring Thermal Conductivity

In this lab, you will study the thermal conductivity of different materials by observing how well graphite and copper wire conduct heat.

OBJECTIVES

- Observe that heat flows in predictable ways, moving from warmer objects to cooler ones.
- Investigate methods of thermal energy transfer, including conduction.

MATERIALS

For each pair

- cup, plastic foam
- graphite lead
- water, very warm
- wire, copper

For each student

- safety goggles

PROCEDURE

1. Gently touch the **copper wire**. Record your observations about the object's temperature in the space below.

   ____

2. Gently touch the **graphite** from a mechanical pencil. Record your observations about the object's temperature in the space below.

   ____

3. Half-fill a **plastic foam cup** with **very warm water**.
4. Place the copper wire and the graphite in the cup of very warm water. Make sure that part of the wire and part of the graphite extend above the surface of the water.
5. After 1 minute, touch the part of the wire that is not submerged in the water. Record your observations about the object's temperature in the space below.

   ____

   ____

   ____

   ____

6. Touch the part of the graphite that is not submerged in the water. Record your observations about the object's temperature in the space below.

   ____

   ____

   ____

Quick Lab continued

7 Describe the flow of thermal energy in this experiment. Which material conducts thermal energy better? How can you tell?

8 Most metals are good conductors of thermal energy. Do you think that graphite is a metal? Explain.

9 Why was it important to make observations about the temperatures of the objects before placing them in the hot water?

FIELD LAB DIRECTED Inquiry **AND** GUIDED Inquiry

Building a Solar Cooker GENERAL

Student pairs
45 minutes

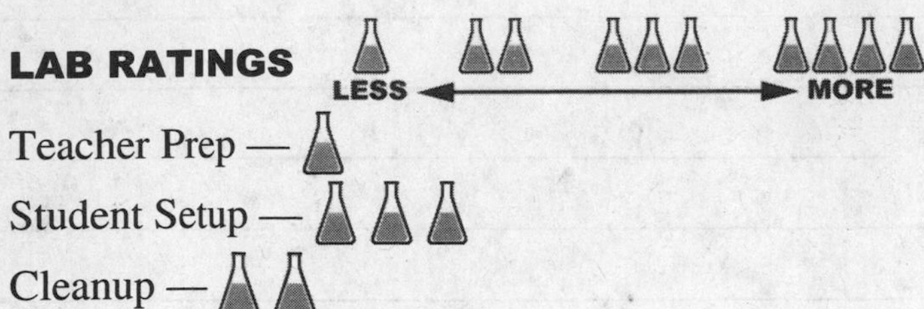

LAB RATINGS LESS ⟷ MORE

Teacher Prep — 1
Student Setup — 3
Cleanup — 2

MATERIALS

For each pair
- box, pizza
- chocolate bar, 1 square
- construction paper, black
- dowel, wooden
- foil, aluminum
- graham crackers (2)
- knife, utility
- marker
- marshmallow, large (1)
- plastic wrap
- ruler
- tape, masking

For each student
- lab apron
- safety goggles

SAFETY INFORMATION

Remind students to review all safety cautions and icons before beginning this lab. Tell students they should always wash their hands before handling food. Stress that while the results of this experiment are safe to consume, students should never taste anything in a science lab without your permission. Check to make sure students do not have food allergies before allowing them to eat the results of this lab. If you have students preparing their own boxes, review the proper way to handle utility knives.

TEACHER NOTES

In this activity, students will design and construct solar cookers and use them to make s'mores. Solar cookers can also be used to boil water, make rice or pasta, and make English muffin pizza. Do not allow students to cook meat in these solar cookers. Foods prepared in this lab should be consumed or tasted in a non-laboratory environment, such as an adjoining (non-laboratory) room, outdoors where the solar cooker is used, a hallway, or in a designated lunchroom. Students should also be instructed to wash their hands before and after consuming the food.

If you do not wish to have students handling knives, cut the boxes for students before class starts.

Tip This activity will better help students understand the transfer of energy through radiation and convection.

Skills Focus Building Models, Making Observations, Analyzing Results

My Notes

MODIFICATION FOR INDEPENDENT Inquiry

Have student pairs design and build their own solar cookers using any materials they wish. Each pair should propose a procedure for testing their cooker design. Allow students to carry out all reasonable procedures. Have each pair share their results with the class.

Field Lab continued

Answer Key for DIRECTED Inquiry

ASK A QUESTION

1. Sample answer: We can use the sun's energy to heat things and to make plants grow. I use the sun's energy in my garden. Because heat radiates from the sun, I can use it to cook food by leaving it out in the sun.

MAKE OBSERVATIONS

6. Accept all reasonable drawings.

9. Accept all reasonable answers and drawings.

10. Accept all reasonable answers.

EVALUATE THE PLAN

11. Accept all reasonable answers.

12. Sample answer: The part under the plastic wrap acted as the oven, while the aluminum foil acted as the heat source.

13. Accept all reasonable answers.

14. Sample answer: time of day, amount of cloud coverage

15. Sample answer: Yes. It might take longer for the food to cook, but a solar cooker could be used in the middle of a sunny day in December.
Teacher Prompt What is the source of energy for the cooker?

DRAW CONCLUSIONS

16. Sample answer: No. The aluminum foil was used to direct the sun's radiant energy to the food cooking inside the pizza box.

17. Sample answer: No. The plastic wrap traps the heat in the pizza box, allowing for convection cooking.

18. Sample answer: An advantage is that it uses a renewable resource and would be cheaper than a regular oven. A disadvantage is that it takes longer to cook food.

19. Sample answer: Quick-cooking food that does not need to reach a high internal temperature would be ideal for a solar cooker. It would not be a good idea to cook raw meat in a solar cooker.

20. Accept all reasonable answers.

21. Accept all reasonable answers.

Connect TO THE ESSENTIAL QUESTION

22. Sample answer: A solar cooker would be good for the environment because, unlike traditional cooking devices, it uses a renewable energy resource.

Field Lab continued

Answer Key for GUIDED Inquiry

ASK A QUESTION

1. Sample answer: We can use the sun's energy to heat things and to make plants grow.
2. Accept all reasonable plans.
3. Sample answer: Some variables include the amount of direct sunlight that day or to an extent, the temperature that day.
4. Sample answer: I will observe how quickly the food cooks. I will compare my data to other students' data.
5. Accept all reasonable answers.
6. Sample answer: I will measure the success of my experiment by how well the food cooks.

MAKE OBSERVATIONS

7. Accept all reasonable designs and drawings.
8. Accept all reasonable answers.

EVALUATE THE PLAN

9. Sample answer: The part under the plastic wrap acted as the oven, while the aluminum foil acted as the heat source.
10. Accept all reasonable answers.
11. Sample answer: time of day, amount of cloud coverage
12. Sample answer: Yes. It might take longer for the food to cook, but a solar cooker could be used in the middle of a sunny day in December.

DRAW CONCLUSIONS

13. Sample answer: The aluminum foil was used to direct the sun's radiant energy to the food cooking inside the pizza box.
14. Sample answer: No. The plastic wrap traps the heat in the pizza box, allowing for convection cooking.
15. Sample answer: An advantage is that it uses a renewable resource and would be cheaper than a regular oven. A disadvantage is that it takes longer to cook food.
16. Sample answer: Quick-cooking food that does not need to reach a high internal temperature would be ideal for a solar cooker. It would not be a good idea to cook raw meat in a solar cooker.
17. Accept all reasonable answers.
18. Accept all reasonable answers.

Connect TO THE ESSENTIAL QUESTION

19. Sample answer: A solar cooker would be good for the environment because, unlike traditional cooking devices, it uses a renewable energy resource.

Name ______________________ Class ______________ Date ____________________

FIELD LAB DIRECTED *Inquiry*

Building a Solar Cooker

In this activity, you will use radiant energy from the sun to cook food. You will build a solar cooker and use your observations to draw conclusions about energy.

OBJECTIVES

- Use the energy from the sun to cook a snack.
- Describe the transfer of energy through radiation.
- Understand the environmental benefits of solar cooking.

MATERIALS

For each pair

- box, pizza
- chocolate bar, 1 square
- construction paper, black
- dowel, wooden
- foil, aluminum
- graham crackers (2)
- knife, utility
- marker
- marshmallow, large (1)
- plastic wrap
- ruler
- tape, masking

For each student

- lab apron
- safety goggles

PROCEDURE

ASK A QUESTION

1. In this activity, you will investigate the following questions: How do you use energy from the sun in your everyday life? What are some other ways you can use the sun's energy? Do you think you can use energy from the sun to cook? Record your thoughts on these questions.

____

____

____

____

____

____

MAKE OBSERVATIONS

2. Use the marker and ruler to draw a 30 cm × 30 cm square in the center of the pizza box lid. Using the utility knife, cut along three sides of the square to create a flap in the box lid.

3. Place the aluminum foil, shiny side out, on the bottom surface of the flap. Make sure to cover the entire flap. Carefully smooth the wrinkles out of the aluminum foil then tape it down.

4. Lift up the flap. Secure a piece of plastic wrap over the opening with tape. Make sure the plastic wrap is tightly secured on all edges.

5. Open the pizza box. Cover the inside bottom of the box with aluminum foil, shiny side out. Carefully smooth the wrinkles out of the aluminum foil and secure it with tape. Cut a 21.5 cm × 21.5 cm square out of black construction paper. Place the square in the center of the pizza box and secure it with tape. Now close the box.

Field Lab continued

6. Open the flap at the top of the box and insert the dowel. Use the dowel as a prop to keep the flap up. Draw a picture of your solar cooker.

7. Take your solar cooker outside and set it in a sunny spot.

8. Open the flap of your solar cooker. Place two graham cracker squares on the construction paper. On one square, place a piece of chocolate. On the other square, place a marshmallow. Close the solar cooker, propping open the flap with the dowel.

9. Check your s'more every 5 minutes (min). Draw what you see.

Time	Drawing
5 minutes	
10 minutes	
15 minutes	
20 minutes	

Field Lab continued

10 How does the s'more change over a 20-min span?

____

____

EVALUATE THE PLAN

11 How long did it take for the chocolate and marshmallow to melt?

____

12 Which part of the solar cooker acted as the oven, and which acted as the heat source? Label them on your picture.

____

____

13 Share your data with another pair of students. What was the overall result of the experiment?

____

____

____

14 Which factors could impact the results of your experiment?

____

____

____

____

____

15 Would this experiment work in December? Why or why not?

____

____

____

____

Field Lab continued

DRAW CONCLUSIONS

16 **Making Conclusions** Explain the role of the aluminum foil in your solar cooker.

17 **Drawing Conclusions** Do you think your solar cooker would be as successful if you removed the plastic wrap? Explain.

18 **Recognizing Costs and Benefits** What is an advantage of using a solar cooker? What is a disadvantage of using a solar cooker?

19 **Recognizing Constraints** Which types of foods would be ideal to cook using a solar cooker? Which types of foods should not be made in a solar cooker?

20 **Analyzing Methods** How could you change the design of your solar cooker to make it more efficient?

Field Lab continued

21 **Constructing Models** What are some other materials you could use to make a solar cooker? Draw your design.

____

____

____

Connect **TO THE ESSENTIAL QUESTION**

22 **Synthesize Information** What impact would solar cookers have on the environment?

____

____

____

Name ______________________ Class ______________ Date ______________

FIELD LAB GUIDED Inquiry

Building a Solar Cooker

In this activity, you will use radiant energy from the sun to cook a snack. You will build a solar cooker and use your observations to draw conclusions about energy.

OBJECTIVES

- Use the energy from the sun to cook a snack.
- Describe the transfer of energy through radiation.
- Understand the environmental benefits of solar cooking.

MATERIALS

For each pair

- box, pizza
- chocolate bar, 1 square
- construction paper, black
- dowel, wooden
- foil, aluminum
- graham crackers (2)
- knife, utility
- marker
- marshmallow, large (1)
- plastic wrap
- ruler
- tape, masking

For each student:

- lab apron
- safety goggles

PROCEDURE

ASK A QUESTION

1. In this activity, you will investigate the following questions: How do you use energy from the sun in your everyday life? What are some other ways you can use the sun's energy? Do you think you can use energy from the sun to cook? Record your thoughts on these questions.

____

____

____

____

____

____

DEVELOP A PLAN

2. In the space below, describe how you will design a solar cooker out of a pizza box, aluminum foil, plastic wrap, black construction paper, and a dowel.

____

____

____

____

____

____

3. What are the variables in your experiment? How will you control them?

____

____

____

____

Field Lab continued

4. What data will you collect during your experiment? What will you do with the data once it has been collected?

____

____

____

____

5. How can you use the data to improve your design?

____

____

____

____

6. How will you measure the success of your experiment?

____

____

____

____

MAKE OBSERVATIONS

7. Show your proposed procedure to your teacher. When your teacher approves your procedure, carry it out. Record your observations in the space below. Draw a picture to show your design and record your observations.

Field Lab continued

EVALUATE THE PLAN

8 How long did it take for the chocolate and marshmallow to melt?

9 Which part of the solar cooker acted as the oven, and which acted as the heat source? Label them on your picture.

10 Share your data with another pair of students. What was the overall result of the experiment?

11 Which factors could impact the results of your experiment?

12 Would this experiment work in December? Why or why not?

DRAW CONCLUSIONS

13 **Making Conclusions** Explain the role of the aluminum foil in your solar cooker.

Field Lab continued

14 **Drawing Conclusions** Do you think your solar cooker would be as successful if you removed the plastic wrap? Explain.

____

____

____

15 **Recognizing Costs and Benefits** What is an advantage of using a solar cooker? What is a disadvantage of using a solar cooker?

____

____

____

____

____

____

16 **Recognizing Constraints** Which types of foods would be ideal to cook using a solar cooker? Which types of foods should not be made in a solar cooker?

____

____

____

____

17 **Analyzing Methods** How could you change the design of your solar cooker to make it more efficient?

____

____

____

Field Lab continued

18 **Constructing Models** What are some other materials you could use to make a solar cooker? Draw your design below.

____

____

____

Connect TO THE ESSENTIAL QUESTION

19 **Synthesize Information** What impact would solar cookers have on the environment?

____

____

____

QUICK LAB DIRECTED Inquiry

Modeling Renewable Energy BASIC

Individual student
15 minutes

LAB RATINGS

LESS ← → MORE

Teacher Prep — 1
Student Setup — 1
Cleanup — 1

MATERIALS

For each student
- blindfold
- bowl
- red beans, 90
- white beans, 10

My Notes

TEACHER NOTES

In this activity, students will use a bowl filled with two different colored beans to represent the effect of using nonrenewable resources on the environment. If you do not have access to beans, this experiment can be done with marbles, or even squares of black and white construction paper.

After students have completed the activity, you may wish to have them repeat it, this time using 80 red beans and 20 white. Ask if they think that is enough of a change to conserve resources. The results will ultimately be the same, so the answer is no. Then, have them repeat the experiment with equal numbers of beans and then with more white beans than red beans and discuss their findings.

Tip Use this activity as part of a conservation unit. Have students brainstorm a way to conserve resources and then make posters educating others about it.

Skills Focus Making Models, Applying Concepts, Evaluating Models

MODIFICATION FOR GUIDED Inquiry

Give student pairs the materials and ask them how they can use them to show what can happen if people continue to use more nonrenewable energy sources than renewable energy sources. After you have approved their procedures, have pairs carry them out. Have pairs share their findings with the class.

MODIFICATION FOR INDEPENDENT Inquiry

Ask each student pair to think of a way to show the impact of using nonrenewable energy resources vs. renewable energy sources. Tell them to include several different variables in their procedure. Allow students to carry out all reasonable procedures. Have pairs share their findings with the class.

Quick Lab continued

Answer Key

2. Accept all reasonable answers.

4. Accept all reasonable answers.

5. Accept all reasonable answers.

6. Sample answer: There were more white beans because we replaced the white beans in the jar; we did not replace the red beans.

7. Sample answer: Nonrenewable resources are fossil fuels, such as natural gas, coal, and oil. Renewable resources are hydroelectric energy and solar energy.

8. Sample answer: This experiment shows that if we keep using nonrenewable resources, we will eventually use them up.

9. Sample answer: If the ratio of red to white beans changed, there would be more beans left at the end of the experiment. There still would be more white beans than red beans.

10. Sample answer: No. The red beans would still be used up more quickly than the white beans.

Name ______________________ Class ______________ Date ________________

QUICK LAB DIRECTED Inquiry

Modeling Renewable Energy

In this lab, you will model the impact of using nonrenewable and renewable energy sources. Through your model you will discover what the consequences of using too many nonrenewable energy sources can be.

OBJECTIVES

- Explain the difference between renewable and nonrenewable energy.
- Make conclusions about the environmental impact of different forms of energy.

MATERIALS

For each student

- blindfold
- bowl
- red beans, 90
- white beans, 10

PROCEDURE

1. Add **90 red beans** and **10 white beans** to the **bowl**. Mix them well. The red beans represent nonrenewable energy sources. The white beans represent renewable energy sources.

2. One student wears the **blindfold** and picks out 10 beans from the bowl. How many red beans did you pick? How many white beans?

   ____

   ____

3. Return only the white beans to the bowl. Mix them well.

4. Repeat steps 2 and 3 ten times. Record your observations after each time.

   ____

   ____

   ____

5. Count how many beans are left. How many beans are red? How many beans are white?

   ____

   ____

   ____

6. Explain why there are more white beans at the end of your experiment.

   ____

   ____

   ____

   ____

   ____

Quick Lab continued

7. Name some energy sources represented by the red beans. Name some energy sources represented by the white beans.

8. What does this model show about the environmental impact of using more nonrenewable than renewable resources?

9. How would the results of your experiment change if you changed the ratio of red beans to white beans to add more white beans?

10. Do you think the results of your experiment would change if you added 10 more red beans and no more white beans? Explain.

QUICK LAB INDEPENDENT Inquiry

Designing a Vehicle Using Alternative Energy BASIC

Student pairs
40 minutes

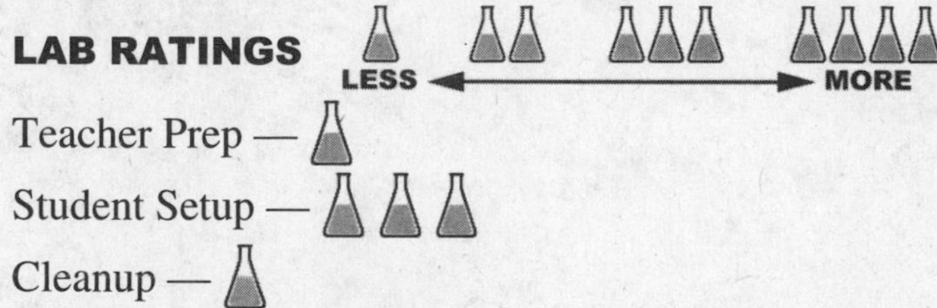

LAB RATINGS LESS ⟷ MORE

Teacher Prep — 1
Student Setup — 3
Cleanup — 1

MATERIALS

For each pair
- building materials, such as spools of thread, blocks, wheels, building toys
- energy source, such as solar cells, battery-operated fans, water wheels
- motors, 1.5–3V DC
- reference materials

For each student
- safety goggles

SAFETY INFORMATION

Remind students to review all safety cautions and icons before beginning this lab. Because students are designing their own experiments and determining the materials they are using, they need to identify potential dangers and account for them. You may wish to review all student plans to make sure safety concerns have been addressed.

My Notes

TEACHER NOTES

In this activity, students will design a toy vehicle that runs on an alternative energy source. Before assigning this lab, gather building materials for students to use. These include but are by no means limited to: solar cells, blocks, spools of thread, wheels, cardboard boxes, aluminum cans, dowels, straws, water wheels, and building toys. Encourage students to use the Design Process worksheet.

Tip Start this discussion by bringing in photos of different cars that use alternative energy sources and discussing the advantages and disadvantages of each. Students may need the entire 40 minutes to complete their vehicles. Allow one class period for research and design.

Skills Focus Designing Technology, Developing Procedures, Comparing Results

MODIFICATION FOR GUIDED Inquiry

Have student pairs design a vehicle that uses wind energy. Allow them to choose the materials they want to build the vehicle. Review all plans and designs and allow pairs to carry out all reasonable plans. Afterward, have a class vehicle show in which each pair shows their vehicle, and discuss the advantages and disadvantages of using wind energy.

Quick Lab continued

Answer Key

1. Accept all reasonable answers.
2. Accept all reasonable answers.
   Teacher Prompt A good plan will have a detailed procedure, describe what a successful outcome would be, include a list of materials, and take into account all variables.
3. Accept all reasonable answers.
4. Accept all reasonable answers.
5. Accept all reasonable answers.
6. Accept all reasonable answers.
7. Accept all reasonable answers.
8. Accept all reasonable answers.
   Teacher Prompt Have a class auto show when this activity is done. Display models in the classroom and have student pairs discuss their design and if it was a success.

Name ______________________ Class ____________ Date ________________

QUICK LAB INDEPENDENT *Inquiry*

Designing a Vehicle Using Alternative Energy

Maybe you have heard on the news how automakers are designing cars that run on alternative energy sources. In this lab, you will design a toy vehicle that runs on an alternative energy source.

OBJECTIVES

- Design a vehicle that runs on an alternative energy source.
- Discuss the advantages and disadvantages of alternative energy sources.

MATERIALS

For each pair

- building materials, such as spools of thread, blocks, wheels, building toys
- energy source, such as solar cells, battery-operated fans, water wheels
- motors, 1.5–3V DC
- reference materials

For each student

- safety goggles

PROCEDURE

1. Choose an alternative energy source. How can you use this energy source to power a vehicle?

   ____

   ____

   ____

2. Write a plan for building your vehicle. Include what materials you will use to build your vehicle and how you will use your energy source. Also include how you will measure your experiment's success.

   ____

   ____

   ____

   ____

   ____

   ____

   ____

   ____

3. Draw a picture of your design.

4. Carry out your plan. Did it work? What variables impacted the success of your experiment?

   ____

   ____

   ____

   ____

Quick Lab continued

5. Modify your design if necessary and retest. Did you get a different result?

6. Why did you choose the energy source you used in this experiment?

7. Did you achieve the results you expected with the energy source? Did the energy source perform differently than you expected?

8. Share your results with other student pairs. Based on your class's findings, which energy source worked best? Which energy source did not work?

EXPLORATION LAB GUIDED Inquiry AND INDEPENDENT Inquiry

Sustainable Resource Management

ADVANCED

Small groups
45 minutes

LAB RATINGS

LESS ← → MORE

Teacher Prep — 1
Student Setup — 2
Cleanup — 1

MATERIALS

For each group
- container
- craft sticks (200, including 10 bunches of 10)
- stopwatch

For each student
- safety goggles

SAFETY INFORMATION

Remind students to review all safety cautions and icons before beginning this lab. Because the simulation may involve rapid handling of materials, remind students to keep the materials under control. For the Independent Inquiry, review the students' plan for safety before they execute it.

My Notes

TEACHER NOTES

In this activity, students will model the unsustainable use of a renewable resource.

Before the activity, explain that a sustainable system is one that does not deplete a resource. For example, a sustainable system for obtaining wood from trees might use a strategy of replacing harvested trees at a fairly constant rate. A small forest of trees might be sustained by adding 25 new trees over a certain period of time. However, things may change if the demand for wood increases. For example, if the local human population doubles in any given time period, twice as many trees will be harvested to meet their demands. This is equal to a 100 percent increase in harvesting from the period before. If the demand becomes too great, the number of harvestable trees will begin to decline.

In the Guided Inquiry, instruct the students to use the materials provided to make a model demonstrating unsustainable forest management. In their model, students should represent trees that are replenished at a constant rate. Students also need to represent a human population that grows exponentially and uses trees at a certain human-to-tree ratio. Students will work in small groups of three or more to develop and run the simulation. The students run the simulation until there are no trees left. The students record what happened in a provided data table, and then construct a column graph of the number of trees in the forest at the end of every year.

In the Independent Inquiry, instruct students to model an exponentially increasing population harvesting renewable resources over time. Students should run the simulation until the resources are exhausted. Results should be communicated in the form of a graph. Students work in small groups to develop and run their simulations.

Tip Ensure that the students are clear on the difference between basic linear ($y = ax$, where a is a constant) and basic exponential ($y = a^x$, where a is a constant) functions.

Skills Focus Developing Models, Collecting Data, Interpreting Results

Exploration Lab continued

MODIFICATION FOR DIRECTED Inquiry

Instruct the students to use 120 craft sticks in a coffee can to model trees in a forest, to add trees at a rate of one every 15 seconds (four per year), and to remove twice the number of trees each minute as were removed the minute before, recording and graphing the results as in the guided inquiry. An interesting variation is to assume that only 10% of the forest's trees reproduce in a given year, so the number of trees added each year is 10% of the trees remaining at the end of the previous year. Either way, using these numbers, the forest is depleted by the eighth year.

Answer Key for GUIDED Inquiry

DEVELOP A PLAN

1. Sample plan:
Starting number of trees: 120
Annual constant tree replenishment rate: 10
How the simulation will be run: We'll start with 120 craft sticks in the coffee can, which will represent the forest. Amy will be the timekeeper and say "time" every 6 seconds. José will be the logger. At the end of every minute, he will take twice as many trees for the population as he did the minute before. Desireé will be the forester and plant one tree every 6 seconds.

FORM A HYPOTHESIS

2. Sample answer: As the number of years increases, the number of trees in the forest will <u>increase, and then decrease</u> because <u>the growing population will overwhelm the planting rate</u>.

TEST THE HYPOTHESIS

4. Sample data:

Tree Harvest over Time

Year	Number of trees at the start of the year	Number of new trees added	Number of trees harvested (one per person)	Number of trees at the end of the year	Cumulative harvest of trees
1	120	10	1	129	1
2	129	10	2	137	3
3	137	10	4	143	7
4	143	10	8	145	15
5	145	10	16	139	31
6	139	10	32	117	63
7	117	10	64	63	127
8	63	10	73 (all remaining, although population = 128)	0	200

Exploration Lab continued

ANALYZE THE RESULTS

5. Sample answer: Our forest failed in the eighth year. At first the number of trees increased, but the doubling population quickly caught up and used up all 200 trees.

6. Graphs will vary based on the experimental data in the tables. Check to see that students correctly applied their data to make the graph.

DRAW CONCLUSIONS

7. Sample answer: Our data supported my hypothesis. The number of trees did increase and then decrease because a resource being replenished at a constant rate can't keep up with an exponential use rate.

8. Sample answer: To get the forest to last for 10 years, we could plant 100 trees a year. But the forest would last only 10 years; it would fail in the eleventh. Or, we could limit the population growth or the tree use to only grow by a factor of 1.5 each year. That might be hard to do. People would have to have fewer babies, stop moving to the area, or conserve more and more.

9. Sample answer: The only way for the forest to be sustainable is for the harvesting rate to be the same as the replenishment rate. We probably can't plant trees at an exponential rate, so we will have to harvest them at the same constant rate that they are planted, even if the population continues to increase.

Connect TO THE ESSENTIAL QUESTION

10. Sample answer: Renewable resources can't be used up at a rate faster than they can be replaced, or the environment will be permanently harmed. For example, if so many trees are harvested from a forest that they can no longer reproduce, the forest will die out. The use of resources has to be carefully managed so that doesn't happen.

11. Sample answer: You can't manage a nonrenewable resource "sustainably" because it doesn't get replaced as it is used up. Even if the people are careful about how much they use, it will eventually be gone. If it gets harder and harder to get, it could start to cost more, and people might start to fight over it. They might become more willing to hurt the environment to get it. It would be important to manage a nonrenewable resource carefully until it could be replaced by a renewable one.

Answer Key for INDEPENDENT Inquiry

DEVELOP A PLAN

1. Sample plan: Resource modeled: Water in a well

Unit of measure for the resource: thousands of liters; 1 milliliter (mL) in the model = 1000 liter (L)

Starting number of resource units: 500 thousand L (500 mL in the model)

Factor by which the population increases annually: 1.5

Annual constant resource replenishment rate: 25 thousand L (25 mL in the model)

Exploration Lab continued

How the simulation will be run: We will model thousands of liters of water in a well with milliliters of water in our simulation. We'll start with 500 mL of water in a small container. Anand will be the timekeeper and say "time" every minute. Natsumi will be the aquifer and will add 25 mL of water to the container every minute. Every minute, Renee, acting as the population, will use a siphon to take 150% of the water she did the minute before.

FORM A HYPOTHESIS

2. Sample answer: As the number of years increases, the amount of water in the well will increase, then decrease because the growing population will overwhelm the renewal rate.

TEST THE HYPOTHESIS

4. Sample data: Unit: thousands of liters of water

Resource Use over Time

Year	Number of resource units at the start of the year	Number of new units added	Number of units used (one per person)	Number of units at the end of the year	Cumulative use of units
1	500	25	1	524	1
2	524	25	2	547.5	2.5
3	547.5	25	4	570.3	4.8
4	570.3	25	8	591.9	8.1
5	591.9	25	16	611.8	13.2
6, etc	...	...	...	...	...

ANALYZE THE RESULTS

5. Sample answer: Our well failed in the sixteenth year. At first the amount of water increased, but the doubling population quickly caught up and used up all the water.

6. Graphs will vary based on the experimental data in the tables.

DRAW CONCLUSIONS

7. Sample answer: Our data supported my hypothesis. The amount of water did increase and then decrease because a resource being replenished at a constant rate can't keep up with an exponential use rate.

8. Sample answer: Our well did last for 10 years, but after that the water level started going down quickly. The population would have had to conserve more and more, and each person would have been getting less and less, or the population would have to stop growing.

Exploration Lab continued

9. Sample answer: The only way for the water supply to be sustainable is for the withdrawal rate to be the same as the replenishment rate. The Earth probably won't produce water for the well any faster than it does already, so the population would have to learn to use the water at the same constant rate that it is available, even if the population continues to increase.

Connect TO THE ESSENTIAL QUESTION

10. Sample answer: Renewable resources can't be used up at a rate faster than they can be replaced, or the environment will be permanently harmed. For example, if a freshwater well near the ocean is overdrawn, saltwater may get into the aquifer and permanently spoil the well. The use of resources has to be carefully managed so that doesn't happen.

11. Sample answer: You can't manage a nonrenewable resource "sustainably" because it doesn't get replaced as it is used up. Even if the people are careful about how much they use, it will eventually be gone. If it gets harder and harder to get, it could start to cost more, and people might start to fight over it. They might become more willing to hurt the environment to get it. It would be important to manage a nonrenewable resource carefully until it could be replaced by a renewable one.

Name ______________________ Class ______________ Date ______________

EXPLORATION LAB GUIDED Inquiry

Sustainable Resource Management

Humans use natural renewable resources such as food, fibers for clothing, building supplies, medicines, and energy. Some resources, such as solar energy, are available at a constant rate regardless of how much humans use. Humans must be careful, however, to manage other kinds of renewable resources so that their use does not exceed their replacement rate. In this activity, you will model a limited renewable resource being used by a growing population.

OBJECTIVE

- Create a model to show how a renewable resource is used by a growing human population.

MATERIALS

For each group
- container
- craft sticks (200, including 10 bunches of 10)
- stopwatch

For each student
- safety goggles

PROCEDURE

Develop a model to simulate the harvest of trees from a forest. Assume that each member of the population needs one tree each year for building materials and heating fuel. During each year, the population doubles, while new trees are added naturally or planted in the forest at a constant rate.

DEVELOP A PLAN

1. Working with your group, review the available materials and the above information to develop a physical model for a population harvesting the trees. Model 1 year with 1 minute on the stopwatch, and begin with a population of one. Run the simulation until the forest disappears. Record your plan below:

   Starting number of trees: ______________________

   Annual constant tree replacement rate: ______________________

   How the simulation will be run: ______________________

   ____

   ____

   ____

   ____

FORM A HYPOTHESIS

2. Complete the sentence below:

   As the number of years increases, the number of trees in the forest will ____________ (increase/decrease) because ______________________

   ____.

Name ______________________ Class ______________ Date ______________

Exploration Lab continued

BUILD A MODEL

3. Work with your group to use the materials to set up your simulation.

TEST THE HYPOTHESIS

4. Follow your plan for the simulation. Use the blank table below or a separate sheet to record your data. You may not need all the columns or rows provided, or you may need to collect more data than shown in the table below.

Tree Harvest over Time					
Year	**Number of trees at the start of the year**	**Number of new trees added**	**Number of trees harvested (one per person)**	**Number of trees at the end of the year**	**Cumulative harvest of trees**
1			1		
2					
3					
4					
5					
6					

ANALYZE THE RESULTS

5. **Describing Events** Describe what happened during your simulation. How many years did your forest last? How many trees were harvested altogether?

____

____

____

____

6. **Constructing Graphs** Make a bar graph of your results. Place years on the *x*-axis and the number of trees remaining at the end of each year on the *y*-axis.

Exploration Lab continued

DRAW CONCLUSIONS

7. **Evaluating Hypotheses** Was your hypothesis supported by your data? Explain why or why not.

____
____
____

8. **Evaluate the Plan** Suggest two different ways that the forest could be managed to last for 10 years. Predict what effect this plan might have on the human population.

____
____
____
____

9. **Evaluate the Plan** Describe a plan of sustainable harvest that could allow the forest to last indefinitely. Predict what effect this plan could have on the human population.

____
____
____
____

Connect TO THE ESSENTIAL QUESTION

10. **Applying Concepts** Explain the relationship between the management of renewable resources and the environment. Give an example from your model of a possible permanent environmental consequence of poor resource management.

____
____
____
____

Exploration Lab continued

11 **Making Inferences** Humans currently depend on being able to collect and use fossil fuels easily and inexpensively. We are using more and more of these nonrenewable resources as our population increases. Sometimes the environment is threatened or harmed when we gather or use these fuels. Some scientists believe that, although we will not "run out" of these resources soon, the portion that was easy to obtain at low cost has already been extracted. How would the management of such nonrenewable resources be different from the management of renewable resources?

____

____

____

____

Name ______________________ Class ______________ Date ______________

EXPLORATION LAB INDEPENDENT Inquiry

Sustainable Resource Management

Humans use natural renewable resources for food, fibers for clothing, building supplies, medicines, and energy. Some resources, such as solar energy, are available at a constant rate regardless of how much humans use. Humans must be careful, however, to manage other kinds of resources so that their use does not exceed the replacement rate. In this activity, you will model a renewable resource being used by a growing population.

OBJECTIVE

- Create a model to show how a renewable resource is used by a growing human population.

MATERIALS

For each group

- materials representing the renewable resource
- stopwatch

PROCEDURE

Develop a model to simulate the use of a renewable resource by a population. Model 1 year with 1 minute on the stopwatch, and begin with a population of one. Assume that each member of the population needs one unit of the resource each year. During each year, the population increases over the previous years' by a factor you determine, while the resource is replaced at a constant rate you set.

DEVELOP A PLAN

 Working with your group, review the available materials and the above information to develop a physical model for a population using a resource. Plan to run your simulation until the resource is used up. Record your plan below, and have your teacher approve it before proceeding:

Resource modeled: ______________________

Unit of measure for the resource: ______________________

Starting number of resource units: ______________________

Factor by which the population increases annually: ______________

Annual constant resource replacement rate: ______________

How the simulation will be run:

____

____

____

____

Teacher approval: ______________________

Name ______________________________ Class ________________ Date ______________________

Exploration Lab continued

FORM A HYPOTHESIS

2 Complete the sentence below:

As the number of years increases, the amount of ____________ (resource) will ____________ (increase/decrease) because ______________________

____.

BUILD A MODEL

3 Work with your group to use the materials to set up your simulation.

TEST THE HYPOTHESIS

4 Follow your plan for the simulation. Use the blank table below or a separate sheet to record your data. You may not need all the columns or rows provided, or you may choose to collect more data than the table has space for.

Resource and its units of measure: ____________________

Resource Use over Time					
Year	Number of resource units at the start of the year	Number of new units added	Number of units used (one per person)	Number of units at the end of the year	Cumulative use of units
1			1		
2					
3					
4					
5					
6					

ANALYZE THE RESULTS

5 **Describing Events** Describe what happened during your simulation. How many years did your resource last? How many units of the resource were used altogether?

____

____

____

6 **Constructing Graphs** Make a graph illustrating your results. Place years on the *x*-axis.

Exploration Lab continued

DRAW CONCLUSIONS

7. **Evaluating Hypotheses** Was your hypothesis supported by your data? Explain why or why not.

8. **Evaluate the Plan** Suggest two different ways that the resource could be managed to last for at least 10 years. Describe the effect this plan might have on the human population.

9. **Evaluate the Plan** Describe a plan of resource use that could allow the resource to last indefinitely. Predict the effect this plan might have on the human population.

Connect TO THE ESSENTIAL QUESTION

10. **Applying Concepts** Explain the relationship between the management of renewable resources and the environment. Give an example from your model of a possible permanent consequence of poor resource management.

11. **Making Inferences** Humans currently depend on being able to collect and use fossil fuels easily and inexpensively. We are using more and more of these nonrenewable resources as our population increases. Sometimes the environment is threatened or harmed when we gather or use these fuels. Some scientists believe that, although we will not "run out" of these resources soon, the portion that was easy to obtain at a low cost has already been extracted. How would the management of such nonrenewable resources be different from the management of renewable resources?

QUICK LAB DIRECTED Inquiry

Investigate the Size of Atomic Particles GENERAL

Student pairs
30 minutes

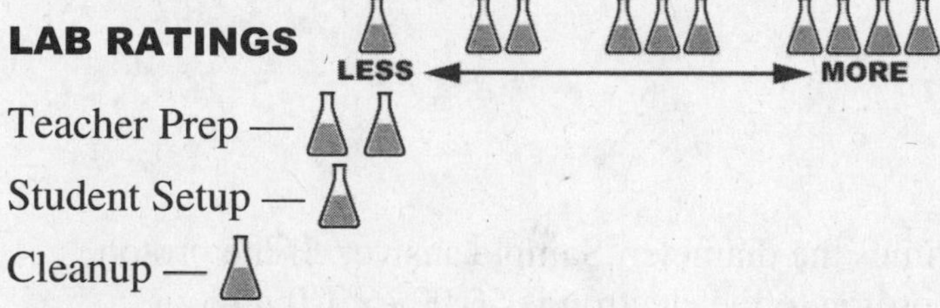

Teacher Prep —
Student Setup —
Cleanup —

MATERIALS

For each pair of students

- calculator
- meterstick
- peas, dried
- pencil
- ruler, metric
- scissors
- yarn, 70 m

My Notes

SAFETY INFORMATION

Remind students to review all safety cautions and icons before beginning this lab. If you wish, you may restrict the use of scissors by cutting the yarn yourself.

TEACHER NOTES

In this activity, students will build a scale model of a proton and an electron in a hydrogen atom. Provide students with information regarding the relative mass of the proton and the electron. The mass of a proton is about 1,800 times greater than the mass of an electron. Then, tell students that the distance of the electron from the proton is 50,000 times the diameter of the proton. Ensure students have enough room to build the scale model. To have enough space, it may be necessary to use a hallway or even a playing field. Alert in advance instructors who might be affected by students working in the vicinity, and take the steps needed to prevent distractions to other classes. If outside space is unavailable, suggest that students use a smaller point that can be drawn, but still visualized, such as a dot of 0.1 millimeter (mm), to represent the proton. This will require the electron to be about 5 meters (m) away (rather than 50 m). Inform the students that if a calculator is unavailable, calculations can be done long-hand. If peas are unavailable as a material, have students suggest an acceptable substitute (any small, spherical object).

Tip Engage students by explaining that this lab demonstrates we're primarily made of empty space!

Student Tip If you can't build the scale model with the available space and materials, consider adjusting the scale.

Skills Focus Devising Procedures, Drawing Conclusions, Calculating Results

Quick Lab continued

MODIFICATION FOR GUIDED *Inquiry*

Allow students to choose the size of the circle they wish to draw in Step 1 of the procedure, and then allow them to follow through on the remainder of the procedure with minimal direction. Students may make a circle that is so large that the length of yarn they need to model the distance to the electron exceeds the length of yarn they have available. Allow students to go back to Step 1 and begin again with a smaller circle, and repeat until they are able to make a viable model.

Answer Key

1. Answers will vary.
2. Answers will vary.
3. The answer should be equal to 50,000 times the diameter. Sample answer: If the proton diameter is 1.0 mm, the distance of the proton to the electron is 50,000 × 1.0 mm, or 50,000 mm. This is the same as 50 m or 0.05 kilometers (km).
   Teacher Prompt Does it make sense to use units of millimeters for your answer?
4. Accept all reasonable answers.
5. Sample answer: The length of yarn needed is 50 m.
   Teacher Prompt What length of yarn do you need to represent the distance of the electron from the proton?
6. Answers will vary. Look for students to realize that the distances between particles in an atom are much larger than the sizes of the particles themselves.
7. Accept all reasonable answers. Sample answer: The pea is 5.0 mm.
   Teacher Prompt What is the size of the pea?
8. Answers will vary. Sample answer: If the proton diameter is 5.0 mm, the distance of the proton to the electron is 50,000 × 5.0 mm, or 250,000 mm. This is the same as 250 m or 0.25 km.
9. Empty space
   Teacher Prompt If the proton is the size of the pea and the electron is 0.25 km away, what occupies the space in between the two?
10. The electron moves around the nucleus in a certain region and does not stay in one place.
    Teacher Prompt What do we know about the behavior of electrons in an atom?

Name ______________________ Class ______________ Date ______________

QUICK LAB DIRECTED Inquiry

Investigate the Size of Atomic Particles

In this lab, you will build a scale model of a hydrogen atom. Your teacher will provide information regarding the relative size of the proton compared with the relative distance of an electron from a proton in a hydrogen atom.

OBJECTIVE

- Build a model to demonstrate aspects of atomic structure.

MATERIALS

For each pair of students

- calculator
- meterstick
- peas, dried
- pencil
- ruler, metric
- scissors
- yarn, 70 m

PROCEDURE

1. Draw a small circle about 1 millimeter (mm) (0.1 centimeter [cm]) in diameter in the space below.

2. Measure and record the diameter of the circle.

   ____

3. Assuming the diameter of the circle represents a proton, calculate the relative distance of the electron from the proton in a hydrogen atom. Show your calculation in the space below.

4. Roll out a length of yarn to reflect the length you just calculated; this will illustrate the relative distance of the electron from the proton.

5. What was the length of yarn you used?

   ____

6. What can you conclude when comparing the size of the proton with the distance of the electron from the proton?

   ____

   ____

7. Measure the diameter of a pea with the metric ruler and record this value.

   ____

Quick Lab continued

8 Assuming the diameter of the pea represents a proton, calculate the relative distance of the electron from the proton in a hydrogen atom.

9 What do you think lies between the proton and the electron in a hydrogen atom?

____

____

10 Is the electron always in one spot in a hydrogen atom, or does its position change?

____

____

QUICK LAB INDEPENDENT *Inquiry*

Investigate Masses of Atomic Particles BASIC

Small groups
30 minutes

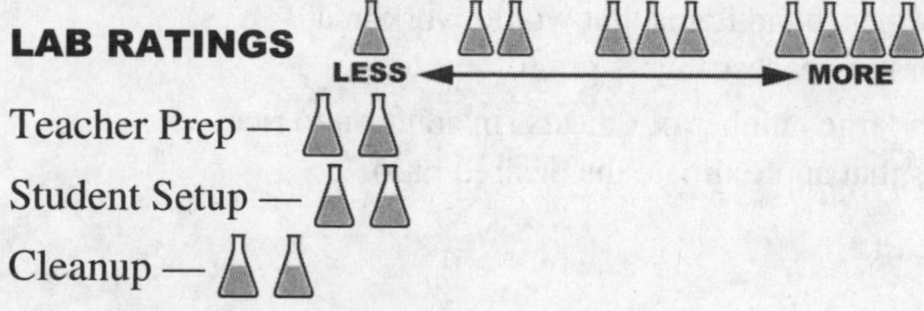

MATERIALS

For each group
- balance
- clay
- containers (2)
- sand
- water

For each student
- lab apron
- safety goggles

SAFETY INFORMATION

Remind students to review all safety cautions and icons before beginning this lab. Make sure students wash their hands thoroughly at the end of the activity. If they use clay, you may wish to have them wear gloves. If they use sand, have them wear safety goggles.

TEACHER NOTES

In this activity, students are challenged to make a model that demonstrates the relative masses of electrons, protons, and neutrons. Ask them the following: Is it possible to use a common, everyday substance to compare the masses of electrons, protons, and neutrons? Make clay, sand, and water available as material options. Provide students with the mass ratios of protons, electrons, and neutrons. The difference in mass between an electron and a proton or neutron is approximately 1:1,800. The electronic balances in your classroom may not be able to measure this range. In these cases, students will need to make smaller units of mass that they can add together to make their models. For example, if they use a small clay ball of 0.1 gram (g) to represent an electron, then four 45 g clay blocks can be put together to represent the mass of a proton.

Tip This activity will help students visualize the difference in mass between an electron and a proton.

Student Tip Think about how you can add materials together to represent the mass of a proton.

Skills Focus Planning Investigations, Devising Procedures, Drawing Conclusions

My Notes

Quick Lab continued

MODIFICATION FOR GUIDED *Inquiry*

Assign students the material they should use for the activity, but allow them to develop their procedure.

An Arborio rice grain weighs about 0.03 g. A tennis ball weighs about 60 g or less. These masses roughly approximate the ratio of an electron to a proton. Since the mass of the rice grain is less than a decigram balance can measure, students can weigh 10, 50, or 100 grains and divide to calculate the approximate mass of one grain. (Let students themselves decide to do this.) You should be able to locate other round items that would work in a similar way. A centigram balance is desirable for masses less than 1 gram.

Instead of having students use clay, provide a large number of objects (in addition to rice and tennis balls) and have students select objects that approximate the desired ratio.

Answer Key

1. Accept all reasonable answers.
2. Accept all reasonable answers.
3. Accept all reasonable answers.
4. Answers will vary. Students will likely run into the problem that limitations of the balance make it impossible to weigh a sample of clay/sand/water that accurately represents an electron and to weigh another sample 1,800 times as large.
   Teacher Prompt What can you do to build up the mass of a proton that is 1,800 times larger than your electron mass?
5. Accept all reasonable answers.
6. Sample answer: The proton has much more mass than the electron.
7. Sample answer: No, I would have seen the same difference in the amount of material, so I would have come to the same conclusion no matter what material I used.

Name ______________________ Class ______________ Date ______________

QUICK LAB INDEPENDENT *Inquiry*

Investigate Masses of Atomic Particles

In this lab, you will make a model that demonstrates the relative mass of electrons, protons, and neutrons. Is it possible to use a common, everyday substance to compare the mass of electrons, protons, and neutrons?

OBJECTIVE

- Use everyday substances to compare the relative masses of the electron and the proton.

MATERIALS

For each group
- balance
- clay
- containers (2)
- sand
- water

For each student
- lab apron
- safety goggles

PROCEDURE

1. As a group, discuss how you will make a model to show two masses that represent large-scale versions of an electron and a proton. Decide what material you will use to make your model and decide what procedure you will follow. Record both in the space below.

2. Have your teacher approve your material choice and procedure.

3. Carry out your procedure and note any observations you make as you work through your process.

4. Did you run into any problems as you worked through your procedure? If so, what problems did you encounter and how did you solve them?

Name ________________________________ Class ________________ Date ______________________

Quick Lab continued

5. Draw a diagram in the space below representing your final model.

6. What conclusion can you draw about the relative mass of an electron and a proton based on your model?

____

____

7. Do you think you would have reached a different conclusion if you had used a different type of material in making your model? Why or why not?

____

____

QUICK LAB GUIDED *Inquiry*

A Model Atom GENERAL

Individual student
15 minutes

LAB RATINGS LESS ⟷ MORE

Teacher Prep — 1
Student Setup — 1
Cleanup — 1

MATERIALS

For each student

- pencils, colored
- periodic table of elements
- plates, paper (3)

My Notes

TEACHER NOTES

In this activity, students will compare the number of valence electrons for adjacent elements on the periodic table. Students will choose one element, compare its valence electron number to horizontally and vertically adjacent elements, and draw a model of each.

Tip This activity may help students understand that different elements have different numbers of valence electrons.

Skills Focus Making Models, Comparing Models

MODIFICATION FOR DIRECTED *Inquiry*

Assign three elements to each student. Choose elements from three different rows, and make sure that two of the elements are in the same column. Make sure that all three elements are located within the first three groups of the periodic table. Instruct students to determine the number of valence electrons for each element and to draw a model of each element. You may wish to show an example of a model so that students know what features to include. Once students have completed their models, have them answer the questions on the Student Page.

Answer Key

3. Answers will vary.
5. Sample answer: There is one more valence electron in the first model.
7. They are the same.
8. Sample answer: The number of valence electrons increases from left to right and does not change as you go up or down.

Name ______________________ Class ______________ Date ______________

QUICK LAB GUIDED Inquiry

A Model Atom

In this lab, you will examine the relationship between an element's location on the periodic table and its number of valence electrons. You will use this information to draw models of three elements and their valence shells.

OBJECTIVE

- Draw models of different elements and their valence shells.

MATERIALS

For each student

- pencils, colored
- periodic table of elements
- plates, paper (3)

PROCEDURE

1. Select any element from the first three periods of the **periodic table of elements**.
2. On a **paper plate**, draw a model of an atom of your chosen element by using **colored pencils**.
3. How many valence electrons does your atom have?

   ____

4. Now, choose an element that appears directly next to your chosen element on the periodic table and draw its model.
5. How does the number of valence electrons vary between the two models?

   ____

   ____

   ____

   ____

   ____

   ____

6. Now, choose an element that appears directly below your first element on the periodic table and draw its model.

Quick Lab continued

❼ How does the number of valence electrons vary between the first and third models?

____

____

____

____

____

____

____

❽ How does the number of valence electrons in an element change as you move across the periodic table? How does it change as you move down the periodic table?

____

____

____

____

____

____

____

____

____

____

____

____

____

____

____

____

____

QUICK LAB DIRECTED *Inquiry*

Predicting Properties GENERAL

Individual student
20 minutes

MATERIALS

For each student

- graph paper
- periodic table

LAB RATINGS LESS ← → MORE

Teacher Prep — 1
Student Setup — 1
Cleanup — 1

My Notes

TEACHER NOTES

In this activity, students will observe trends in the periodic table by graphing values for atomic radii. They will interpret trends in graphed data to predict the atomic radii values for missing elements. Values of atomic radii vary in a predictable way across the periodic table. Generally, radii decrease across each row (period) and increase down each column (group). The radius increases dramatically between the noble gas at the end of each row and the alkali metal at the beginning of the next row. Values of atomic radii in the data table have been rounded up to make graphing easier. You can provide students with copies of the periodic table if they do not have one in their textbooks.

Student Tip Determine the scale for your line graph by looking at the range of values on the data table.

Skills Focus Constructing Graphs, Identifying Patterns, Making Inferences

MODIFICATION FOR GUIDED *Inquiry*

Have students determine the best type of graph for the data in the table. Students should design their own graphs at an appropriate scale and with the correct axis labels. Graphs should represent the trend in atomic radii as it relates to the structure of the atomic table. Students should be able to use their graphs to answer the questions in Steps 2–5.

Quick Lab continued

Answer Key

1. Sample graph:

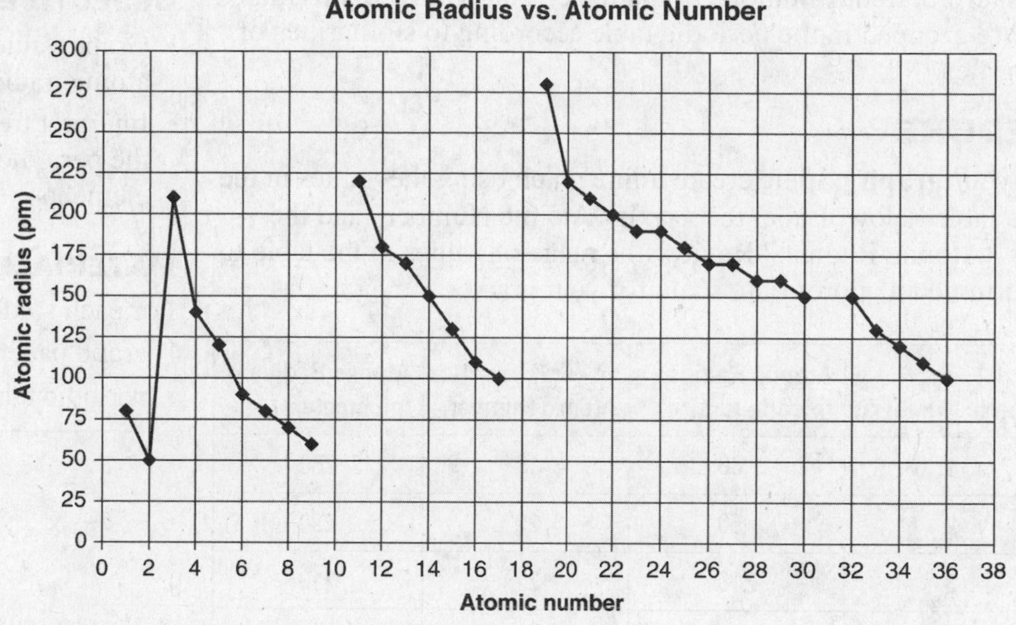

2. Sample answer: The line drops steadily and then jumps and begins to drop again in a zigzag pattern.

3. Sample answer: The zigzags in the graph relate to the periods in the table. Each jump in the line marks the beginning of a new period in the table.

Teacher Prompt What happens to the graph at elements 3, 11, and 19? What is significant about these elements? Sample answer: The line of the graph jumps at elements 3, 11, and 19, which is significant because those elements mark the beginning of a new period in the table.

4. Sample answer: The values for atomic radii generally decrease across a period and increase down a group.

5. Sample answer: 50, 90, 150

Teacher Prompt Based on the element's location in the periodic table, would the atomic radius be larger or smaller than the previous element Sample answer: The atomic radius would be smaller, because atomic radius decreases across a period in the periodic table.

Name ______________________ Class ______________ Date ____________________

QUICK LAB DIRECTED *Inquiry*

Predicting Properties

In this lab, you will create a graph of atomic radius values and use the graph to interpret trends in the periodic table. You will recognize that elements are grouped in the periodic table according to similarities of their properties.

OBJECTIVES

- Graph values for atomic radii.
- Interpret trends in the periodic table of elements.

MATERIALS

For each student

- graph paper
- periodic table

PROCEDURE

1. On your **graph paper**, create a line graph using the values in the data table below. Label the x-axis "Atomic Number" and the y-axis "Atomic Radius." Review the range of values in the table to determine an appropriate scale for your graph.

Atomic Number	Atomic Radius (picometers)	Atomic Number	Atomic Radius (picometers)
1	80	19	280
2	50	20	220
3	210	21	210
4	140	22	200
5	120	23	190
6	90	24	190
7	80	25	180
8	70	26	170
9	60	27	170
10	?	28	160
11	220	29	160
12	180	30	150
13	170	31	?
14	150	32	150
15	130	33	130
16	110	34	120
17	100	35	110
18	?	36	100

Quick Lab continued

2. Describe the pattern you see in the graph.

3. Compare your graph to the **periodic table of elements**. How does the pattern relate to the structure in the periodic table?

4. What trends do you observe about the the relationship between atomic radius and atomic number in the periodic table?

5. Based on these trends, what are the approximate values of the atomic radii of elements 10, 18, and 20?

QUICK LAB DIRECTED Inquiry

Recognizing Patterns GENERAL

Individual student
15 minutes

LAB RATINGS

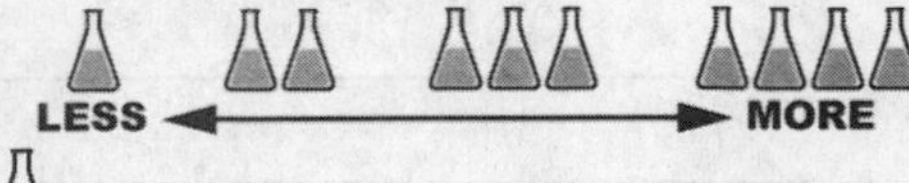

Teacher Prep —
Student Setup —
Cleanup —

MATERIAL

For each student

- periodic table of elements

My Notes

TEACHER NOTES

In this activity, students will organize a given set of elements by atomic number in order to fill out a table. They will then use the information given about the elements to predict what other elements belong in the table. Do not provide students with a periodic table until they have reached the final step in the exercise.

Skills Focus Identifying Patterns

MODIFICATION FOR GUIDED Inquiry

Make copies of the periodic table for each student. Before giving students the tables, use corrective fluid or a black marker to cover the atomic numbers of various elements. Challenge students to figure out the missing atomic numbers and write them in the appropriate spaces.

Answer Key

1–3.

15 P Phosphorus 30.9	16 S Sulfur 32.0	17 Cl Chlorine 35.5
33 As Arsenic 74.9	34 Se Selenium 79.0	35 Br Bromine 79.9
51 Sb Antimony 121.8	52 Te Tellurium 127.6	53 I Iodine 126.9

Name ______________________ Class ______________ Date ______________

QUICK LAB DIRECTED Inquiry

Recognizing Patterns

In this lab, you will construct a table that organizes elements according to atomic number. You will then use the table to predict the atomic numbers and identities of other elements.

OBJECTIVE

- Predict the atomic numbers of elements in a table.

MATERIAL

For each group

- periodic table of the elements

PROCEDURE

1. Fill out the empty cells in the table below using the elements given. Place elements in the table from left to right in order of increasing atomic number. Be sure to label each element with its correct symbol, atomic number, and mass.

	(shaded)	
(shaded)	(shaded)	(shaded)

Elements:
Phosphorus (P, 15, 30.9)
Arsenic (As, 33, 74.9)
Sulfur (S, 16, 32.0)
Bromine (Br, 35, 79.9)
Chlorine (Cl, 17, 35.5)

2. Using the data from the first two rows, predict the atomic numbers of the elements in the shaded cells. Write the numbers in the appropriate shaded cells.

3. Now look at a periodic table of elements. Complete the table with the names, symbols, and atomic masses of the elements in the shaded cells.

QUICK LAB GUIDED Inquiry

What's in a Change? GENERAL

Small groups
20 minutes

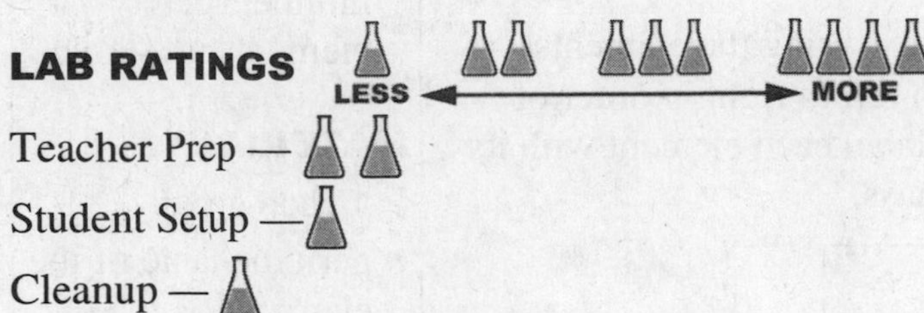

LAB RATINGS

LESS ⟷ MORE

Teacher Prep —
Student Setup —
Cleanup —

MATERIALS

For each group
- colored pencils
- hydrogen molecule model (2)
- oxygen molecule model (1)
- plain paper

For each student
- safety goggles

My Notes

SAFETY INFORMATION

Remind students to review all safety cautions and icons before beginning this lab. Instruct students to not eat the marshmallows and to use caution not to poke themselves with the toothpicks.

TEACHER NOTES

In this activity, students will model a chemical reaction between hydrogen and oxygen and predict how those molecules will combine to form water.

Prepare the model hydrogen and oxygen molecules in advance. Hydrogen molecules can be modeled using one toothpick connecting two mini-marshmallows. Oxygen molecules can be modeled using two toothpicks connecting two regular-size marshmallows. To protect and contain models, prepare activity packs for each student group using a sealable plastic bag containing two hydrogen molecules and one oxygen molecule.

Tip This activity may help students understand the law of conservation of mass.

Skills Focus Making Models, Evaluating Models

MODIFICATION FOR DIRECTED Inquiry

Instead of asking students to figure out how to build a water molecule, provide them with instructions for using the materials in the hydrogen and oxygen models to build the water model. Provide step-by-step directions that describe the arrangement of the atoms and bonds. Then, have students construct a water molecule and answer the questions on the student activity sheet.

Quick Lab continued

Answer Key

1. Answers will vary but should correctly represent the chemical characteristics of each molecule (number of bonds, atoms).
2. Answers will vary but should contain two small hydrogen atoms and one large oxygen atom connected by a single bond.
4. Sample answer: I had to take the original models apart and rearrange the parts to make the new model. Taking the models apart represents the breaking of chemical bonds.
5. Sample answer: The toothpicks and marshmallows are arranged and connected differently.
6. Sample answer: a chemical reaction
7. Sample answer: None of the toothpicks or marshmallows was destroyed; the toothpicks and marshmallows were just reorganized.

Name ________________________ Class ______________ Date ________________

QUICK LAB GUIDED Inquiry

What's in a Change?

In this lab, you model a chemical reaction between hydrogen and oxygen molecules by combining them to form water. You will explore the law of conservation of mass by demonstrating that mass is conserved when substances undergo physical and chemical changes.

OBJECTIVES

- Model a chemical reaction.
- Model a water molecule.
- Describe the law of conservation of mass.

MATERIALS

For each group

- colored pencils
- hydrogen molecule model (2)
- oxygen molecule model (1)
- plain paper

For each student

- safety goggles

PROCEDURE

1. Examine the **model hydrogen and oxygen molecules**. Using **colored pencils**, sketch each molecule on your **paper**. Label your sketch with the different parts of the molecules and the chemical formula for each molecule.

2. Recall that the chemical formula for water is H_2O. Observe your hydrogen and oxygen molecules, and predict how you could combine them to make a water molecule. On your paper, sketch a diagram of what you think a water molecule might look like.

3. Use your hydrogen and oxygen models to build a new model of a water molecule.

4. What did you have to do to make a water molecule from the hydrogen and oxygen molecules? What chemical process does this model?

____

____

____

____

Quick Lab continued

5 How is the water molecule different from the oxygen and hydrogen molecules?

6 What process took place when you combined the hydrogen and oxygen into water?

7 How does this activity illustrate the law of conservation of mass?

QUICK LAB GUIDED Inquiry

Sharing Electrons GENERAL

Individual student

20 minutes

LAB RATINGS LESS ←→ MORE

Teacher Prep — 1

Student Setup — 1

Cleanup — 1

MATERIALS

For each student

- paper
- pencil, colored
- periodic table, copy
- tape, masking

My Notes

SAFETY INFORMATION

Remind students to review all safety cautions and icons before beginning this lab. Instruct students to use caution and to respect each other's personal space when they are moving about the classroom.

TEACHER NOTES

In this activity, students will choose 1 element from the first 3 periods of the periodic table. Students will draw a Bohr model representing an atom of their chosen element. Then, they will tape their drawing to the front of their body and circulate among each other. As they move throughout the classroom, they will search for atoms with which their atom could bond.

For this lab, students should not necessarily be able to identify whether an atom will form ionic, covalent, or metallic bonds. In other words, they may not yet be able to distinguish between instances in which atoms will gain or lose electrons and instances in which atoms share electrons.

Tip Make sure students are comfortable with the idea of valence electrons. You may wish to have a sample Bohr model on display for your students to view.

Skills Focus Constructing Models, Evaluating Predictions

MODIFICATION FOR DIRECTED Inquiry

Rather than allowing students to choose any element from the first three periods of the periodic table, assign half of the class one preselected element and the other half of the class another preselected element. These elements should be ones whose atoms are likely to form bonds with each other, such as sodium, with one valence electron, and chlorine, with seven valence electrons. Then, students with drawings of atoms of one element will pair with students of the other element and will explain how and why the bond between their atoms occurs. If your students do this lab at the directed inquiry level, they can still complete Steps 2–8 in the Procedures section.

Quick Lab continued

Answer Key

1. Answers may vary. Student answers should name one element from the first three periods of the periodic table and correctly identify how many total electrons an atom of the element contains.

Teacher Prompt Where do you look on the periodic table to find information about the number of electrons that atoms of an element contain?

3 Answers will vary. Because students are only using atoms from the first three periods, the outermost energy level will have a maximum of eight electrons. So, the outermost energy level will have between one and eight electrons. Students who select one of the elements from the first period will only have one or two electrons in total.

4. Answers may vary. Student responses should indicate that atoms with a full outermost energy level tend to not form bonds, while atoms that do not have a full outermost energy level tend to form bonds.

6. Answers may vary. Student pairs will contain two elements with atoms that are likely to bond (such as sodium and chloride).

7. Sample answer: My atom, beryllium, bonded with oxygen because oxygen atoms need two more valence electrons to have a full outermost energy level, while beryllium atoms need two fewer electrons to have a full outermost energy level.

8. Accept all reasonable answers.

Teacher Prompt Think about which element you thought your atom might bond with. Were there other correct answers that you didn't consider?

Name ______________________ Class ______________ Date ______________

QUICK LAB GUIDED *Inquiry*

Sharing Electrons

During this lab, you will choose one element from the first three periods of the periodic table. You will draw a Bohr model of an atom based on your chosen element. You will show how many valence electrons are in the outermost energy level of your atom and will then search for another atom (drawn by one of your classmates) with which to bond.

OBJECTIVES

- Draw a model of an atom using information from the periodic table.
- Predict how an atom can form bonds with other atoms.

MATERIALS

For each student

- paper
- pencil, colored
- periodic table, copy
- tape, masking

PROCEDURE

1. Select an element from one of the first three periods of the periodic table. Write the element and the total number of electrons it contains, on the line below.

   ____

2. Draw a model to show the electrons of one atom of your chosen element. Use a separate piece of paper and make your drawing large and clear. Remember that a Bohr model shows the nucleus of the atom in the center of the model and all of the electrons. For the element you have chosen, the first energy level can hold two electrons, and the second and third levels can each hold eight.

3. How many valence electrons are in your atom's outermost energy level?

   ____

4. Make a prediction about whether your atom will form bonds with other atoms.

   ____

5. Use the tape to attach your drawing to the front of your shirt, dress, or sweater.

6. Circulate around the room and search for another atom that will likely bond with your atom. When you find one, write down your partner's element name and the number of valence electrons in that atom.

   ____

Name ______________________ Class ______________ Date ________________

Quick Lab continued

7. Why was your atom able to bond with your partner's atom?

____

____

8. Review your original prediction. Were you correct? If not, revise your prediction to reflect what actually happened between your atom and your partner's atom.

____

____

S.T.E.M. LAB GUIDED *Inquiry* **AND** INDEPENDENT *Inquiry*

Build a Bohr Model GENERAL

Small groups
45 minutes

LAB RATINGS LESS ⟷ MORE

Teacher Prep — 2
Student Setup — 2
Cleanup — 2

SAFETY INFORMATION

Remind students to review all safety cautions and icons before beginning this lab. In the Independent Inquiry section of this lab, groups may use slightly different methods to construct the models; remind them to always use caution when working with sharp objects or glue.

TEACHER NOTES

In this activity, students will use a variety of materials to create a Bohr model of an atom from elements in the first three periods of the periodic table. For both levels of the lab, encourage students to be innovative with their designs, but offer more direction on the placement of electrons for the Guided Inquiry level. After students have created a Bohr model of their atom, they will answer several analysis questions to help them understand how valence electrons determine how atoms of some elements can bond with atoms of other elements.

Tip If your students have not yet worked with modeling atoms, it may be helpful to have a sample Bohr model on display. If so, challenge students to do more than simply copy the display model; innovation with materials is one of the skills students should develop as they proceed through this lab.

Student Tip Remember that Bohr models show all the electrons in an atom, not just the valence electrons. Also, remember that Bohr models show the nucleus in the center of the model. Think about how your model will display these different aspects of an atom.

Skills Focus Devising Procedures, Creating Models

MATERIALS

For each group

- aluminum foil
- ball, foam
- cardboard
- clay, modeling
- glue, white
- gumdrops
- hole punch
- marker
- marshmallows, large
- marshmallows, miniature
- paper brad
- paper, construction
- paper, tissue
- periodic table, copy
- pipe cleaners
- plate, paper
- scissors
- string

For each student

- safety goggles

My Notes

S.T.E.M. Lab continued

MODIFICATION FOR DIRECTED Inquiry

Rather than allowing student groups to select an element from the first three periods of the periodic table, preselect one atom for groups to model. Lead student groups through each step of the modeling process. It may also be helpful to have a premade Bohr model on display for students to simulate. Students completing this inquiry level can still answer the questions in the procedures, although they may need more extensive teacher prompting and instruction.

Answer Key for GUIDED Inquiry

ASK A QUESTION

1. Sample answer: A Bohr model will help us see the number of valence electrons an atom has, which helps us predict what kinds of bonds an atom might make.

BUILD A MODEL

2. Accept all reasonable answers.

MAKE OBSERVATIONS

4. Accept all reasonable answers.
Teacher Prompt Does your atom have more than one energy level? If so, what do the other energy levels look like?

FORM A HYPOTHESIS

5. Sample answer: Our chosen element, nitrogen, has five valence electrons. It could form bonds by gaining three electrons.

6. Sample answer: Nitrogen atoms could bond with atoms that have three valence electrons, like those of aluminum or boron.

7. Accept all reasonable answers. Students should understand that they cannot visually see things on an atomic level, which is why modeling is so important.

DRAW CONCLUSIONS

8. Answers may vary.
Teacher Prompt Can you see if other groups used the materials in a different way? Are there other ways to use the materials that could make your model more accurate?

9. Accept all reasonable answers.
Teacher Prompt What makes an atom stable?

10. Sample answer: Sodium chloride illustrates the ideas from this lab because it is a compound made up of two different elements that are bonded together. Sodium has one valence electron and chlorine has seven. The sodium atom gives up its one valence electron, and the chlorine atom gains one electron when they bond.

S.T.E.M. Lab continued

11. Accept all reasonable answers.
Teacher Prompt Can Bohr models really show us the physical arrangement of particles in an atom?

Connect TO THE ESSENTIAL QUESTION

12. Sample answer: An atom's valence electrons determine whether it will share, lose, or gain electrons. This determines whether it can bond to another atom and how it will bond.

Answer Key For INDEPENDENT Inquiry

ASK A QUESTION

1. Sample answer: A Bohr model will help us see the number of valence electrons an atom has, which helps us predict what kinds of bonds an atom might make.

BUILD A MODEL

2. Accept all reasonable answers.

MAKE OBSERVATIONS

4. Accept all reasonable answers.
Teacher Prompt Does your atom have more than one energy level? If so, what do the other energy levels look like?

FORM A HYPOTHESIS

5. Sample answer: Our chosen element, nitrogen, has five valence electrons. It could form bonds by gaining three electrons.

6. Sample answer: Nitrogen atoms could bond with atoms that have three valence electrons, like those of aluminum or boron.

7. Accept all reasonable answers. Students should understand that they cannot visually see things on an atomic level, which is why modeling is so important.

DRAW CONCLUSIONS

8. Answers may vary.
Teacher Prompt Can you see if other groups used the materials in a different way? Are there other ways to use the materials that could make your model more accurate?

9. Accept all reasonable answers.
Teacher Prompt Are there ways you could have used the materials you left out? What is your rationale for your material selection?

10. Accept all reasonable answers.
Teacher Prompt What makes an atom stable?

S.T.E.M. Lab continued

11. Sample answer: Sodium chloride illustrates the ideas from this lab because it is a compound made up of two different elements that are bonded together. Sodium has one valence electron and chlorine has seven. The sodium atom gives up its one valence electron. The chlorine atom gains one electron when they bond.

12. Accept all reasonable answers.
Teacher Prompt Can Bohr models really show us the physical arrangement of particles in an atom?

Connect TO THE ESSENTIAL QUESTION

13. Sample answer: An atom's valence electrons determine whether it will share, lose, or gain electrons. This determines whether it can bond to another atom and how it will bond.

S.T.E.M. LAB GUIDED Inquiry

Build a Bohr Model

In this lab, you will work in small groups to create a Bohr model of a selected atom. You will have many different materials available, but your group must decide how to assemble the materials to create your model. When creating your model, your group should try to use all the materials provided. Remember that atoms of elements in the first period of the periodic table have one energy level that can contain a maximum of two electrons. In the second period, atoms have two energy levels. The second energy level can contain a maximum of eight electrons. Atoms of elements in the third period have three energy levels. For elements in the third period, the third energy level can also hold a maximum of eight electrons. Your group will determine where all the electrons in your model belong and will make predictions about how your atom could bond with other atoms.

OBJECTIVES

- Create a Bohr model of an atom.
- Distinguish the valence electrons.
- Analyze how valence electrons affect how atoms bond with other atoms.

MATERIALS

For each group

- aluminum foil
- ball, foam
- cardboard
- clay, modeling
- glue, white
- gumdrops
- hole punch
- marker
- marshmallows, miniature
- paper brad
- paper, construction
- paper, tissue
- periodic table, copy
- pipe cleaners
- plate, paper
- scissors
- string

For each student

- safety goggles

PROCEDURE

ASK A QUESTION

1. How will building a Bohr model help you understand the bonding of atoms?

____

____

BUILD A MODEL

2. Select an element from the first three periods of the periodic table. Write your choice below.

____

Name ______________________ Class ____________ Date ________________

S.T.E.M. Lab continued

❸ Work with your group to build a Bohr model of your atom. Remember that Bohr models show the nucleus in the center of the model, and each energy level is represented as a ring around the nucleus, as shown in the image below.

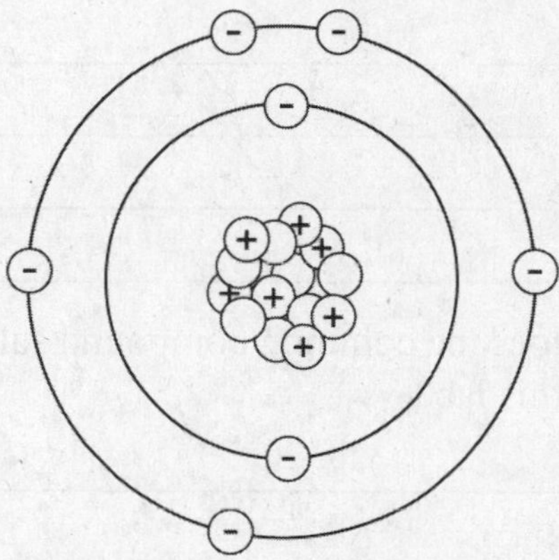

MAKE OBSERVATIONS

❹ How many valence electrons are in your model?

____

FORM A HYPOTHESIS

❺ Given the number of valence electrons, how will atoms of your element react with other atoms? Write a hypothesis below and be sure it includes a "because" statement.

____

____

❻ Study the periodic table and determine at least two other elements whose atoms could form a bond with your atom. Write the elements below.

____

❼ What would you need to test your hypothesis?

____

DRAW CONCLUSIONS

❽ **Analyzing Models** How accurately did your model represent your chosen element?

____

S.T.E.M. Lab continued

9 **Explaining Hypotheses** Explain why you believe your atom would bond with the atoms you identified in Step 6. Be sure to include what will happen to the valence electrons. If you believe your atom would not form bonds, explain why.

____

____

____

____

10 **Applying Conclusions** How does the common compound salt (sodium chloride) illustrate the ideas in this lab?

____

____

____

____

____

11 **Describing Constraints** In what ways do Bohr models fail to accurately represent atoms?

____

____

Connect TO THE ESSENTIAL QUESTION

12 **Applying Concepts** What did you find to be the determining characteristic of an atom that defines how it bonds with another atom?

____

____

Name ______________________________ Class ________________ Date ______________________

S.T.E.M. LAB INDEPENDENT *Inquiry*

Build a Bohr Model

In this lab, you will work in small groups to create a Bohr model of a selected atom. You will have many different materials available, but your group must decide how to assemble the materials to create your model. Your group may choose not to use all the materials that are available; you will be asked to provide justification for choosing the materials you use in your models. Your group will determine where all the electrons in your model belong, and you will make predictions about how your atom could bond with other atoms.

OBJECTIVES

- Create a Bohr model of an atom.
- Distinguish the valence electrons.
- Analyze how valence electrons affect how atoms bond with each other.

MATERIALS

For each group

- aluminum foil
- ball, foam
- cardboard
- clay, modeling
- glue, white
- gumdrops
- hole punch
- marker
- marshmallows, large
- marshmallows, miniature
- paper brad
- paper, construction
- paper, tissue
- periodic table, copy
- pipe cleaners
- plate, paper
- scissors
- string

For each student

- safety goggles

PROCEDURE

ASK A QUESTION

1. How will building a Bohr model help you understand the bonding of atoms?

____

____

BUILD A MODEL

2. Select an element from the first three periods of the periodic table. Write your choice below.

____

3. Work with your group to build a Bohr model of an atom of the element you chose. Remember that Bohr models show the nucleus in the center of the model, and each energy level is represented as a ring around the nucleus.

MAKE OBSERVATIONS

4. How many valence electrons are in your model?

____

FORM A HYPOTHESIS

5. Given the number of valence electrons, how will the atoms of your element react with other elements? Write a hypothesis below and be sure it includes a "because" statement.

6. Study the periodic table and determine at least two other elements with which your element could form a bond. Write the elements below.

7. What would you need to test your hypothesis?

DRAW CONCLUSIONS

8. **Analyzing Models** How accurately did your model represent your chosen element?

9. **Defending Methods** Explain why you selected the materials you used and why you chose not to use other materials.

10. **Explaining Hypotheses** Explain why you believe your atom would bond with the atoms you identified in Step 6. Be sure to include what will happen to the valence electrons. If you believe your element is stable, explain why.

11. **Applying Conclusions** How does the common compound salt (sodium chloride) illustrate the ideas in this lab?

S.T.E.M. Lab continued

12 **Describing Constraints** In what ways are Bohr models not fully accurate representations of atoms?

____

____

____

____

Connect TO THE ESSENTIAL QUESTION

13 **Applying Concepts** What did you find to be the determining characteristic of an atom that defines how it bonds with another atom?

____

____

QUICK LAB DIRECTED Inquiry

Growing Crystals GENERAL

Small groups
20 minutes

LAB RATINGS

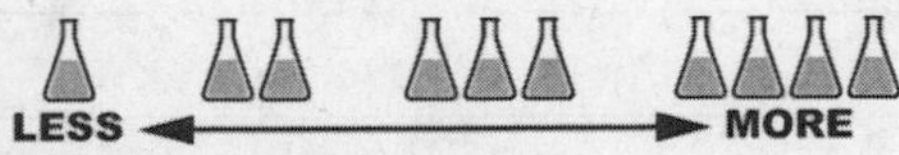

Teacher Prep —
Student Setup —
Cleanup —

SAFETY INFORMATION

Remind students to review all safety cautions and icons before beginning this lab.

TEACHER NOTES

In this activity, students will notice that crystals grow in shapes other than simple cubic structures. For preparation, use a beaker to combine the salt and hot water. Stir until the salt is dissolved. To prevent crystallization up the sides of the cup, smear petroleum jelly around the inside of the cup just above the water line.

Skills Focus Making Observations, Making Predictions, Comparing Results

MODIFICATION FOR INDEPENDENT Inquiry

Have students research crystal formation and develop a set of procedures to grow their own crystals. Allow students to proceed with all reasonable experiments.

MATERIALS

For each group

- beaker, 250 mL
- cup, foam
- Epsom salt (30 mL)
- paper clip
- pencil
- string, 30 cm
- water (75 mL)

For each student

- gloves
- lab apron
- safety goggles

My Notes

Answer Key

5. Answers will vary.
6. Sample answer: Regularly—the crystals are long and needlelike.
7. Sample answer: The size of the crystals is different, but the shape is the same.
8. Sample answer: All crystals will be the same shape.
9. Sample answer: My classmates' crystals have the same shape as my group's crystals.
10. Sample answer: The crystals have the same shape, but the original crystals were much smaller. They were probably smaller because they grew more quickly.

QUICK LAB DIRECTED *Inquiry*

Growing Crystals

In this lab, you will grow and examine your own ionic crystals.

OBJECTIVE

- Describe how crystals form in solution.

MATERIALS

For each group

- beaker, 250 mL
- cup, foam
- Epsom salt (30 mL)
- paper clip
- pencil
- string, 30 cm
- water (75 mL)

For each student

- gloves
- lab apron
- safety goggles

PROCEDURE

1. Tie one end of a 30 cm **string** to a **paper clip**.
2. Wrap the other end of the string around a **pencil** so that the clip hangs low in the **cup** while the pencil rests across the top of the cup.
3. Carefully pour 50 mL of warm **Epsom salt solution** into the cup.
4. Lower the paper clip into the solution, and rest the pencil on top of the cup.

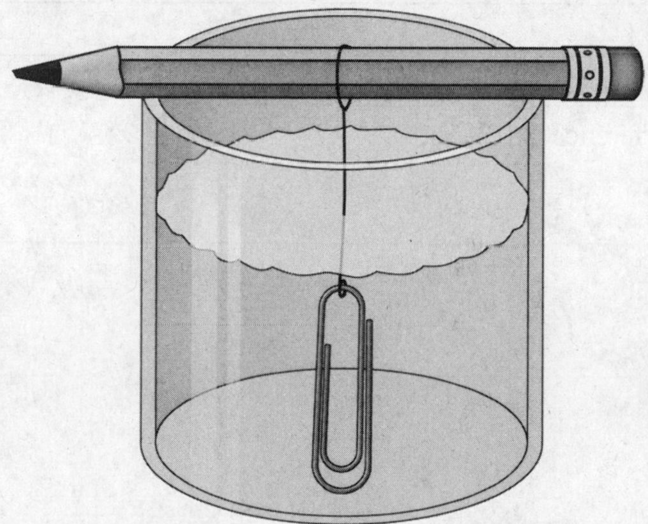

Quick Lab continued

5 Place the cup in a safe location. Observe every day for a week. Write your observations in the space below. When instructed, remove the paper clip and examine it closely.

6 Describe what the crystals look like. Are they regularly formed? Explain.

7 Compare the shape of the largest crystal to that of the smallest. Sketch each and describe any similarities and differences.

Name _______________ Class _______________ Date _______________

Quick Lab continued

8. Predict the shape of your classmates' crystals.

____

____

9. Compare your sketch to those of your classmates. Describe similarities and differences.

____

____

____

10. Compare the shape of the original salt crystals with your grown crystals. Explain any differences.

____

____

____

QUICK LAB DIRECTED Inquiry

Modeling Bonding GENERAL

Large group
20 minutes

LAB RATINGS LESS ⟷ MORE

Teacher Prep — 3
Student Setup — 1
Cleanup — 1

MATERIALS

For each group

- atom name tag
- Bonding Time worksheet
- pencil
- reference materials

My Notes

SAFETY INFORMATION

Although there are no safety icons for this activity, remind students to walk carefully in the circles. You may wish to do this activity outdoors and not attempt this in a crowded classroom.

TEACHER NOTES

In this activity, students wear name tags representing different atoms. Before class, assemble the name tags by copying the Name Tag Template on the page following the answer key on name tag label paper. You could also enlarge the tags on the template and make a name tag by punching two holes at the top of each card and looping yarn through them.

Tell students to form two same-sized circles, with one circle inside the other. Have the outside circle walk clockwise and the inside circle walk counterclockwise and instruct both circles to stop when you say so. Have students stop every 30 seconds, and then give them each a minute to fill in their charts. Repeat this activity 10 times.

Tip This activity gives students an understanding of positive and negative charges and how "opposites attract."

Skills Focus Making Models

MODIFICATION FOR GUIDED Inquiry

Have student think of a way to model ionic bonds. Students should then do research and design a model. Allow students to build any reasonable model and have them share their models with the class.

Answer Key

1. Answers will vary.

4. Answers will vary.

5. Answers will vary.

Quick Lab continued

Al^{3+} **(Aluminum)**	Ca^{2+} **(Calcium)**
Cu^{2+} **(Copper)**	H^{+} **(Hydrogen)**
Fe^{2+} **(Iron)**	Mg^{2+} **(Magnesium)**
K^{+} **(Potassium)**	Na^{+} **(Sodium)**
C_2^{2-} **(Carbide)**	Cl^{-} **(Chloride)**
F^{-} **(Fluoride)**	H^{-} **(Hydride)**
CO_3^{2-} **(Carbonate)**	HCO_3^{-} **(Hydrogen Carbonate)**
NO_3^{-} **(Nitrate)**	PO_4^{3-} **(Phosphate)**
OH^{-} **(Hydroxide)**	SO_4^{2-} **(Sulfate)**

Name ______________________ Class ____________ Date ________________

QUICK LAB DIRECTED Inquiry

Modeling Bonding

Chemical bonds hold atoms together. Ions form ionic bonds. Positive ions can only bond with negative ions, and negative ions can only bond with positive ions.

OBJECTIVE

- Model the formation of an ionic bond.

MATERIALS

For each student

- atom name tag
- Bonding Time worksheet
- pencil
- reference materials

PROCEDURE

1. Wear the name tag your teacher gives you. What is the atom on your name tag? Does it have a positive or negative ion?

   ____

   ____

   ____

2. With your class, form two circles, one inside the other. Walk around the circle. If you are in the outside circle, walk clockwise. If you are in the inside circle, walk counter clockwise. When your teacher says "stop," look at the name tag of the student opposite you.

3. Ask yourself if the atom on your name tag can bond with the atom of the student across from you. If not, do nothing.

4. If yes, fill out the information in the Bonding Time worksheet. Write the compound and make up a name for it.

5. Research one of the bonds in your worksheet to see what happens when this bond forms. Share your findings with the class.

   ____

   ____

   ____

   ____

   ____

   ____

Bonding Time

Positive Ion	Negative Ion	Compound	Compound Name

EXPLORATION LAB DIRECTED Inquiry AND GUIDED Inquiry

Chemical Bonds GENERAL

Small groups
45 minutes

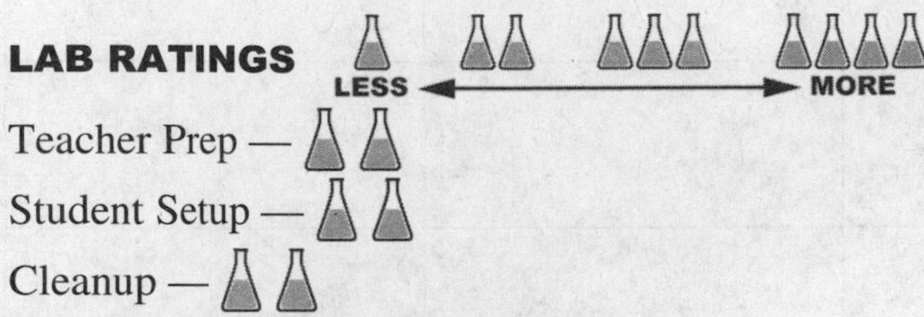

LAB RATINGS LESS ⟷ MORE

Teacher Prep — 2
Student Setup — 2
Cleanup — 2

SAFETY INFORMATION

Remind students to review all safety cautions and icons before beginning this lab. Students should wear safety goggles and aprons throughout the investigation. Have students wipe up any water that spills during the conductivity test. Be sure that proper oversight is used when students are working with Bunsen burners. Have students with long hair tie it back to avoid any possibility of it getting too close to the flame. Instruct students to keep test tubes pointed away from everyone (including themselves) during heating. Be sure students always use the test tube clamp when heating each substance. Instruct students to allow the heated test tubes to cool until the next class period before cleaning them. Have students wash and dry their hands after completing this inquiry.

TEACHER NOTES

In this lab, students will discover how the chemical bonds that hold substances together relate to the physical properties of those substances. They will observe the physical structure and test the melting point, solubility, and electrical conductivity of three substances in an attempt to classify them as having ionic, covalent, or metallic bonds.

If time is limited, assemble the conductivity meters ahead of time and place the samples in labeled cups. Prior to the investigation, have students read through the investigation and prepare their data tables.

Tip Make sure that students understand the difference between ionic, covalent, and metallic bonds; additionally, discuss how bond strength affects the interaction of matter with the surrounding world.

Skills Focus Practicing Lab Techniques, Making Observations, Recognizing Patterns

MODIFICATION FOR INDEPENDENT Inquiry

Have students prepare their own data tables rather than providing one.

MATERIALS

For each group

- balance
- battery, 6-V lantern
- beaker, 50 or 100 mL
- Bunsen burner
- copper strip
- cups, plastic (3)
- cylinder, graduated, 50 mL
- Epsom salts
- iron filings
- light bulb and socket
- magnifying lens
- marker or wax pencil
- sparker for lighting Bunsen burner
- spoons, plastic (3)
- stopwatch
- sugar, table
- test tubes (3)
- test tube clamp
- test tube rack
- water, distilled
- wire leads with alligator clips (3)
- zinc strip

For each student

- gloves
- lab apron
- safety goggles

Exploration Lab continued

Answer Key for DIRECTED Inquiry

PROPERTIES OF SUBSTANCES

Property	Epsom salts ($MgSO_4$)	Sugar ($C_{12}H_{22}O_{11}$)	Iron filings (Fe)
Physical appearance	Answers will vary	Answers will vary	Answers will vary
Crystal shape	Prism	Cubelike	Irregular
Conductivity of solid	No	No	Yes
Conductivity in water	Yes	No	No
Melts in flame	No	Yes	No
Solubility in water	Yes	Yes	No
Bond type	Ionic	Covalent	Metallic

MAKE OBSERVATIONS

7. See table.

8. See table.

9. See table.

11. Sample answer: No, water by itself does not conduct a current.

13. See table.

14. See table.

16. See table. Neither sugar nor iron filings in water conduct a current. The sugar dissolves but the iron does not dissolve in water.

18. See Table 1.

ANALYZE THE RESULTS

20. Sample answer: Each substance had a unique set of properties. Sugar had a low melting point and low conductivity. Epsom salts only had high conductivity when dissolved in water. They had a high melting point. The iron filings did not dissolve in water and had high conductivity as a solid. They also had a high melting point.

DRAW CONCLUSIONS

21. Sample answer: Sugar is a covalent compound because it contains covalent bonds. Epsom salts are ionic because they contain magnesium and sulfate ions held together by ionic bonds. Iron is a metallic compound because it is composed of atoms of one metal held together by metallic bonds.

22. Sample answer: Ionic compounds are soluble in water, have low conductivity as a solid but high conductivity when dissolved in water. They have high melting points. Covalent compounds have low conductivity both as a solid and when dissolved in water. They have low melting points. Metallic compounds have high conductivity as a solid, don't dissolve in water, and have high melting points.

Exploration Lab continued

23. Sample answer: Yes, other ionic compounds should behave like Epsom salts, other covalent compounds should behave like sugar, and other metallic compounds should behave like iron. The types of bonds in each group of compounds determine these properties.

Connect TO THE ESSENTIAL QUESTION

24. Sample answer: The chemical bonds affect the behavior of a substance. Ionic compounds behave differently than covalent compounds or metallic substances because of the types of bonds holding the atoms together.

Answer Key for GUIDED Inquiry

MAKE OBSERVATIONS

7. Accept all reasonable answers.

8. Accept all reasonable answers.

DEVELOP A PLAN

9. Accept all reasonable answers.

MAKE OBSERVATIONS

10. Accept all reasonable answers.

ANALYZE THE RESULTS

11. Sample answer: Each substance had a unique set of properties. Sugar had a low melting point and low conductivity. The Epsom salts only had high conductivity when dissolved in water. They had a high melting point. The iron filings did not dissolve in water and had high conductivity as a solid. They also had a high melting point.

DRAW CONCLUSIONS

12. Sample answer: Sugar is a covalent compound; it contains covalent bonds. Epsom salts are ionic; they contain magnesium and sulfate ions held together by ionic bonds. Iron is a metallic compound; it contains atoms of one metal held together by metallic bonds.

13. Sample answer: Ionic compounds are soluble in water, have low conductivity as a solid but high conductivity when dissolved in water. They have high melting points. Covalent compounds have low conductivity both as a solid and when dissolved in water. They have low melting points. Metallic compounds have high conductivity as a solid, don't dissolve in water, and have high melting points.

14. Sample answer: Yes, other ionic compounds should behave like Epsom salts, other covalent compounds should behave like sugar, and other metallic compounds should behave like iron. The types of bonds in each group of compounds determine these properties.

Connect TO THE ESSENTIAL QUESTION

15. Sample answer: The chemical bonds affect the behavior of a substance. Ionic compounds behave differently than covalent compounds or metallic substances because of the types of bonds holding the atoms together.

Name ______________________ Class ______________ Date ______________

EXPLORATION LAB DIRECTED Inquiry

Chemical Bonds

In this lab, you will learn how chemical bonds affect the way matter behaves. You will compare melting point, conductivity, and physical appearance of three substances that differ in the types of chemical bonds that make up their structures. One substance is ionic, another is covalent, and a third is metallic. You will look for patterns in these physical properties in order to draw conclusions about how their bond structures relate to these properties.

OBJECTIVE

- Observe physical properties of three different substances and relate these properties to their bond structure.

MATERIALS

For each group

- balance
- battery, 6-V lantern
- beaker, 50 or 100 mL
- Bunsen burner
- copper strip
- cups, plastic (3)
- cylinder, graduated, 50 mL
- Epsom salts
- iron filings
- light bulb and socket
- magnifying lens
- marker or wax pencil
- sparker for lighting Bunsen burner
- spoons, plastic (3)
- stopwatch
- sugar, table
- test tubes (3)
- test tube clamp
- test tube rack
- water, distilled
- wire leads with alligator clips (3)
- zinc strip

For each student

- gloves
- lab apron
- safety goggles

PROCEDURE

ASK A QUESTION

1. In this lab you will be doing some experiments to answer the following questions: How do the physical properties of ionic, covalent, and metallic substances compare? Do these properties relate to the type of bonds present in these substances?

BUILD A CONDUCTIVITY METER

2. To help answer the questions posed above, you and your partner will build a conductivity meter to function as part of your procedure for testing and comparing ionic, covalent, and metallic substances.

3. Study the figure below. Assemble the necessary materials to make a similar conductivity meter for your own use.

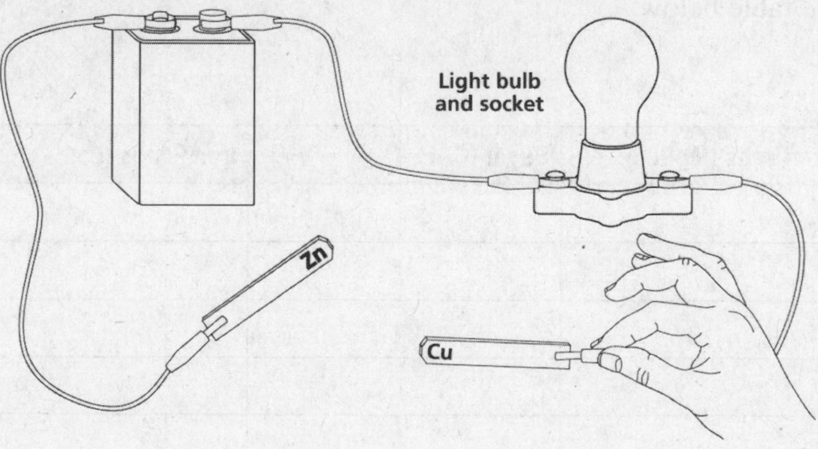

Exploration Lab continued

4 Be sure the meter works properly. To do this, touch the two metal strips together. Does the bulb light? If not, check all of your connections carefully.

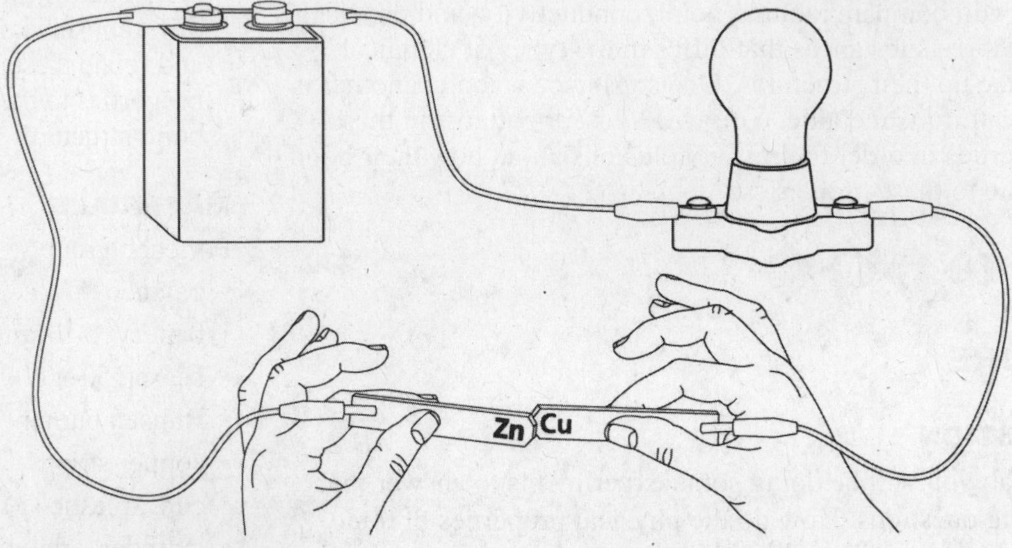

MAKE OBSERVATIONS

5 Obtain the following materials: Epsom salts ($MgSO_4$), sugar ($C_{12}H_{22}O_{11}$), and iron filings (Fe).

6 Use a separate spoon to measure out 5 grams (g) of each substance. Place each substance into a separate plastic cup. Label each cup with its contents.

7 Use a plastic spoon to place a tiny sample of the Epsom salts and sugar on a piece of black construction paper. Place a tiny sample of the iron filings on a piece of white paper. Record your observations of the physical appearance of each substance in the table below.

PROPERTIES OF SUBSTANCES

Property	Epsom salts ($MgSO_4$)	Sugar ($C_{12}H_{22}O_{11}$)	Iron filings (Fe)
Physical appearance			
Crystal shape			
Conductivity of solid			
Conductivity in water			
Melts in flame			
Solubility in water			
Bond type			

Name ______________________ Class ____________ Date ________________

Exploration Lab continued

8. Observe the substances with a magnifying lens. Do you see any patterns of shape among the grains? Record your observations in the table.

9. Place each substance between the metal strips. Does the bulb light as you bring the strips together? Record your observations in the table.

10. Fill a beaker with 30 milliliters (mL) of distilled water. Place the two metal strips of the conductivity tester into the water.

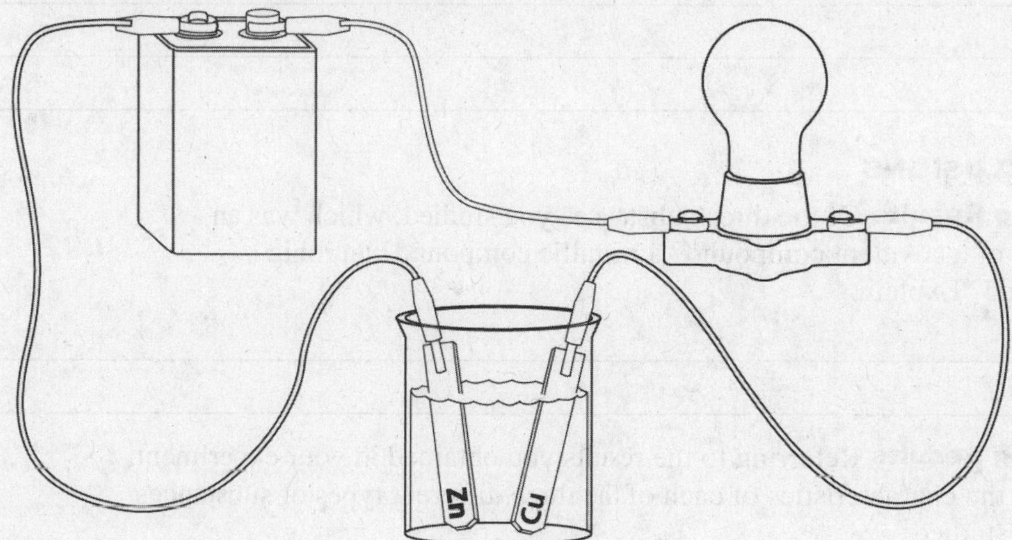

11. Does the bulb light? Record your observations here.

____

12. Add about half of the Epsom salts from Step 6 to the water. Retain the remainder of the substance in the cup.

13. Stir with the plastic spoon to mix completely. Does the substance dissolve in water? Record your observations in the table.

14. Repeat the conductivity test as you did in Step 11. What happens when you put the metal strips into the water? Record your observations in the table.

15. Rinse and dry the beaker.

16. Repeat Steps 12 through 15 for each of the other substances. Save the remainder of each substance for a later test. Clean and dry the beaker between each material conductivity test, being careful to dispose of the iron filings in the trash.

17. Put the remainder of each substance into a clean, dry test tube. Label each tube near the top with the permanent marker. Light the Bunsen burner.

18. Use the test tube clamp to hold each test tube while you heat it over the flame. Hold the tube over the Bunsen burner for two minutes. Do you notice any signs of melting? Record your observations in the table.

Exploration Lab continued

19 Place the test tube in the test tube rack, being careful not to touch the tube in the process. Allow time for the tube to cool before handling.

ANALYZE THE RESULTS

20 **Analyzing Observations** What general pattern of physical properties did you find?

____

____

____

DRAW CONCLUSIONS

21 **Applying Results** Of the three substances you studied, which was an example of a covalent compound? a metallic compound? an ionic compound? Explain.

____

____

22 **Applying Results** Referring to the results you obtained in your experiment, describe the characteristics of each of the three different types of substances that you studied.

____

____

23 **Applying Results** Would you expect other substances to have similar properties to the properties you observed for these three substances? Explain.

____

____

Connect TO THE ESSENTIAL QUESTION

24 **Interpreting Conclusions** How do a compound's chemical bonds affect its melting point and its conductivity?

____

____

____

Name ______________________________ Class ________________ Date ________________________

EXPLORATION LAB GUIDED *Inquiry*

Chemical Bonds

In this lab, you will learn how chemical bonds affect the way matter behaves. You will compare melting point, conductivity, and physical appearance of three substances that differ in the types of chemical bonds that make up their structures. One substance is ionic, another is covalent, and a third is metallic. You will look for patterns in these physical properties in order to draw conclusions about how their bond structures relate to these properties.

OBJECTIVE

- Observe physical properties of three different substances and relate these properties to their bond structure.

MATERIALS

For each group

- balance
- battery, 6-V lantern
- beaker, 50 or 100 mL
- Bunsen burner
- copper strip
- cups, plastic (3)
- cylinder, graduated, 50 mL
- Epsom salts
- iron filings
- light bulb and socket
- magnifying lens
- marker or wax pencil
- paper, black construction
- paper, white
- sparker for lighting Bunsen burner
- spoons, plastic (3)
- stopwatch
- sugar, table
- test tubes (3)
- test tube clamp
- test tube rack
- water, distilled
- wire leads with alligator clips (3)
- zinc strip

For each student

- gloves
- lab apron
- safety goggles

PROCEDURE

ASK A QUESTION

1. In this lab you will be doing some experiments to answer the following questions: How do the physical properties of ionic, covalent, and metallic substances compare? Do these properties relate to the type of bonds present in these substances?

BUILD A CONDUCTIVITY METER

2. To help answer the questions posed above, you and your partner will build a conductivity meter to function as part of your procedure for testing and comparing ionic, covalent, and metallic substances.

3. Study the figure below. Assemble the necessary materials to make a similar conductivity meter for your own use.

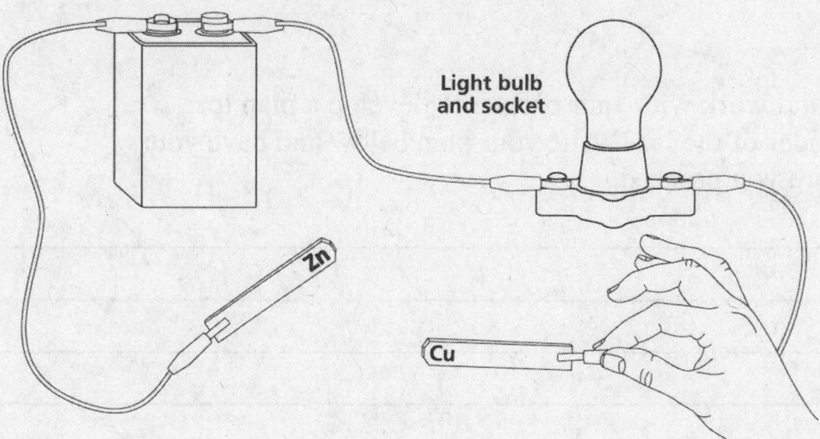

Exploration Lab continued

4. Be sure the meter works properly. To do this, touch the two metal strips together. Does the bulb light? If not, check all of your connections carefully.

MAKE OBSERVATIONS

5. Obtain the following materials: Epsom salts ($MgSO_4$), sugar ($C_{12}H_{22}O_{11}$), and iron filings (Fe).

6. Use a separate plastic spoon to measure out 5 grams (g) of each substance. Place each substance into a separate plastic cup. Label each cup with its contents.

7. Use a plastic spoon to place a tiny sample of the Epsom salts and sugar on a piece of black construction paper. Place a tiny sample of the iron filings on a piece of white paper. record your observations of the appearance of each substance in the table below.

PROPERTIES OF SUBSTANCES

Property	Epsom salts ($MgSO_4$)	Sugar ($C_{12}H_{22}O_{11}$)	Iron filings (Fe)
Physical appearance			
Crystal shape			
Conductivity of solid			
Conductivity in water			
Melts in flame			
Solubility in water			
Bond type			

8. Observe the substances with a magnifying lens. Do you see any patterns of shape among the grains? Record your observations in the table above.

DEVELOP A PLAN

9. Study the table above and work with your partner to develop a plan for carrying out the remainder of the lab. Write your plan below and have your teacher approve it before you proceed.

____

____

____

____

____

____

____

____

Exploration Lab continued

MAKE OBSERVATIONS

10 Carry out your plan from Step 9 in order to complete all of the observations you need to fill in the table.

ANALYZE THE RESULTS

11 **Analyzing Observations** What general pattern of physical properties did you find?

____

____

____

DRAW CONCLUSIONS

12 **Applying Results** Of the three substances you studied, which was an example of a covalent compound? a metallic compound? an ionic compound? Explain.

____

____

13 **Applying Results** Referring to the results you obtained in your experiment, describe the characteristics of each of the three different types of substances that you studied.

____

____

14 **Applying Results** Would you expect to find that other substances had similar properties to the properties you observed for these three substances? Explain.

____

____

Connect TO THE ESSENTIAL QUESTION

15 **Interpreting Conclusions** How do a compound's chemical bonds affect its melting point and its conductivity?

____

____

____

QUICK LAB DIRECTED Inquiry

Breaking Bonds in a Chemical Reaction GENERAL

Student pairs
20 minutes

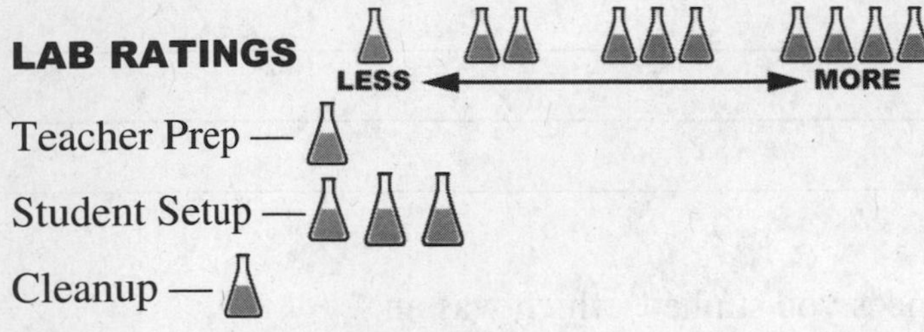

MATERIALS

For each pair
- baking soda
- Bunsen burner
- test tube
- test-tube holder
- wooden splint

For each student
- heat-resistant gloves
- lab apron
- safety goggles

My Notes

SAFETY INFORMATION

Remind students to review all safety cautions and icons before beginning this lab. Review with students the proper way to use a Bunsen burner and how to hold the test tube away from themselves while heating chemicals. If you prefer, you can divide the class into two groups and allow each group to observe while you heat the baking soda and perform the splint test.

TEACHER NOTES

In this activity, students will break down the bonds in baking soda by applying heat to a test tube of baking soda. This is a decomposition reaction. Before beginning this activity, ask students if they have ever used baking soda while baking. Explain that baking soda is often used in baking recipes that call for acidic foods, such as citrus juice, buttermilk, or yogurt. When the baking soda comes in contact with the acid in the batter, it begins to form carbon dioxide. As the batter bakes, the heat causes the gas bubbles to expand, causing the baked good to rise.

Tip Use this activity to discuss the difference between physical and chemical changes. When compounds undergo chemical changes, the substances being mixed change chemically. Therefore, the new substances cannot be separated without breaking chemical bonds.

Skills Focus Making Observations, Writing Chemical Equations

MODIFICATION FOR INDEPENDENT Inquiry

Have student pairs ask a question about breaking bonds during a chemical reaction and write a hypothesis to answer their question. Students should then do research and design an experiment to prove their hypothesis. Allow students to carry out any reasonable and safe procedures. Have students share their results with the class.

Quick Lab continued

Answer Key

1. Sample answer: It is white and powdery.
2. Accept all reasonable answers.
3. Sample answer: Fire needs oxygen. In a test tube filled with carbon dioxide there is not enough oxygen for the fire to keep burning.
4. Accept all reasonable answers.
5. Sample answer: It did not change.
6. Water vapor
7. $2NaHCO_3 \rightarrow CO_2 + Na_2CO_3 + H_2O$
   Teacher Prompt Remind students that when writing an equation both sides of the equation need to be equal.
8. The baking soda
9. The carbon dioxide, the water, and the Na_2CO_3

Name ______________________________ Class ________________ Date ______________________

QUICK LAB DIRECTED Inquiry

Breaking Bonds in a Chemical Reaction

Chemical bonds hold atoms together in compounds. When these bonds break, a chemical change occurs. In this lab, you will observe what happens when you break a chemical bond.

OBJECTIVES

- Observe how a chemical bond is broken during a chemical change.
- Write a chemical equation.

MATERIALS

For each student pair
- baking soda
- Bunsen burner
- test tube
- test-tube holder
- wooden splint

For each student
- heat-resistant gloves
- lab apron
- safety goggles

PROCEDURE

1. Put 2 centimeters of **baking soda** into the **test tube**. Describe what it looks like.

____

____

____

____

2. Hold the test tube over the flame. Make sure that you hold the mouth of the test tube away from all people. Record your observations.

____

____

____

____

3. You can test for carbon dioxide by lighting a **wooden splint** and placing it in the test tube. If the flame goes out, there is carbon dioxide present. Explain why that happens.

____

____

____

____

____

Name ______________________ Class ______________ Date ______________

Quick Lab continued

4 Test for carbon dioxide. Record your observations.

5 How did the color of the baking soda change?

6 What was on the inside walls of the test tube?

7 The chemical formula for baking soda is $NaHCO_3$. Use this formula to write an equation for this chemical reaction.

8 Name the reactant(s) in this experiment.

9 Name the product(s) in this experiment.

QUICK LAB DIRECTED Inquiry

Catalysts and Chemical Reactions GENERAL

Small groups
20 minutes

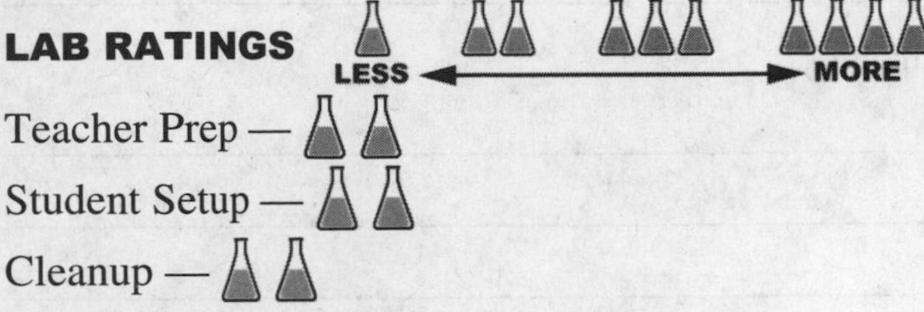

MATERIALS

For each group
- funnel
- glass stirring rod
- graduated cylinder, 10 mL
- hydrogen peroxide, 3% solution
- liver cubes, small (2)
- mortar and pestle
- pen or marker
- spoon
- tape, masking
- test tubes, 10 mL (3)
- test-tube rack
- tweezers

For each student
- gloves
- lab apron
- safety goggles

SAFETY INFORMATION

Remind students to review all safety cautions and icons before beginning this lab. Use hydrogen peroxide solutions with concentrations of no more than 3%. You may want to prepare the three test tubes containing hydrogen peroxide for each team. If students prepare their own test tubes, warn them that hydrogen peroxide is a bleaching agent that can damage clothing and irritate the skin. Be sure that students use running water to rinse any skin area that comes in contact with hydrogen peroxide. When students have completed this activity, solutions may be washed down the sink if your school drains are connected to a sanitary sewer system with a treatment plant. Liver pieces should be disposed of properly and not poured down the sink. Students should clean the lab area and wash their hands thoroughly.

My Notes

TEACHER NOTES

In this activity, students will investigate how a catalyst affects a chemical reaction. They will also compare how the surface area of the catalyst affects the rate of the reaction. In this experiment, students will observe the reaction in which hydrogen peroxide, H_2O_2, decomposes into oxygen, O_2, and water, H_2O. An enzyme present in liver cells acts as a catalyst for this reaction. The liver sample pieces should be approximately one gram. If liver is not available, potato will work just as well.

Tip This activity will help students name some factors that can affect the rate of a chemical reaction.

Student Tip Make your hand into a fist. Now stretch it out and extend your fingers. When does your hand have more surface area?

Skills Focus Practicing Lab Techniques, Drawing Conclusions

Quick Lab continued

MODIFICATION FOR GUIDED Inquiry

Measure 5 milliliters (mL) of the hydrogen peroxide solution into a test tube and show it to the class. Explain that you are now observing the decomposition of hydrogen peroxide into oxygen and water. Ask students to develop a procedure to investigate whether an enzyme in liver, which acts as a catalyst, will affect this chemical reaction. Students may also consider whether the surface area of the catalyst will affect the reaction. Allow students to carry out their procedures once you have approved them. Remind students of the importance of having a control test tube in the experiment.

Answer Key

5. Accept all reasonable answers.
6. The test tubes with the liver have more vigorous bubbling, which indicates a faster reaction rate.
   Teacher Prompt Did you notice a change in the hydrogen peroxide after you added the liver? If so, how? What did this change tell you about the reaction rate?
7. Ground liver produces a faster reaction because more catalyst is exposed to the hydrogen peroxide.
   Teacher Prompt How much of the liver cube was exposed to the hydrogen peroxide? When you ground the liver cube, how did the number of liver cells exposed to the hydrogen peroxide change?
8. Test tube 3 is a control test tube. It is used to compare the rate of bubbling with liver to the rate without liver.

Name ______________________ Class ______________ Date ________________

QUICK LAB DIRECTED Inquiry

Catalysts and Chemical Reactions

In this lab, you will investigate how the presence and surface area of a catalyst affects the rate of a chemical reaction. You will observe hydrogen peroxide, H_2O_2, as it decomposes into oxygen, O_2, and water, H_2O. An enzyme present in liver cells acts as a catalyst for this reaction.

OBJECTIVES

- Identify factors that can affect the rate of a chemical reaction.
- Describe the role of catalysts.

MATERIALS

For each group
- funnel
- glass stirring rod
- graduated cylinder, 10 mL
- hydrogen peroxide, 3% solution
- liver cubes, small (2)
- mortar and pestle
- pen or marker
- spoon
- tape, masking
- test tubes, 10 mL (3)
- test-tube rack
- tweezers

For each student
- gloves
- lab apron
- safety goggles

PROCEDURE

1. Put a small piece of masking tape near the top of each test tube, and label the tubes "1," "2," and "3."
2. Using the funnel and graduated cylinder, measure 5 milliliters (mL) of the hydrogen peroxide solution into each test tube. Place the test tubes in the test-tube rack.
3. Grind one liver cube with the mortar and pestle.
4. Use the tweezers to place the cube of liver in test tube 1. Place the ground liver in test tube 2. Use the glass stirring rod to push the liver into the hydrogen peroxide solution in both test tubes. Leave test tube 3 alone.
5. Observe the reaction rate (the amount of bubbling) in all three test tubes. Record your observations in the table below.

OBSERVATIONS OF REACTION RATES

Test tube 1	
Test tube 2	
Test tube 3	

6. How does the presence of the liver affect the reaction of hydrogen peroxide?

____

____

____

Quick Lab continued

7. Which type of liver (whole or ground) produces a faster reaction? Why?

____

____

____

____

8. What is the purpose of test tube 3?

____

____

____

EXPLORATION LAB DIRECTED *Inquiry* **AND** GUIDED *Inquiry*

Change of Pace GENERAL

Small groups
Two 45-minute periods

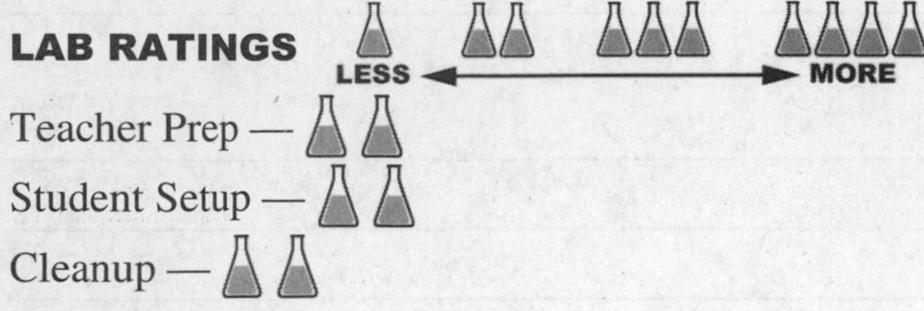

MATERIALS
- aluminum foil strips, 5 cm × 1 cm each (3)
- funnels (2)
- graduated cylinder, at least 30 mL (2)
- hydrochloric acid, 1.0 M, 0.5 M, and 0.1 M concentrations (15 mL each)
- sandpaper
- scissors
- stopwatch
- test tube rack
- test tubes, at least 30 mL (3)
- water

For each student
- gloves
- lab apron
- safety goggles

My Notes

SAFETY INFORMATION

Remind students to review all safety cautions and icons before beginning this lab. The reaction between aluminum foil and hydrochloric acid produces heat. Make sure students use caution when handling graduated cylinders. Hydrochloric acid may cause damage to skin, eyes, and clothes. Students should wear gloves, goggles, and aprons at all times during this experiment.

Only hydrochloric acid of concentrations 1.0 M or less should be used. HCl is corrosive. In case of an acid spill, flush the area with a solution of baking soda and water to neutralize the acid. Then, rinse the area and wipe up with a wet washcloth or sponge.

TEACHER NOTES

In this activity, students will explore how changing surface area and concentration can affect the rate of a chemical reaction. They will investigate ways to increase or decrease the rate of the reaction between aluminum foil and hydrochloric acid (HCl). The speed at which a chemical reaction occurs is called the *rate* of the reaction. Sometimes you want a reaction to take place rapidly, such as when you are removing tarnish from your jewelry. Other times you want a reaction to happen slowly, as when you are depending on a battery as a source of electrical energy. Therefore, it is important to know how the rate of a chemical reaction can be controlled. Aluminum can react with the oxygen in air to form aluminum oxide, which forms a very thin coating on the surface of the foil. This coating is fairly non-reactive, so be sure to use fresh (new) aluminum foil in the experiment. Aluminum may not react with HCl instantly, so advise students to be patient and remain observant because when it does begin to react, it may be quick and dramatic. Please note that using 1 M of HCl means that the reaction will take at least one hour. If you are limited to shorter class periods, create the set-ups for your first class ahead of time. That class will create the set-ups for the next class, and so on.

Exploration Lab continued

Although the experiment calls for 15 mL HCl, students should use as much HCl as necessary to fill the test tube about halfway. To dispose of HCl, flush it down the sink with plenty of running water. After HCl has been poured off, any remaining aluminum foil or solids may be disposed of in the garbage.

In the interest of time, you may wish to do Part I and Part II of the Directed Inquiry version in two separate class periods.

Tip Introduce this activity by asking students to visualize a sugar cube dissolving in a glass of water. Ask them to think about ways to make the sugar dissolve more quickly.

Student Tip Which will dissolve more quickly in a glass of water: a sugar cube or a packet of sugar? Why?

Skills Focus Developing Hypotheses, Explaining Events

MODIFICATION FOR INDEPENDENT Inquiry

Ask students to design their own experiment to investigate ways to speed up or slow down a reaction. Students may propose to explore temperature, concentration, surface area, or other factors related to reaction rate. They should propose an experimental setup and procedure, including all materials and safety precautions required. Students should decide which data they will need to collect and how they will record and analyze those data. With teacher approval, they should carry out their investigations and present their results in a lab report.

Answer Key for DIRECTED Inquiry

FORM A HYPOTHESIS

2. Accept all reasonable answers, but students should point out that changes in surface area will affect reaction rate.

MAKE OBSERVATIONS

5. Answers will vary, but the sample with the most surface area should have the fastest reaction rate, the most bubbles, and the most heat.

ANALYZE THE RESULTS

6. Sample answer: We crushed one strip into a tiny ball, folded one strip, and used sandpaper on another strip. We crushed and folded the two pieces to decrease the exposed surface area. We used sandpaper to remove the protective oxidize coating so that the acid could come into contact with the aluminum better.
7. Sample answer: The foil that had been sanded reacted the fastest, and the foil ball reacted the slowest. The sanded foil had the protective oxidized coating removed.

Exploration Lab continued

DRAW CONCLUSIONS

8. Answers will vary.
9. Sample answer: You can change the surface area of a material to change its reaction rate. The more surface area there is, the more molecules of the material can react and the faster the reaction rate.

FORM A HYPOTHESIS

11. Accept all reasonable answers, but students should point out that concentration affects reaction rate.

MAKE OBSERVATIONS

13. Answers will vary, but the 1.0 M solution should have the fastest reaction rate, the most bubbles, and the most heat.

ANALYZE THE RESULTS

14. Sample answer: The 1.0 M solution had the fastest reaction rate, and the 0.1 M solution had the slowest reaction rate.
15. Sample answer: you could observe the bubbles and the amount of heat produced by the reaction. The reaction with the most bubbles and the most heat would be the most active, so it would have the fastest reaction rate.

DRAW CONCLUSIONS

16. Answers will vary.
17. Sample answer: A higher concentration has a faster reaction rate because there are more molecules available to react.

Connect TO THE ESSENTIAL QUESTION

18. Sample answer: yes, because if you double the amount of a weaker concentration, it will be the same as half the amount of a stronger concentration

Answer Key for GUIDED Inquiry

FORM A HYPOTHESIS

2. Answers will vary, but should address the fact that changes in the surface area of the foil and the concentration or amount of the HCl will change the reaction rate.

DEVELOP A PLAN

3. Accept all reasonable answers.

Exploration Lab continued

MAKE OBSERVATIONS

4. Answers will vary, but trials should test only one variable at a time.

ANALYZE THE RESULTS

5. Sample answer: We crushed the aluminum foil into a ball, sanded its surface, and cut it into pieces.

6. Sample answer: The sanded foil reacted the fastest, and the foil ball reacted the slowest. The sanded sample had the protective oxidized coating removed and the foil ball had the least surface area, so it reacted the most slowly.

7. Sample answer: We changed the strength of the HCl solution by adding water to it.

8. Sample answer: The trial with the 1.0 M HCl reacted the fastest, and the trial with the most diluted HCl solution reacted the slowest. The higher concentration HCl had more acid to react with the foil than the watered-down HCl, so it reacted more quickly. We could tell because there were more bubbles and more heat in the reaction with the stronger HCl.

DRAW CONCLUSIONS

9. Answers will vary.

Connect TO THE ESSENTIAL QUESTION

10. Sample answer: You can increase its surface area. The more surface area there is, the more of a material is exposed, so more of it can react. Therefore, it has a quicker reaction rate.

11. Sample answer: You can change the strength of a solution or the amount that you use. The higher the concentration or quantity of a solution, the faster the reaction rate.

Name ______________________________ Class __________________ Date ________________________

EXPLORATION LAB DIRECTED Inquiry

Change of Pace

In this activity, you will investigate the ways in which surface area and concentration of reactants can affect the rate of a chemical reaction. You will explore ways to increase or decrease the rate of the reaction between aluminum foil and hydrochloric acid (HCl).

The speed at which a chemical reaction occurs is called the *rate* of the reaction. Sometimes you want a reaction to take place rapidly, such as when you are polishing silver. Other times you want a reaction to happen slowly, like when you are depending on a battery as a source of electrical energy. Therefore, it is important to know how the rate of a chemical reaction can be controlled.

OBJECTIVES

- Describe the factors that affect the rate of a chemical reaction.
- Compare different ways to change the rate of a chemical reaction.

MATERIALS

- aluminum foil strips, 5 cm × 1 cm each (3)
- funnels (2)
- graduated cylinder, at least 30 mL (2)
- hydrochloric acid, 1.0 M, 0.5 M, and 0.1 M concentrations (15 mL each)
- sandpaper
- scissors
- stopwatch
- test tube rack
- test tubes, at least 30 mL (3)
- water

For each student

- gloves
- lab apron
- safety goggles

PROCEDURE

ASK A QUESTION

1. Given three identical pieces of **aluminum foil**, how can you change each one to react at different speeds in 15 mL of **1.0 M hydrochloric acid**? Discuss your ideas within your group.

FORM A HYPOTHESIS

2. Write a hypothesis to address the question above. Explain your reasoning.

____

____

____

MAKE OBSERVATIONS

3. Prepare each of the three strips of aluminum foil so that they will have a different reaction rate with the 1.0 M hydrochloric acid. You might crush one into a ball, fold one up, use scissors to cut one into pieces, use **sandpaper** to rough the surface, or any other ideas you might have for ways to change the reaction rate with the acid.

Exploration Lab continued

4. Prepare the **test tubes** by placing them in the **test tube rack** and adding the hydrochloric acid. Use the **graduated cylinder** and the **funnel** to carefully measure out 15 mL of 1.0 M acid. Then, pour it into the first test tube. Repeat for all three test tubes.

5. Place one foil sample into one of the test tubes, and observe the reaction. Use the **stopwatch** to measure how long it takes for the reaction to begin and how long it lasts. Observe how strongly the reaction bubbles and how much heat it creates. Record your observations below, and make sure to record how you changed the aluminum foil in each test. When the reaction is complete, test your next piece of aluminum foil in the next test tube, until all your samples have been tested.

Sample A

____

____

____

____

____

Sample B

____

____

____

____

____

Sample C

____

____

____

____

____

Name ______________________ Class ______________ Date ______________

Exploration Lab continued

ANALYZE THE RESULTS

6 **Describing Methods** What did you do with each of your strips of aluminum to make them react differently? Why did you choose those methods?

7 **Analyzing Data** The amount of aluminum was the same in each of the tests. Which test reacted the fastest? Which reacted the slowest? Why?

DRAW CONCLUSIONS

8 **Evaluating Hypotheses** Do your results support the hypothesis that you made? Explain.

Exploration Lab continued

9 **Applying Concepts** What can you can do to a material to make its reaction rate slower or faster? Explain your answer.

____

____

____

____

____

ASK A QUESTION

10 Given three identical pieces of aluminum foil, how can you change hydrochloric acid to change the reaction rate with each piece? Discuss your ideas within your group.

FORM A HYPOTHESIS

11 Write a hypothesis to address the question above. Explain your reasoning.

____

____

____

MAKE OBSERVATIONS

12 Prepare the three test tubes by placing them in the test tube rack and filling them with different concentrations of hydrochloric acid. Use a graduated cylinder and funnel to carefully measure out 15 mL of hydrochloric acid in 1.0 M, **0.5 M**, and **0.1 M concentrations**, one for each test tube. Be sure to rinse and dry the graduated cylinder between measurements so as not to change the concentration of the hydrochloric acid sample.

13 Place a strip of foil in the first test tube, and observe the reaction. Use the **stopwatch** to measure how long it takes for the reaction to begin and how long it lasts. Observe how strongly the reaction bubbles and how much heat it creates. Record your observations below. When the reaction is complete, test the next concentration in the next test tube, until all the samples have been tested.

1.0 M Hydrochloric Acid

0.5 M Hydrochloric Acid

0.1 M Hydrochloric Acid

ANALYZE THE RESULTS

14. **Comparing Results** Which concentration of hydrochloric acid reacted the fastest? Which reacted the slowest?

15. **Describing Observations** If you didn't have the stopwatch, how else could you tell which concentration reacted the fastest or the slowest?

Exploration Lab continued

DRAW CONCLUSIONS

⑯ **Evaluating Hypotheses** Do your results support the hypothesis that you made? Explain.

____

____

____

____

____

⑰ **Applying Concepts** How does the concentration of a solution affect the reaction rate? Explain your answer.

____

____

____

____

____

Connect TO THE ESSENTIAL QUESTION

⑱ **Applying Concepts** Would 15 mL of 1.0 M hydrochloric acid have the same reaction rate as 30 mL of 0.5 M hydrochloric acid? Explain your answer.

____

____

____

____

____

Name ______________________________ Class ________________ Date ______________________

EXPLORATION LAB GUIDED Inquiry

Change of Pace

In this activity, you will explore ways to increase or decrease the rate of the reaction between aluminum foil and hydrochloric acid (HCl). The speed at which a chemical reaction occurs is called the *rate* of the reaction. Sometimes you want a reaction to take place rapidly, such as when polishing silver. Other times you want a reaction to happen slowly, like when you are depending on a battery as a source of electrical energy. Therefore, it is important to know how the rate of a chemical reaction can be controlled.

OBJECTIVES

- Describe the factors that affect the rate of a chemical reaction.
- Compare different ways to change the rate of a chemical reaction.

MATERIALS

- aluminum foil strips, 5 cm × 1 cm each (3)
- funnels (2)
- graduated cylinder, at least 30 mL (2)
- hydrochloric acid, 1.0 M, 0.5 M, and 0.1 M concentrations (15 mL each)
- sandpaper
- scissors
- stopwatch
- test tube rack
- test tubes, at least 30 mL (3)
- water

For each student

- gloves
- lab apron
- safety goggles

PROCEDURE

ASK A QUESTION

1. Given aluminum foil and hydrochloric acid, how can you change each one to change the rate of a chemical reaction between them? Consider some ideas, and discuss them within your group.

FORM A HYPOTHESIS

2. Write a hypothesis to address the question above. Explain your reasoning.

____

____

____

____

____

____

____

____

____

____

____

Exploration Lab continued

DEVELOP A PLAN

3. Examine the materials your teacher has provided. Think about ways to use those materials to test your hypothesis. Write a step-by-step procedure for testing your hypothesis. Remember that there are two variables in this investigation—aluminum foil and HCl—but for accurate results you should test only one variable at a time. Which variables will you control? How will you control them? How will you collect and record data? Write your procedure below. Include sketches if you wish.

____

____

____

____

____

____

____

____

____

____

____

MAKE OBSERVATIONS

4. With teacher approval, carry out your procedure to test your hypothesis. Record your observations and data below. Pay particular attention to the number of bubbles formed by the reaction. You may wish to make a table to record your data.

____

____

____

____

____

____

____

____

Exploration Lab continued

ANALYZE THE RESULTS

5 **Describing Methods** What did you do with each of your strips of aluminum to make them react differently? Why?

____

____

____

____

____

6 **Analyzing Data** The amount of aluminum was the same in each test. Which test reacted the fastest? Which reacted the slowest? Why?

____

____

____

____

____

7 **Describing Methods** hat did you to to the HCl to change the reaction rate with aluminum foil?

____

____

____

____

____

8 **Analyzing Data** Which test reacted the fastest? Which reacted the slowest? How do you know?

____

____

____

____

____

DRAW CONCLUSIONS

9 **Evaluating Hypotheses** Do your results support the hypothesis that you made? Explain.

____

____

____

____

____

Connect TO THE ESSENTIAL QUESTION

10 **Applying Concepts** What can you can do to a material to change its reaction rate? Explain your answer.

____

____

____

____

____

11 **Applying Concepts** What can you do to a solution to change its reaction rate? Explain your answer.

____

____

____

____

____

QUICK LAB DIRECTED Inquiry

Natural vs. Synthetic Fibers GENERAL

Student pairs
15 minutes

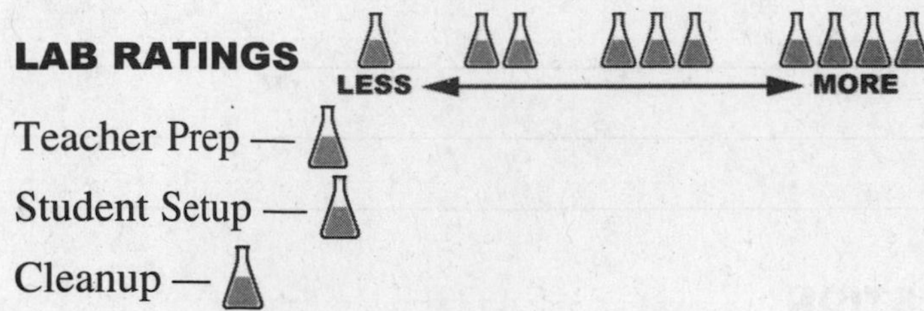

MATERIALS

For each pair
- cotton fabric
- cover slip
- eyedropper
- microscope
- microscope slide
- nylon fabric
- tweezers
- water

For each student
- safety goggles

SAFETY INFORMATION

Remind students to review all safety cautions and icons before beginning this lab. Have students wear safety goggles when using the tweezers to pull a fiber from the cloth. Once they have prepared their wet mounts, students can remove the goggles to carry out their microscopic observations.

My Notes

TEACHER NOTES

In this activity, students will investigate the differences between a natural fiber (cotton) and a synthetic fiber (nylon). Each has advantages for clothing manufacturers. Cotton has a soft feel and is very comfortable to wear but requires more care and ironing. Nylon is more durable, requires little or no ironing, and is more versatile. Review with the students how to prepare a wet-mount slide. They should also be reminded to always use the lowest-power objective when first locating the object under the microscope.

Tip This activity introduces students to the concept of polymers, which are organic compounds whose molecules are extremely long and made up of repeating units. Show students a rubber band and explain that the rubber is a natural polymer called latex. Tell students that they will be examining fabrics made of polymers, one natural and one synthesized by humans. Have students compare the stretchiness of the fabrics they examine with that of a rubber band.

Student Tip Encourage students to try stretching the fabrics as they make observations and to try wetting the fabrics to see how well they hold water.

Skills Focus Examining Samples, Constructing Drawings, Making Observations

MODIFICATION FOR GUIDED Inquiry

Have students research the difference between natural and synthetic fibers. Students should develop a list of materials they would like to observe and the procedures they will use to determine the nature of each material. Allow students to move forward with all reasonable procedures.

Quick Lab continued

Answer Key

1. Sample answers: Cotton: softer, thicker, wrinkly. Nylon: feels smoother, more like plastic.

4. Sample answers: Cotton fiber is made of smaller fibers and looks like a twined rope. Nylon is made of individual solid fibers.

6. Accept all reasonable answers.

7. Sample answer: Scientists want to develop new synthetic fibers because they want fibers with specific properties.

Name ______________________ Class ______________ Date ________________

QUICK LAB DIRECTED Inquiry

Natural vs. Synthetic Fibers

In this activity, you will look at the properties of two kinds of fibers. Cotton is made up of natural fibers. Nylon is made up of synthetic fibers. The fibers in cotton and nylon are both made of organic molecules called polymers. A polymer is a very long molecule made up of smaller, repeating units called monomers. Cotton fibers are made up of cellulose, a polymer of glucose, which is a type of sugar. Nylon fibers are made up of polyamide, which is polymer that is made commercially using chemical reactions. In nylon, the polymer is made of monomers that contain nitrogen. The differences in the monomers give different polymers different properties. Other examples of natural polymers are starch, glycogen, and keratin. Other examples of synthetic polymers are polyester, polyurethane, polyvinyl chloride (PVC), and polycarbonate.

OBJECTIVES

- Describe the structure of a polymer.
- Compare fibers made of a natural polymer with fibers made of a synthetic polymer.

MATERIALS

For each pair
- cotton fabric
- cover slip
- eyedropper
- microscope
- microscope slide
- nylon fabric
- tweezers
- water

For each student
- safety goggles

PROCEDURE

1. Examine a swatch of cotton fabric and one of nylon fabric. Write your observations of each fabric's physical properties such as flexibility, texture, and odor.

   ____

   ____

   ____

   ____

2. Pull one fiber off each swatch. Place each fiber on a separate microscope slide.
3. Add a drop of water to the fiber on each slide. Cover the drop and fiber on each slide with a cover slip.
4. Examine each fiber under a microscope. Record your observations on the lines below.

   ____

   ____

   ____

   ____

Quick Lab continued

5. In the space below, sketch the fibers.

6. From your observations, deduce some of the well-known properties of each: softness, breathability, stretchiness, and durability.

____

____

____

7. Synthetic fibers are a big business. New ones are still being developed. Why do you think scientists want to develop new synthetic fibers?

____

____

____

____

____

____

QUICK LAB DIRECTED *Inquiry*

Investigate Organic Molecules GENERAL

Small groups
15 minutes

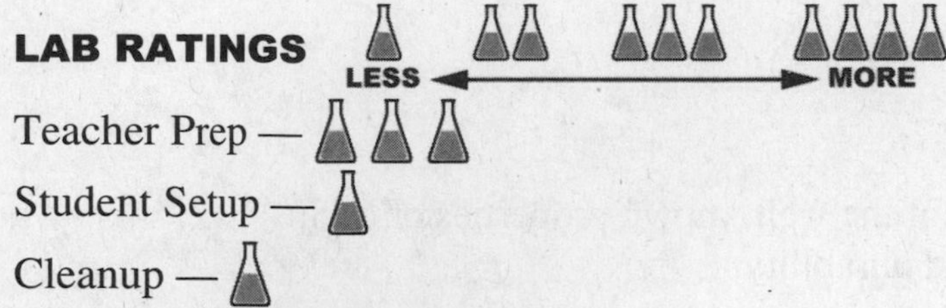

SAFETY INFORMATION

Remind students to review all safety cautions and icons before beginning this lab. Caution students not to get iodine on their skin or clothes because it stains. Tell students not to clean up any iodine that spills, but rather to inform you of the spill. When students have completed the inquiry, have them pour the solutions down a drain and discard the bread and tofu in the proper waste container. Ask students to rinse the jar lids with running water. Be sure that they do not splash water as they are rinsing the lids. Also, have students wash and dry their hands upon completion of this activity.

MATERIALS

For each group

- beaker or test tube rack
- bread
- cornstarch solution
- eyedroppers (4)
- iodine solution
- jar lids, small (5)
- liquid gelatin
- stopwatch or clock/watch with second hand
- sugar solution
- tofu

For each student

- lab apron
- safety goggles

TEACHER NOTES

In this activity, students learn that carbohydrates are made up of one or more basic units called monomers. They will then test common food items for the presence of starch, which is a complex carbohydrate that is a polymer of glucose.

Prepare the cornstarch solution by dissolving 1 tablespoon (tbsp) of cornstarch in 250 milliliters (mL) water. Prepare a liquid gelatin solution by adding twice the volume of hot water listed on the gelatin package directions to one package of gelatin crystals. Allow time for the solution to cool to room temperature before the activity begins. It is best to use packaged unflavored gelatin because it contains no added sugar. Prepare the table sugar solution by dissolving 1 (tbsp) of table sugar in 250 mL water. Prepare the iodine solution by mixing 15 mL iodine and 0.5 grams (g) potassium iodide with 100 mL of water. (It is simpler to use Lugol's iodine and reduces prep time.)

Provide each group with four test tubes, each containing one of the four solutions. Label each test tube with the solution it contains. Place the four test tubes in either a test tube rack or a small beaker.

Tip This activity enables students to practice testing for the presence of chemical substances. A dilute solution of Lugol's iodine will react with the starch, amylose, which is a straight-chain polymer of glucose, to produce a blue-black color. Potatoes also test positive for amylose. You do not get the same results if you use fruits and grains in which the primary form of starch is amylopectin, which contains branched chains of glucose units.

My Notes

______

______

______

______

______

Quick Lab continued

Skills Focus Recording Observations, Making Predictions, Making Inferences

MODIFICATION FOR GUIDED *Inquiry*

Have students make a list of other types of foods they would like to test for starch. Allow students to bring samples from home to test in class.

Answer Key

1. Comparison of Three Common Carbohydrates

Carbohydrate	Chemical name	Kind of sugar	Molecular formula
Blood sugar	glucose	monosaccharide, or simple sugar	$C_6H_{12}O_6$
Table sugar	sucrose	disaccharide, or double sugar	$C_{12}H_{22}O_{11}$
Cornstarch	amylose	polysaccharide, or complex carbohydrate	$C_n(H_2O)_{n-1}$

2. 2:1, or 2 hydrogen atoms to 1 oxygen atom

4. Iodine turned blue-black with cornstarch but not with sugar or gelatin.

5.

Food item	Iodine test results	Chemical name
cornstarch	turns blue-black	amylose
table sugar	no color change	sucrose
gelatin	no color change	protein
bread	turns blue-black	amylose
tofu	no color change	protein

7. Sample answer: Only the bread contains starch because only it caused iodine to turn blue-black.

8. Sample answer: The cornstarch solution is cloudy, but the sugar solution is not. The cornstarch is less soluble than the sugar.

9. Sample answer: Plants store excess sugars made during photosynthesis as starch. Starch molecules have hundreds of glucose units in them. Starch does not dissolve as easily as sugar because it is a much larger molecule.

10. Sample answer: No, because iodine did not change to blue-black in either gelatin or tofu.

Name ______________________ Class ______________ Date ______________

QUICK LAB DIRECTED Inquiry

Investigate Organic Molecules

Carbohydrates are one of the major types of organic compounds in living things. The sugar dissolved in blood, or blood sugar, is an example of a simple sugar or monosaccharide. The chemical name of blood sugar is glucose. Glucose is used by all living things as a source of energy needed for cellular work. Fructose, or fruit sugar, is another simple sugar.

The chemical formula for both glucose and fructose is $C_6H_{12}O_6$. Common table sugar is sucrose, which is a disaccharide. Sucrose molecules have two simple-sugar units—one glucose unit and one fructose unit. When the two combine, a water molecule (H_2O) is released, giving sucrose the formula $C_{12}H_{22}O_{11}$.

Starch is a kind of complex carbohydrate called a polysaccharide. Molecules of complex carbohydrates are polymers and are made of long chains of repeating units of monosaccharides linked together.

In this activity, you will compare the molecular structure of three carbohydrates and test five food items for the presence of starch. The kind of starch you will test is called amylose. Each molecule of amylose is a long, straight chain of hundreds of glucose units. Plants store excess sugar made during photosynthesis as starch. Grains such as corn, wheat, and rice contain starch. Enlarged stems and roots such as potatoes, yams, and carrots also contain starch.

OBJECTIVES

- Recognize the structures of different types of carbohydrates.
- Test common substances for the presence of starch.

MATERIALS

For each group

- beaker or test tube rack
- bread
- cornstarch solution
- eyedroppers (4)
- iodine solution
- jar lids, small (5)
- liquid gelatin
- stopwatch or clock/watch with second hand
- sugar solution
- tofu

For each student

- lab apron
- safety goggles

PROCEDURE

 Complete the table below.

Carbohydrate	Chemical name	Kind of sugar	Molecular formula
Blood sugar			
Table sugar			
Cornstarch			$C_n(H_2O)_{n-1}$

2. What is the ratio of hydrogen (H) to oxygen (O) in a carbohydrate?

____

❸ Place a dropper of cornstarch solution, a dropper of table sugar solution, and a dropper of liquid gelatin into three separate jar lids. Be sure to use a separate dropper for each solution.

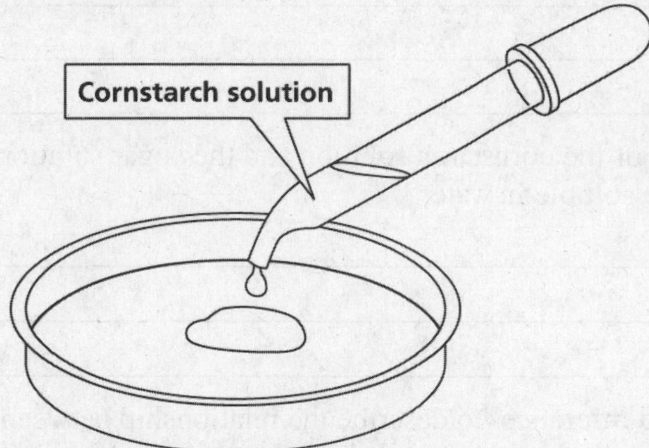

❹ Use the fourth dropper to add a drop of iodine solution to the cornstarch, sugar, and gelatin samples.

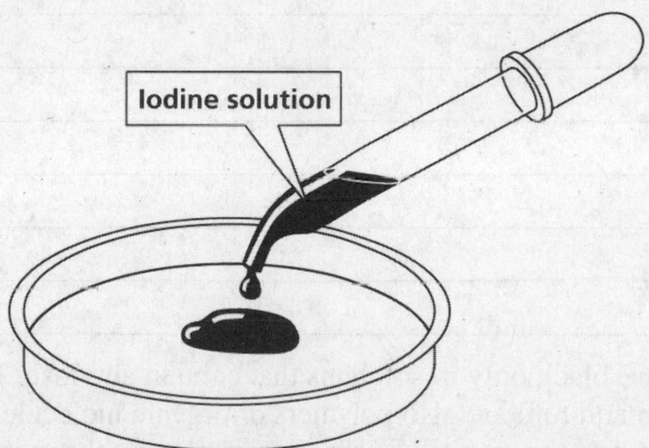

❺ Examine the jar lids after one minute. Record your observations in the table.

Food Item	Iodine Test Results	Chemical Name
cornstarch		
table sugar		
gelatin		protein
bread		
tofu		protein

❻ Using the remaining two jar lids, repeat Steps 3 and 4 with a small sample of the bread and tofu.

Quick Lab continued

7. Iodine can be used to detect the presence of starch. Do either bread or tofu contain starch? How do you know?

8. Compare the appearances of the cornstarch solution and the sugar solution. Which appears to be more soluble in water?

9. Use your observations and inferences to describe the relationship between starch and glucose.

10. Iodine turns blue-black only in solutions that contain amylose. The proteins found in gelatin and tofu are also polymers of organic molecules. Based on this information and the results of your tests, is glucose the monomer in protein? Explain your answer.

EXPLORATION LAB DIRECTED *Inquiry* **AND** GUIDED *Inquiry*

Investigate Carbon Bonding GENERAL

Student pairs

45 minutes

LAB RATINGS

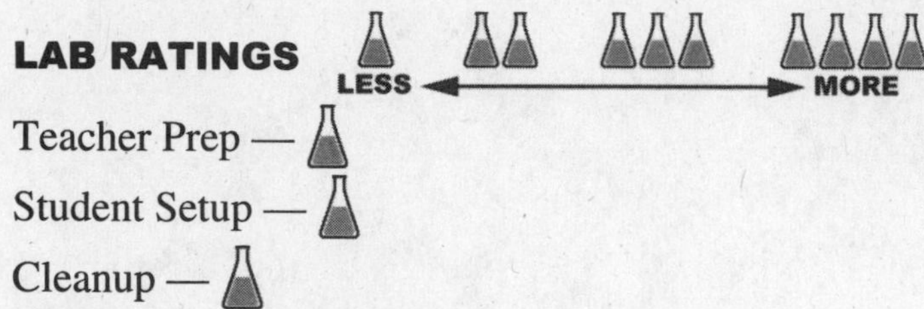

Teacher Prep —

Student Setup —

Cleanup —

SAFETY INFORMATION

Remind students to review all safety cautions and icons before beginning this lab. Advise students to be careful when inserting the toothpicks into the foam balls to avoid any hand injury.

TEACHER NOTES

In this activity, students work in pairs to build models of organic molecules. The models they build will not illustrate all of the principles of covalent bonding in carbon compounds. For example, organic molecules have a three-dimensional structure that is created, in part, by the angles between the bonds formed by carbon atoms. When a carbon atom forms four single bonds, for instance, the bonds are distributed about the core of the atom at angles greater than 90 degrees. The carbon atom and its four single covalent bonds form a 3-D structure called a tetrahedron. It is important that students focus only on the number of covalent bonds that each carbon atom forms, the kinds of covalent bonds, and arrangement of the atoms of the different elements in each structure they model. If enough foam balls are not available, small and large marshmallows, gumdrops, and so on can be used.

Tip This activity may help students understand how carbon atoms bond to each other and to hydrogen and oxygen to form several kinds of organic molecules. Remind students to sketch each model they make before re-using the materials to build another model.

Student Tip Each time you construct a model, be sure that each carbon atom in the molecule has four toothpicks (bonds) attached to it.

Skills Focus Modeling Structures, Interpreting Models, Making Predictions

MATERIALS

For each pair

- foam balls, medium (2)
- foam balls, large (6)
- foam balls, small (12)
- marking pen
- toothpicks (20)

For each student

- safety goggles

My Notes

Exploration Lab continued

Answer Key for DIRECTED Inquiry

1. a. C_2H_6; b. C_2H_4; c. C_2H_2; d. C_2H_6O; e. $C_2H_4O_2$; f. C_6H_{12}

MAKE OBSERVATIONS

4. Accept all reasonable responses.

ANALYZE THE RESULTS

5. one; two; three

6. one; two

7. 6; 12; 18

8. oxygen

9. Sample answer: the molecule with the triple bond because the structure is more rigid

10. Both have the formula $C_6H_{12}O_6$.

11. Sample answer: The carbon atom with a double bond to an oxygen atom is at the end of a glucose molecule, but it is the next to the last carbon is in the fructose molecule.

DRAW CONCLUSIONS

12. Sample answer: Having only single bonds between carbon atoms makes an organic molecule an alkane. Having a double bond between two carbon atoms makes an organic molecule an alkene. Having a triple bond between two carbon atoms makes an organic molecule an alkyne. Having an oxygen atom joined to a carbon atom with a single bond makes an organic molecule an alcohol. Having one oxygen atom joined to a carbon atom with a single bond and another oxygen atom joined to the same carbon atom with a double bond makes an organic molecule an organic acid.

13. $500 \times 6 = 3{,}000$ carbon atoms

Connect TO THE ESSENTIAL QUESTION

14. Sample answer: Carbon atoms bond to each other with three different kinds of covalent bonds, and organic molecules can have one to several hundred carbon atoms. This means that a very large number of different organic molecules can be made with carbon.

Answer Key for GUIDED Inquiry

1. a. C_2H_6; b. C_2H_4; c. C_2H_2; d. C_2H_6O; e. $C_2H_4O_2$; f. C_6H_{12}

MAKE OBSERVATIONS

4. Accept all reasonable responses.

MAKE A PREDICTION

6. Sample hypothesis: If I use all of the model atoms to model an organic molecule, then I can make four different kinds of organic molecules.

Exploration Lab continued

TEST THE PREDICTION

7. Accept all reasonable responses.

8. one; two; three

9. one; two

10. 6; 12; 18

11. oxygen

12. Sample answer: Compare: Both have the same formula, $C_6H_{12}O_6$. Contrast: The carbon atom with a double bond to an oxygen atom is at the end of a glucose molecule, but it is the next to the last carbon is in the fructose molecule.

DRAW CONCLUSIONS

13. Sample answer: Having only single bonds between carbon atoms makes an organic molecule an alkane. Having a double bond between two carbon atoms makes an organic molecule an alkene. Having a triple bond between two carbon atoms makes an organic molecule an alkyne. Having an oxygen atom joined to a carbon atom with a single bond makes an organic molecule an alcohol. Having one oxygen atom joined to a carbon atom with a single bond and another oxygen atom joined to the same carbon atom with a double bond makes an organic molecule an organic acid.

14. $500 \times 6 = 3{,}000$ carbon atoms

Connect TO THE ESSENTIAL QUESTION

15. Sample answer: Carbon atoms bond to each other with three different kinds of covalent bonds, and organic molecules can have one to several hundred carbon atoms. This means that a very large number of different organic molecules can be made with carbon.

16. Sample answer: The ability of carbon to form a very large number of different kinds of organic molecules probably has something to do with the many different kinds of living things.

Name ______________________ Class ______________ Date ______________

EXPLORATION LAB DIRECTED Inquiry

Investigate Carbon Bonding

In this lab, you will use models to explore the chemical bonds that form between carbon atoms in organic molecules. Carbon atoms form a kind of bond called a covalent bond, in which valence electrons are shared by two atoms. A carbon atom has four valence electrons, so a carbon atom forms four chemical bonds. A hydrogen atom forms only one covalent bond with another atom. An oxygen atom forms two covalent bonds with other atoms. Covalent bonds in which two atoms share two electrons are called single bonds. A bond in which four electrons are shared is called a double bond. A bond in which six electrons are shared is called a triple bond. A carbon atom must share all of its valence electrons to form a neutral compound. To understand how carbon atoms form compounds, you will use foam balls to model atoms and toothpicks to model chemical bonds.

OBJECTIVES

- Model the single, double, and triple bonds between two carbon atoms.
- Model carbon chains and rings.
- Model simple molecules in basic categories of organic compounds.

MATERIALS

For each pair

- foam balls, medium (2)
- foam balls, large (6)
- foam balls, small (12)
- marking pen
- toothpicks (20)

For each student

- safety goggles

PROCEDURE

1. The figure below shows examples of six different kinds of organic molecules. Write the chemical formula for each kind of organic molecule shown below.

Examples of Basic Kinds of Organic Compounds

Alkane	Alkene	Alkyne
H–C(H)(H)–C(H)(H)–H	$H_2C=CH_2$	H–C≡C–H

Formula: **a.** ______________ **b.** ______________ **c.** ______________

Exploration Lab continued

Alcohol	Organic Acid	Six-Carbon Ring
H H | | H–C–C–O–H | | H H	H | O H–C–C// | \\ H O–H	H H H \ / H | C | H–C / \ C–H | | H–C \ / C–H | C | H / \ H H H

Formula: **d.** ______________ **e.** ______________ **f.**

BUILD A MODEL

2. Label the large foam balls "C" for carbon, the small foam balls "H" for hydrogen, and the medium foam balls "O" for oxygen.
3. Construct a model of each molecule shown above.

MAKE OBSERVATIONS

4. Draw and label your models in the space below.

Exploration Lab continued

ANALYZE THE RESULTS

5 **Interpreting Models** How many bonds were there between the two carbon atoms in the first model? in the second model? in the third model?

____

____

6 **Interpreting Models** How many oxygen atoms bonded with a carbon atom in your model of the alcohol? the organic acid?

____

____

7 **Interpreting Models** In the six-carbon ring, what is the total number of carbon atoms? hydrogen atoms? single bonds?

____

____

8 **Identifying Patterns** Which other kind of atom, besides another carbon atom, can a carbon atom form a double bond with?

____

9 **Making Predictions** In which molecule might the carbon atoms be more tightly held together? Why?

____

____

____

____

____

Glucose

```
O   H
 \\ /
  C
  |
H-C-OH
  |
HO-C-H
  |
H-C-OH
  |
H-C-OH
  |
  CH2OH
```

Fructose

```
  CH2OH
  |
  C=O
  |
HO-C-H
  |
H-C-OH
  |
H-C-OH
  |
  CH2OH
```

Exploration Lab continued

⑩ **Interpreting Structures** The structures of molecules of glucose and fructose are shown above. What is the chemical formula for each molecule?

____

⑪ **Analyzing Structures** How is the structure of a glucose molecule different from the structure of a fructose molecule?

____

____

____

DRAW CONCLUSIONS

⑫ **Forming Conclusions** What do you think makes an organic molecule an alkane? an alkene? an alkyne? an alcohol? an organic acid?

____

____

____

⑬ **Applying Concepts** You learned that starch and cellulose are polymers that contain hundreds of glucose units. If one starch molecule contains 500 glucose units, how many carbon atoms are in the starch molecule?

____

____

____

Connect TO THE ESSENTIAL QUESTION

All organic molecules contain carbon atoms bonded to other carbon atoms except methane (CH_4) gas which has only one carbon atom.

⑭ **Defending Concepts** Defend the statement that follows: Carbon has the ability to form an enormous number of different organic compounds.

____

____

____

____

____

____

Name ________________________ Class ______________ Date ________________

EXPLORATION LAB GUIDED *Inquiry*

Investigate Carbon Bonding

In this lab, you will use models to explore the chemical bonds that form between carbon atoms in organic molecules. Carbon atoms form a kind of bond called a covalent bond in which valence electrons are shared by two atoms. A carbon atom has four valence electrons, so a carbon atom forms four chemical bonds. A hydrogen atom forms only one covalent bond with another atom. An oxygen atom forms two covalent bonds with other atoms. Covalent bonds in which two atoms share two electrons are called single bonds. A bond in which four electrons are shared is called a double bond. A bond in which six electrons are shared is called a triple bond. A carbon atom must share all of its valence electrons to form a neutral compound. To understand how carbon atoms form compounds, you will use foam balls to model atoms and toothpicks to model chemical bonds.

OBJECTIVES

- Model the single, double, and triple bonds between two carbon atoms.
- Model carbon chains and rings.
- Model simple molecules in basic categories of organic compounds.

MATERIALS

For each pair

- foam balls, medium (2)
- foam balls, large (6)
- foam balls, small (12)
- marking pen
- toothpicks (20)

For each student

- safety goggles

PROCEDURE

1. The figure below shows examples of six different kinds of organic molecules. Write the chemical formula for each kind of organic molecule shown below.

Examples of Basic Kinds of Organic Compounds

Alkane	Alkene	Alkyne
H–C(H)(H)–C(H)(H)–H	$H_2C{=}CH_2$	H–C≡C–H

Formula: a. ______________ b. ________________ c. ________________

Exploration Lab continued

Alcohol	Organic Acid	Six-Carbon Ring
H–C–C–O–H (with H above and below each C)	H–C–C(=O)–O–H (with H above and below the first C)	Six C atoms in a ring, each bonded to two H

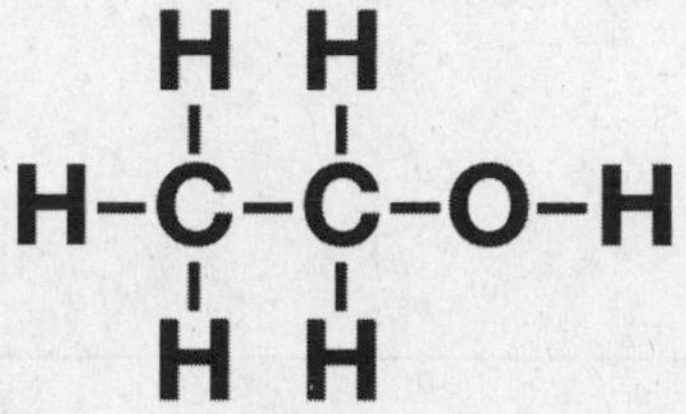

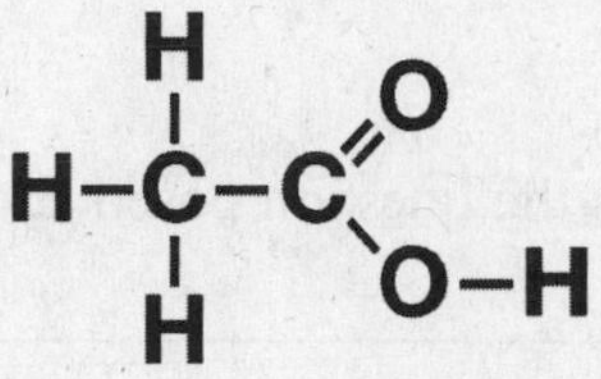

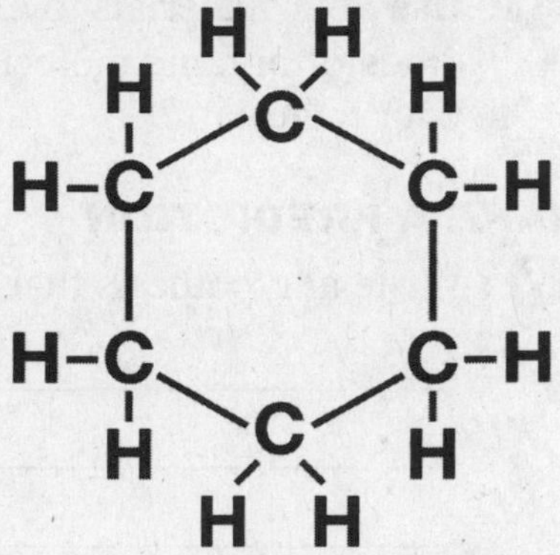

Formula: **d.** ____________ **e.** ____________ **f.** ____________

BUILD A MODEL

2 Label the large foam balls "C" for carbon, the small foam balls "H" for hydrogen, and the medium foam balls "O" for oxygen.

3 Construct a model of each molecule shown above.

MAKE OBSERVATIONS

4 Draw and label your models in the space below.

Exploration Lab continued

ASK A QUESTION

5 Use your materials to explore the question that follows: How many different kinds of organic molecules can be made by using all of the model atoms in your materials?

MAKE A PREDICTION

6 Write a hypothesis that answers the question posed above.

____

____

____

____

____

TEST THE PREDICTION

7 Build as many different molecules as you can with the materials. Draw each model you made in the space below.

____

____

____

____

____

____

____

____

____

____

____

____

ANALYZE THE RESULTS

8 **Interpreting Models** How many bonds were there between the two carbon atoms in your model of an alkane? in your model of an alkene? in your model of an alkyne?

____

____

9 **Interpreting Models** How many oxygen atoms bonded with a carbon atom in your model of an alcohol? an organic acid?

____

____

10 **Interpreting Models** In the six-carbon ring, what is the total number of carbon atoms? hydrogen atoms? single bonds?

____

____

11 **Identifying Patterns** Which other kind of atom, besides another carbon atom, can a carbon atom form a double bond with?

____

Glucose	Fructose
O=C–H (aldehyde)	CH_2OH
H–C–OH	C=O
HO–C–H	HO–C–H
H–C–OH	H–C–OH
H–C–OH	H–C–OH
CH_2OH	CH_2OH

12 **Analyzing Structures** Compare and contrast the glucose molecule and the fructose molecule.

____

____

____

____

____

Exploration Lab continued

DRAW CONCLUSIONS

13 **Forming Conclusions** What makes an organic molecule an alkane? an alkene? an alkyne? an alcohol? an organic acid?

14 **Applying Concepts** You learned that starch and cellulose are polymers that contain hundreds of glucose units. If one starch molecule contains 500 glucose units, how many carbon atoms are in the starch molecule?

Connect TO THE ESSENTIAL QUESTION

All organic molecules contain carbon atoms bonded to other carbon atoms except methane (CH_4) gas, which has only one carbon atom.

15 **Defending Concepts** Defend the statement that follows: Carbon has the ability to form an enormous number of different organic compounds.

16 **Recognizing Relationships** All of the functional parts of living organisms are made of organic compounds. Why do you think there are so many different kinds of living things?

QUICK LAB INDEPENDENT Inquiry

Modeling Isotopes and Radioactive Decay ADVANCED

Student pairs
30 minutes

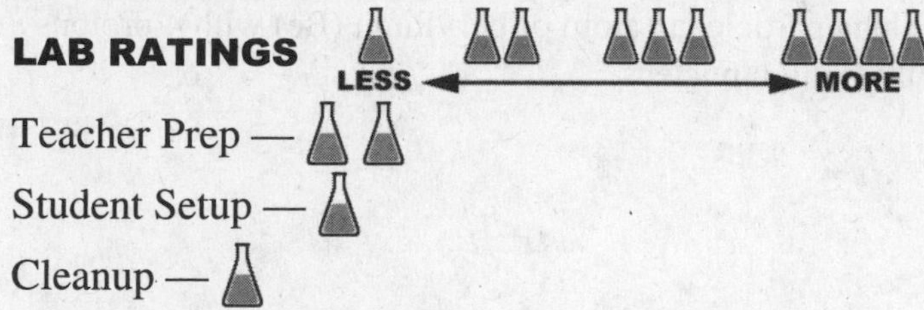

Teacher Prep —
Student Setup —
Cleanup —

MATERIALS

For each group
- beads of one color (18)
- beads of another color (21)
- empty film canisters (3)

For each student
- safety goggles

SAFETY INFORMATION

Remind students to review all safety cautions and icons before beginning this lab. Be sure that students pick up any beads that fall on the floor to prevent anyone from slipping on them.

My Notes

TEACHER NOTES

In this activity, students will work in pairs to model the nucleus of an atom of each of carbon's three isotopes. Students will be given the materials for modeling but will decide for themselves how the materials should be used. Students may wonder why they have only two kinds of subatomic particles to model. Explain that electrons, the third type of subatomic particle, are involved in chemical bonding but are not a part of what distinguishes isotopes of the same element. Students will model alpha decay of carbon-14 in the second portion of this lab. You may wish to explain to interested students that carbon-14 does not actually undergo alpha decay. Instead, it undergoes beta decay, releasing an electron and energy. The atoms that typically undergo alpha decay are larger than carbon atoms and contain many subatomic particles, which make them more difficult to model using beads. If empty film canisters are not available, supply some other type of small container such as zipper bags or even paper cups. A periodic table of elements should be available for students to refer to.

Tip This activity may help students understand how the nuclei of isotopes of the same element differ. Students should understand that the number of protons in an atom's nucleus determines the elemental identity of an atom.

Student Tip Sketch the contents of the nucleus of each isotope of carbon before assembling the models. This will help you decide which color of beads to use for each type of particle found in the nucleus.

Skills Focus Modeling Structures, Developing Methods, Interpreting Results

MODIFICATION FOR INDEPENDENT Inquiry

Have students research an isotope of an element that undergoes alpha decay. Have students design a model that could be used to show the decay series of the isotope.

Quick Lab continued

Answer Key

1. The nucleus of a carbon-12 atom has 6 protons and 6 neutrons.
2. Sample answer: red beads; blue beads
3. Sample answer: We removed two red beads, which represent protons, and two blue beads, which represent neutrons.
4. helium (He)
5. Sample answer: If a carbon-14 atom lost an alpha particle, an atom of beryllium (Be) with 4 protons and 6 neutrons would be formed along with the helium nucleus.
6. 6

Name ______________________________ Class ________________ Date ________________________

QUICK LAB INDEPENDENT *Inquiry*

Modeling Isotopes and Radioactive Decay

In this lab, you will use the materials provided by your teacher to model three isotopes of carbon. The most common isotope of carbon is carbon-12. The other two are carbon-13 and carbon-14. Of these three, only carbon-14 is radioactive.

Some radioactive isotopes release alpha particles. An alpha particle consists of two protons and two neutrons. You will model alpha decay using one of your model isotopes.

OBJECTIVES

- Model different isotopes of one element.
- Use a model to demonstrate radioactive decay.

MATERIALS

For each group

- beads of one color (18)
- beads of another color (21)
- empty film canisters (3)

For each student

- safety goggles

PROCEDURE

1. How many protons and neutrons are in the nucleus of a carbon-12 atom?

   ____

2. Decide how to use the materials that your teacher has provided to model the three isotopes of carbon. Build the three model isotopes. What did you use to model protons?

   ____

   What did you use to model neutrons?

   ____

3. Use one of your model isotopes to model the process of alpha decay. Describe what you did in the space below.

   ____

   ____

   ____

Quick Lab continued

4. An alpha particle is the same as the nucleus of an atom of a certain element. Which element is this?

____

5. If carbon-14 were able to undergo alpha decay, what atoms would be formed? Explain your answer.

____

____

____

6. How many electrons do atoms of each isotope of carbon have?

____

QUICK LAB DIRECTED Inquiry

Modeling a Nuclear Chain Reaction ADVANCED

Small groups
30 minutes

MATERIALS
For each group
- dominoes (15)

My Notes

LAB RATINGS LESS ⟷ MORE

Teacher Prep — 1
Student Setup — 2
Cleanup — 1

TEACHER NOTES

In this activity, students will work in small groups to model an uncontrolled nuclear fission chain reaction. Uranium-235 is unstable and can split into two smaller nuclei with the release of two or three neutrons depending on the split. In this activity, a model will be developed in which each fission event releases two neutrons, each of which is represented by a domino.

Tip This activity may help students understand the basic concepts of nuclear fission chain reactions. Emphasize that neutrons released by the fission of one nucleus (a falling domino) collide with other nuclei. In the process, energy is released. Each time one nucleus splits (domino falls), two more nuclei split and more energy is released. Therefore, the reaction not only perpetuates itself once it begins, but the amount of energy released by the reaction is multiplied with each round of fission until all the fuel (the dominoes) is used up.

Student Tip Think of a falling domino as a nucleus that is "falling apart." The result is a release of energy.

Skills Focus Modeling Concepts, Making Observations, Interpreting Results

MODIFICATION FOR INDEPENDENT Inquiry

Have students rearrange the dominoes to show a controlled chain reaction. Have students time each of the model chain reactions and describe the differences.

Quick Lab continued

Answer Key

3. Sample answer: This models an uncontrolled chain reaction because each domino causes two more dominoes to fall.
4. neutrons being released in a fission reaction
5. smaller nuclei, neutrons, and energy
6. Sample answer: Absorption of neutrons could be modeled by putting a hand between some of the dominoes so that they do not tip over other dominoes.
7. Sample answer: If nuclear chain reactions in nuclear power plants were not controlled, they could produce too much energy and present a safety hazard.

Name ______________________________ Class ________________ Date ______________________

QUICK LAB DIRECTED Inquiry

Modeling a Nuclear Chain Reaction

Uranium-235 decays by nuclear fission. When a uranium-235 nucleus splits into two smaller nuclei, it releases two or three neutrons that can cause neighboring nuclei to undergo fission. This fission can result in a nuclear chain reaction. In this lab, you will build a model of a nuclear chain reaction using dominoes.

OBJECTIVES

- Model uncontrolled and controlled nuclear chain reactions.
- Evaluate the benefits and risks of nuclear energy.

MATERIALS

For each group

- dominoes (15)

PROCEDURE

1. Set up the dominoes to model a fission reaction that results in release of two neutrons at each fission event.

2. Repeat Step 1 if some of the dominoes do not fall. You may have to adjust the setup a few times.

3. Which type of chain reaction, controlled or uncontrolled, does the model show? Explain your answer.

   ____

   ____

   ____

4. What did the falling dominoes represent?

   ____

5. What is released at each step of the reaction?

   ____

Quick Lab continued

6. In a nuclear power plant, a nuclear chain reaction is controlled by using a material that absorbs some of the neutrons that are produced. Explain how you could change your model to show a controlled nuclear chain reaction.

____

____

____

7. Why do you think it is important to be able to control nuclear chain reactions in a nuclear power plant?

____

____

____

QUICK LAB DIRECTED *Inquiry*

Investigate Solutions GENERAL

Small groups
15 minutes

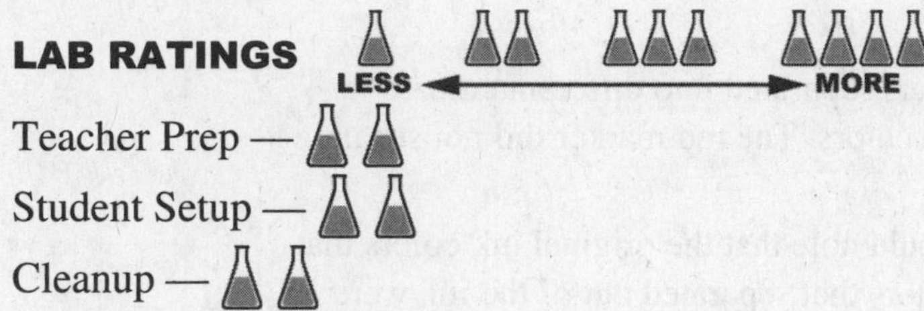

LAB RATINGS

Teacher Prep —
Student Setup —
Cleanup —

MATERIALS

For each group
- cups, plastic (3)
- eyedropper
- filters, coffee (3)
- markers, different-colored (3)
- rubber bands (3)
- water

For each student
- lab apron
- protective gloves
- safety goggles

SAFETY INFORMATION

Remind students to review all safety cautions and icons before beginning this lab. Remind students that they should always wear gloves and safety goggles when working with solutions. Have students wash and dry their hands upon completion of this inquiry.

TEACHER NOTES

In this activity, students will explore the properties of solutions by exploring how ink solutions separate into different-colored solutes. Students will place ink from different-colored markers on coffee filters and then pour water onto the filters to observe the solutes of each ink solution. Provide each group with a primary-colored marker (red, blue, or yellow), a secondary-colored marker (green, orange, or purple), and either a brown or black marker. The markers should be water soluble. Review the terms *solute* and *solvent* with students before the lab.

My Notes

Tip Be sure to test the markers before the class begins to make sure that they contain water-soluble ink and that students will see a separation of colors. Generic brand markers might separate more easily than brand-name markers.

Student Tip Be sure to place a thick coat of ink on each coffee filter. You might want to color over the same area ten times with the marker.

Skills Focus Explaining Observations

MODIFICATION FOR GUIDED *Inquiry*

Once students are familiar with the concepts of solutions, solvents, and solutes, challenge them to use the materials to answer the question, "How can we separate a solution into its solutes?" Prompt students by explaining that the ink in some colored markers is a solution. Challenge them to write out a set of procedures that will allow them to explore this question. After the investigation, have students identify the solutes and solvents of each solution.

Quick Lab continued

Answer Key

3. Accept all reasonable answers.
   Teacher Prompt Have you ever accidently spilled water on a drawing made with markers? What happens to the ink?
5. Accept all reasonable answers.
6. Accept all reasonable answers.
7. Sample answer: The green and brown markers separated into different colors; however they did not separate into the same colors. The red marker did not separate into any colors.
8. Accept all reasonable answers. Students should note that the original ink colors that separated out were the solutions, and the colors that separated out of the ink were the solutes. For example, green ink is a solution, and blue and yellow dyes are the solutes in that solution.
   Teacher Prompt What is the definition of a solution? What is the definition of a solute?
9. Sample answer: Water is the solvent because it dissolved the solutes.

QUICK LAB DIRECTED Inquiry

Investigate Solutions

In this lab, you will explore the properties of solutions by adding drops of water to ink from colored markers. Many colors of ink are solutions that are made up of different colored dyes. Water helps to separate the different colored dyes in an ink solution.

OBJECTIVES

- Separate different-colored ink solutions using a filter.
- Describe common characteristics of solutions.
- Identify solvents and solutes.

MATERIALS

For each group
- cups, plastic (3)
- eyedropper
- filters, coffee (3)
- markers, different-colored (3)
- rubber bands (3)
- water

For each student
- lab apron
- protective gloves
- safety goggles

PROCEDURE

1. Use one of the markers to draw a solid rectangle on one of the coffee filters that is 3 cm × 3 cm. Place the filter over the top of the cup so that the colored rectangle is over the opening of the cup. Secure the filter in place by putting the rubber band over the filter and cup.
2. Repeat Step 1 for each of the different markers so that each coffee filter has a different-colored rectangle on it. Place each coffee filter over the top of a plastic cup.
3. Make a prediction about what you think will happen to the colored rectangles when you add a few drops of water to each.

   ____

   ____
4. Use the eyedropper to place several drops of water onto each colored rectangle. Make sure that any drops of water that pass through the filter fall into the plastic cups.

Quick Lab continued

5 Observe each filter over the course of five minutes. Record your observations in the table below.

OBSERVATIONS OF DIFFERENT-COLORED INK

Original marker color	Observations after 1 minute	Observations after 3 minutes	Observations after 5 minutes

6 Was your original prediction correct? Explain.

____

____

7 What were the similarities and differences between the inks you used in this experiment?

____

____

____

8 Identify the solutes and the solutions in this investigation.

____

____

____

9 A solvent is any substance in which another substance dissolves. What was the solvent in this experiment?

____

QUICK LAB DIRECTED Inquiry

Solution Concentration GENERAL

Small groups
25 minutes

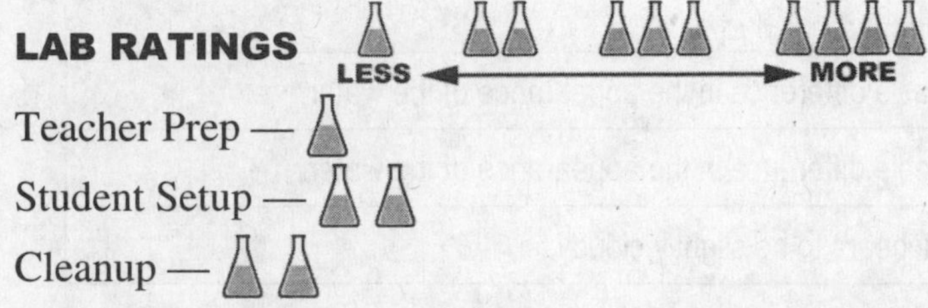

Teacher Prep —
Student Setup —
Cleanup —

MATERIALS

For each group
- balance
- beakers (4)
- cup, plastic
- hot plate
- rod, stirring
- sugar, granulated, 225 g
- water, 1 L

For each student
- lab apron
- protective gloves
- safety goggles

SAFETY INFORMATION

Remind students to review all safety cautions and icons before beginning this lab. Remind students that they should not taste any substances used in the lab, and advise them to use caution when handling the hot plate. Caution students to use heat-resistant gloves when touching the heated beakers. Be sure that all the beakers have completely cooled before students wash them.

TEACHER NOTES

In this activity, students will explore the concept of concentration by dissolving different amounts of sugar into beakers of warm water. They will then organize the solutions by their concentrations.

Student Tip To measure the sugar, place a cup on the balance and measure the mass of the cup. Add the value of the cup mass to the mass of sugar that you wish to measure. For example, if the cup is 3 grams and you wish to measure 12 grams of sugar, you will obtain a value of 15 grams. Move the balance slider to the calculated amount. (For example, move the balance slider to 15 grams.) Then, slowly pour sugar into the cup until the scale is balanced.

Skills Focus Making Observations, Organizing Results

My Notes

MODIFICATION FOR GUIDED Inquiry

Challenge students to create solutions with different concentrations. Provide students with the materials and have them decide on the amounts of sugar that they will add to each solution. Allow them to brainstorm a set of procedures that they will follow to create the solutions. After you approve the procedures, have students carry out their investigations. Students should create their own data table to display their results.

Quick Lab continued

Answer Key

5. Sample answers:

CONCENTRATIONS OF SUGAR WATER

Solution	Sugar	Water	Observations
1	12 grams	100 mL	No noticeable difference in the appearance of the water.
2	24 grams	100 mL	No noticeable difference in the appearance of the water.
3	48 grams	100 mL	Solution appears to be slightly cloudy.
4	136 grams	100 mL	Solution is a bit cloudy and has the consistency of a syrup.

6. Sample answer: Solution 1 is the most dilute because it has the least amount of sugar dissolved in water.

7. Sample answer: Solution 4 is the most concentrated because it has the most amount of sugar dissolved in water.

8. Sample answer: Solution 1, Solution 2, Solution 3, Solution 4. The more concentrated the solution, the more syrupy it appears.

9. Sample answer: In order to create a saturated solution, I would add the 12 g of sugar at a time and continue to stir the solution until sugar will no longer dissolve in it. **Teacher Prompt** What is the definition of a saturated solution?

10. Sample answer: The sugar would not dissolve as quickly or as easily into the solvent. **Teacher Prompt** How easily does sugar dissolve in hot liquids, such as coffee or tea? How easily does sugar dissolve in cold liquids, such as lemonade?

Name ______________________ Class ______________ Date ________________

QUICK LAB DIRECTED *Inquiry*

Solution Concentration

In this lab, you will explore the concept of solution concentration by mixing different amounts of sugar into water. Once you have made your solutions, you will observe them and organize them according to their concentration.

OBJECTIVES

- Create solutions with different concentrations.
- Analyze the properties of solutions with different concentrations.

MATERIALS

For each group
- balance
- beakers (4)
- cup, plastic
- hot plate
- rod, stirring
- sugar, granulated, 225 g
- water, 1 L

For each student
- lab apron
- protective gloves
- safety goggles

PROCEDURE

1. Set up the hot plate. Fill one beaker with 100 milliliters (mL) of water. Place the beaker on top of the hot plate and turn on the hot plate.
2. Measure 12 grams of sugar using the balance.
3. Then, add the sugar to water in the beaker. Use the stirring rod to stir until the sugar has completely dissolved. Use heat-resistant gloves to remove this beaker from the hot plate and set it aside.
4. Repeat Steps 1–3 for the remaining three beakers. Measure and pour the following amounts of sugar into each beaker: 24 grams, 48 grams, 136 grams.
5. Observe each of the beaker solutions and record your observations in the table below.

COMPOSITIONS OF SUGAR WATER SOLUTIONS

Solution	Sugar	Water	Observations
1	12 grams	100 mL	
2	24 grams	100 mL	
3	48 grams	100 mL	
4	136 grams	100 mL	

6. Which solution is the most dilute and why?

____

____

Name ______________________ Class ______________ Date ______________

Quick Lab continued

7. Which solution is the most concentrated and why?

____

____

8. Organize your solutions in order of least concentrated to most concentrated. What differences can you observe among the different solutions?

____

____

9. How would you know if you have created a saturated solution? Write down the steps you would take to create a saturated solution of sugar and water.

____

____

____

____

10. How might your results have varied if you had not used the hot plate in this experiment?

____

____

EXPLORATION LAB GUIDED *Inquiry* **AND** INDEPENDENT *Inquiry*

Investigate Solubility ADVANCED

Small groups
45 minutes

MATERIALS

For each group
- balance
- basin, plastic
- beaker
- cups, clear plastic
- filters, coffee
- hot plate
- spoon, plastic
- stopwatch
- table salt
- tap water
- thermometer
- water, cold
- water, hot

For each student
- lab apron
- protective gloves
- safety goggles

LAB RATINGS

LESS ⟷ MORE

Teacher Prep — 2 flasks
Student Setup — 3 flasks
Cleanup — 2 flasks

SAFETY INFORMATION

Remind students to review all safety cautions and icons before beginning this lab. Students should always use caution when working with solutions, especially when heating them. Be sure that students take extra care when using the hot plates to heat the solutions. Warn students not to touch the beaker until it has completely cooled.

TEACHER NOTES

In this activity, students will explore the properties of solutions. Students will first show that a simple filtration step will not allow a solution to be separated into its components. They will go on to show that a solution can be separated by heating the solution to remove the solvent by evaporation, leaving the solute behind. Then, students will explore the relationship between solubility and temperature by measuring the time it takes for a known quantity of salt to dissolve in water at various temperatures.

Students should develop their own procedural steps for both levels of the lab; however, as they are all investigating the same questions, the methods should be similar. For the first part, students should filter a saltwater solution through a coffee filter. To show that the solution can be separated by heating, students should make another solution and heat it with the hot plate and show that the water can be evaporated by heating, leaving the salt behind. To show that rates of solubility can vary with different temperatures, students should prepare several solutions (always using the same amount of salt) but dissolve the salt at different temperatures. In the Independent Inquiry option, students will be challenged to decide the specific materials they will need; these materials should be very similar to the materials indicated below.

Tip Approve students' plans before allowing them to conduct their investigations. Circulate as students are working to help answer any questions that they may have.

Student Tip It is helpful to remember the difference between solutions and mixtures when you conduct your investigations.

My Notes

Exploration Lab continued

Skills Focus Practicing Lab Techniques, Answering Questions, Forming Predictions

MODIFICATION FOR DIRECTED Inquiry

Rather than challenging students to develop their own procedures, give groups a pre-made handout with clearly defined procedural steps to aid their investigations. This way, students can concentrate on exploring the properties of solutions rather than developing the methods for which to explore solutions.

Answer Key for GUIDED Inquiry

ASK A QUESTION

1. Accept all reasonable answers. Students should write down any pre-existing knowledge they have about solutions.

DEVELOP A PLAN

2. Accept all reasonable answers. Students should use the materials above, such as the coffee filter, water, and salt to demonstrate that filtration does not separate the solution.

FORM A PREDICTION

3. Sample answer: I think that if we filter the solution through a coffee filter, some of the salt will separate out of the solution and will remain in the coffee filter.

TEST THE PREDICTION

4. Accept all reasonable answers. If students' original predictions were incorrect, students should revise their predictions.

DEVELOP A PLAN

5. Accept all reasonable answers. Students should develop a plan to show that the salt will separate out of a solution when enough heat is applied. They should use materials such as water, salt, a thermometer, and a hot plate.
6. Accept all reasonable answers. Students' plans should demonstrate that the rate of solubility will vary at different temperatures. They should take careful care to control certain variables (such as the amount of salt used) when other variables (such as the temperature) change.
   Teacher Prompt Think about how you will make sure your results are valid. How can using the balance aid you in this part of the lab?

FORM A PREDICTION

7. Sample answer: I think that the salt will separate from the solution at a very high heat (boiling water). I also think that if the temperature increases, so will the rate of solubility.

TEST THE PREDICTION

8. Accept all reasonable answers. Students should revise their predictions about heat and solutions if needed.

Exploration Lab continued

ANALYZE THE RESULTS

9. Sample answer: We could not separate the solute from the solvent by filtering. When we heated the solution enough, the salt eventually separated out. When we gradually increased the temperature of the water, the same amount of salt dissolved faster as the temperature increased.

10. Sample answer: The solute is the salt, and the solvent is the water.

11. Accept all reasonable answers.

DRAW CONCLUSIONS

12. Accept all reasonable answers. Students should understand that filtration does not separate the parts of a solution.

13. Accept all reasonable answers.

14. Sample answer: When the temperature increases, so does the rate of solubility of a solution.

Connect TO THE ESSENTIAL QUESTION

15. Sample answer: Solutions are homogeneous mixtures of a solute and a solvent. The solute and solvent cannot be separated by filtration but can be separated using a state change that removes the solvent by evaporation. The addition of heat tends to make the solute dissolve faster in the solvent.

Answer Key for INDEPENDENT Inquiry

ASK A QUESTION

1. Accept all reasonable answers. Students should write down any pre-existing knowledge they have about solutions.

DEVELOP A PLAN

2. Answers may vary. Students should develop procedures to investigate three distinct problems: what happens when a solution is filtered, what happens to the parts of a solution when it is heated, and what happens to the rate of solubility when the temperature changes. Accept student answers that detail how their experiments will explore these questions.

FORM A PREDICTION

3. Accept all reasonable answers.

TEST THE PREDICTION

4. Accept all reasonable answers. Students should revise their predictions about filtration, heat, and solutions if needed.

Exploration Lab continued

ANALYZE THE RESULTS

5. Sample answer: We could not separate the solute from the solvent by filtering. When we heated the solution enough, the salt eventually separated out. When we gradually increased the temperature of the water, the same amount of salt dissolved faster as the temperature increased.
6. Sample answer: The solute is the salt, and the solvent is the water.
7. Accept all reasonable answers.

DRAW CONCLUSIONS

8. Accept all reasonable answers. Students should understand that filtration does not separate the parts of a solution, but increasing the temperature of a solution can separate it into its parts and increase the rate of solubility.
9. Sample answer: When the temperature increases, so does the rate of solubility of a solution.

Connect TO THE ESSENTIAL QUESTION

10. Sample answer: Solutions are homogeneous mixtures of a solute and a solvent. The solute and solvent cannot be separated by filtration but can be separated using a state change that removes the solvent by evaporation. The addition of heat tends to make the solute dissolve faster in the solvent.

Name ______________________ Class ______________ Date ______________

EXPLORATION LAB GUIDED Inquiry

Investigate Solubility

In this lab, you will explore the properties of solutions. This lab will instruct you to investigate different problems, using the materials provided. You will work with your group to develop procedures to investigate the problems, then conduct investigations to learn more about solutions, solvents, solutes, solubility, and temperature.

OBJECTIVES

- Explore the properties of solutions.
- Identify solutes and solvents.
- Describe the relationship between temperature and the rate of solubility.

MATERIALS

For each group
- balance
- basin, plastic
- beaker
- cups, clear plastic
- filters, coffee
- hot plate
- spoon, plastic
- stopwatch
- table salt
- tap water
- thermometer
- water, cold
- water, hot

For each student
- lab apron
- protective gloves
- safety goggles

PROCEDURE

ASK A QUESTION

1. Solubility is the ability of one substance to dissolve in another at a given temperature and pressure. As a group, discuss what you know about solutions, and record it here.

   ____

   ____

   ____

   ____

DEVELOP A PLAN

2. In the first part of this lab, your group will demonstrate that a solution cannot be separated by filtering it. Using materials provided, generate a list of steps you will follow to explore this concept. Write your detailed plan below, and identify the constants and variables. Include how you will organize or display your results.

   ____

   ____

   ____

   ____

   ____

   ____

   ____

Exploration Lab continued

FORM A PREDICTION

3 What do you think will happen when you carry out your procedures?

TEST THE PREDICTION

4 Work with your group to carry out the procedures as you wrote them. Be sure to follow all proper lab techniques. Did the results of your investigation support your prediction?

DEVELOP A PLAN

5 In this part of the lab, your group is tasked with showing that a solution can be separated with heat. Again, use materials provided to help you generate a list of procedure steps that you will follow to investigate this idea.

6 Also in this part of the lab, your group will explore the relationship between temperature and the rate of solubility. How will your group show that the rate of solubility is affected by temperature? Using materials provided, write your detailed plan below, and identify the constants and variables.

Exploration Lab continued

FORM A PREDICTION

7. What do you think will happen to a solution when you apply heat to it? What do you think will happen to the rates of solubility at different temperatures? Write your predictions to both questions below.

____

____

____

____

TEST THE PREDICTION

8. Work with your group to carry out the procedures as you wrote them. Again, follow all proper lab techniques. Did the results of your investigation support your prediction?

____

ANALYZE THE RESULTS

9. **Explaining Results** What happened when you filtered the solution? What happened when you heated the solution? What happened to the rates of solubility of the solution at different temperatures? Explain.

____

____

____

____

10. **Describing Concepts** In your experiments, what were the parts of your solution? Identify both the solute and the solvent.

____

____

11. **Analyzing Methods** Critically assess your procedures. If you were to repeat this experiment, what could you do differently to improve your method?

____

____

____

Exploration Lab continued

DRAW CONCLUSIONS

12 **Explaining Events** What did the first part of the lab teach you about solutions? Explain why the solution did not change when you filtered it.

13 **Interpreting Results** What did the second part of the lab teach you about solutions? Explain why heat is important to understanding the properties of solutions.

14 **Recognizing Concepts** What is the relationship between temperature and the rate of solubility?

Connect TO THE ESSENTIAL QUESTION

15 **Applying Concepts** What did this investigation allow you to observe about the properties of solutions?

Name ______________________ Class ______________ Date ________________

EXPLORATION LAB INDEPENDENT *Inquiry*

Investigate Solubility

In this lab, you will explore the properties of solutions. This lab will instruct you to investigate different problems, and you will work with your group to develop the materials and procedures necessary to explore the questions. Once you develop a list of steps, you will follow them and investigate the questions in the lab.

OBJECTIVES

- Explore the properties of solutions.
- Identify solutes and solvents.
- Describe the relationship between temperature and the rate of solubility.

MATERIALS

to be determined by student groups

For each student

- lab apron
- protective gloves
- safety goggles

PROCEDURE

ASK A QUESTION

1. Solubility is the ability of one substance to dissolve in another at a given temperature and pressure. Work with your group to write down how you think the solubility of a solution might be affected by temperature.

____

____

____

____

DEVELOP A PLAN

2. In this lab, your group will have several challenges. First, you will investigate if a solution can be filtered to separate its components. Next, you will investigate if the components of a solution can be separated by using heat. Finally, you will investigate how the rate of solubility of a solution changes with its temperature. Work with your group to develop a set of procedures to investigate these three problems. Develop a list of materials you will need and the steps you will follow. Identify your variables and your constants for each part of your investigation and include how you will organize or display your results.

____

____

____

____

____

____

____

Exploration Lab continued

FORM A PREDICTION

3. What do you think will happen when you carry out your procedures?

____

____

TEST THE PREDICTION

4. Work with your group to carry out the procedures as you wrote them. Be sure to follow all proper lab techniques. Did the results of your investigation support your prediction?

____

____

ANALYZE THE RESULTS

5. **Explaining Results** What happened when you filtered the solution? What happened when you heated the solution? What happened to the rates of solubility of the solution at different temperatures? Explain.

____

____

____

6. **Describing Concepts** In your experiment, what were the parts of your solution? Identify both the solute and the solvent.

____

____

7. **Analyzing Methods** Critically assess your procedures. If you were to repeat this experiment, what could you do differently to improve your method?

____

____

DRAW CONCLUSIONS

8 **Interpreting Results** What did this lab teach you about solutions? Explain why heat is important to understanding the properties of solutions. Explain what happened to the parts of the solution when it was filtered.

___

___

___

9 **Recognizing Concepts** What is the relationship between temperature and the rate of solubility?

___

___

Connect TO THE ESSENTIAL QUESTION

10 **Applying Concepts** What did this investigation allow you to observe about the properties of solutions?

___

___

___

QUICK LAB DIRECTED Inquiry

Household Acids and Bases BASIC

Small groups
15 minutes

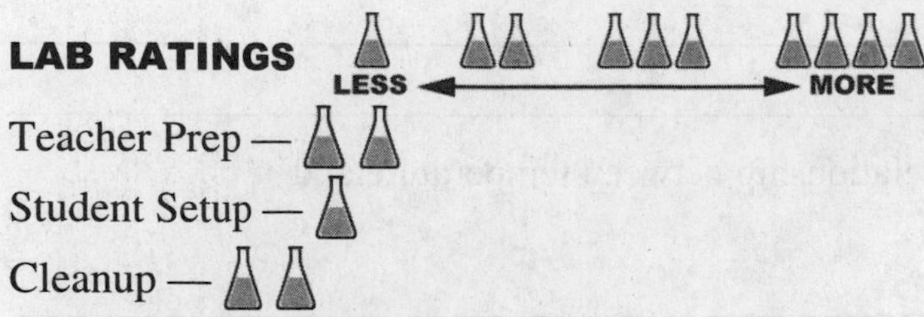

SAFETY INFORMATION

Remind students to review all safety cautions and icons before beginning this lab. Some substances may cause eye or skin irritation or may stain clothing. Aprons, gloves, and goggles should be worn at all times. All spills should be wiped up immediately.

TEACHER NOTES

In this activity, students will use litmus paper to identify acids and bases. Use common substances such as lemon juice, shampoo, coffee, milk, soft drinks, milk of magnesia, and vinegar. Label each sample so students can keep track of substances in their data tables. Students may use test tubes or plastic cups to hold substances. Samples may be poured down the sink when the activity is finished. Remind students to clean the stirring rod.

Skills Focus Practicing Lab Techniques, Making Observations, Making Inferences

MODIFICATION FOR GUIDED Inquiry

Have students develop their own procedures for determining the pH of sample substances. Allow them to carry out all reasonable procedures.

MATERIALS

For each group
- glass stirring rod
- litmus paper, red and blue (at least 4 strips each)
- paper towels
- plastic cup
- test substances (8)
- watch glass
- water (1 cup)

For each student
- gloves
- lab apron
- safety goggles

My Notes

____

____

____

____

____

Answer Key

2. Answers will vary.
5. Sample answer: If I used only red litmus paper, I could not distinguish between acidic and neutral solutions. If I used only blue litmus paper, I could not distinguish between basic and neutral solutions. So, I must use both red and blue litmus paper.
6. An acid has a pH less than 7. A base has a pH greater than 7. A neutral substance has a pH of 7. Students' answers for their specific substances will vary.

Name ______________________ Class ______________ Date ______________

QUICK LAB DIRECTED Inquiry

Household Acids and Bases

In this activity, you will use blue and red litmus paper to identify acidic and basic substances. Blue litmus paper will turn red under acidic conditions, and red litmus paper will turn blue under basic conditions. Neutral substances do not change the color of red or blue litmus paper.

OBJECTIVE

- Identify acidic and basic substances.

MATERIALS

For each group

- glass stirring rod
- litmus paper, red and blue (at least 4 strips each)
- paper towels
- plastic cup
- test substances (8)
- watch glass
- water (1 cup)

For each student

- gloves
- lab apron
- safety goggles

PROCEDURE

1. Obtain samples of eight **test substances** from your teacher.
2. Place one piece of **red litmus paper** and one piece of **blue litmus paper** on a clean **watch glass**. Test the pH of a substance by dipping a **glass stirring rod** into it and then touching the stirring rod to a piece of litmus paper. Place only one drop of each substance on the litmus paper so that the litmus paper may be used for multiple tests. Observe any color changes in the litmus paper, and record your observations in the table below.

Substance	Effects on Blue Litmus Paper	Effects on Red Litmus Paper	Acid, Base, or Neutral
1			
2			
3			
4			
5			
6			
7			
8			

Quick Lab continued

3. Clean the stirring rod thoroughly by dipping it in a **cup** of **water** and wiping it dry with a **paper towel**.

4. Repeat Steps 2 and 3 with each sample substance. Use new pieces of litmus paper as needed.

5. Why were both red and blue litmus paper used?

____

____

____

____

____

6. What is the pH range of acids? Of bases? What is the pH of a neutral substance? Infer the pH range of each of the substances you tested.

____

____

____

____

____

____

____

QUICK LAB DIRECTED Inquiry

Making Salt ADVANCED

Small groups

20 minutes, plus 10 minutes the following day

LAB RATINGS

LESS ↔ MORE

Teacher Prep — 2

Student Setup — 2

Cleanup — 2

SAFETY INFORMATION

Remind students to review all safety cautions and icons before beginning this lab. Students should wear safety goggles, protective gloves, and an apron. In case of an acid or a base spill, first dilute the spill with water. Then, while wearing disposable plastic gloves, mop up the spill with damp cloths designated for spill cleanup. Students should also have access to a safety shower and eyewash station, and they should know how to operate this safety equipment.

Caution students not to taste the salt that forms after the water has evaporated.

MATERIALS

For each group

- beakers, (3)
- cylinder, graduated, 50 mL
- eyedroppers (2)
- hydrochloric acid solution, 0.1 M
- magnifying lens
- petri dish
- phenolphthalein solution, in dropper bottle
- sodium hydroxide solution, 0.1 M
- stirring rod
- water, distilled

For each student

- gloves
- lab apron
- safety goggles

TEACHER NOTES

In this activity, students will investigate a neutralization reaction between an acid, hydrochloric acid (HCl), and a base, sodium hydroxide (NaOH). After students titrate the solution, they will place it in a petri dish and allow the water to evaporate overnight. They will then observe the salt crystals in the dish the next day. Concentrations of hydrochloric acid and sodium hydroxide should be 0.1 M. Provide each group of students with a beaker containing 30 mL of each solution. Students should use only premixed solutions of phenolphthalein (2 g mixed into 100 mL of 95% ethanol, diluted with 100 mL of water).

To dispose of the hydrochloric acid, titrate with 0.1 M NaOH as required until the pH is between 6 and 8, and then pour the solution down the drain. For the sodium hydroxide, titrate with 0.1 M HCl until the pH is between 5 and 9, and then pour down the drain. Unused indicators should be tightly covered and returned to the storage shelf.

Tip It may be helpful for students to see the equation for the reaction:

$HCl + NaOH \rightarrow H_2O + NaCl$.

Student Tip What are some physical properties of salt? Look for these properties as you observe the products of this reaction.

Skills Focus Practicing Lab Techniques, Making Observations

My Notes

Quick Lab continued

MODIFICATION FOR GUIDED Inquiry

Provide students with the materials listed and have students follow the procedure to prepare the neutralization reaction. Have student groups describe how they will observe the products of the neutralization reaction, and have them describe how they will record their observations.

Answer Key

7. Accept all reasonable answers. Students should observe white cubic crystals.

8. Sample answer: The phenolphthalein serves an an indicator, allowing us to observe when the solution became neutral.
Teacher Prompt What do indicator solutions tell us?

9. Sample answer: The crystals were most likely salt.

10. Sample answer: The purpose of leaving the solution out all night was so the water would evaporate out of the solution.

11. Sample answer: This was a neutralization reaction because the pH of the acid/base solution was neutral, and the products were water and salt.
Teacher Prompt What are the products of a neutralization reaction? What were the products of the chemical reaction between hydrochloric acid and sodium hydroxide?

Name ______________________ Class ______________ Date ______________

QUICK LAB GUIDED *Inquiry*

Making Salt

Two products of a neutralization reaction are water and a salt. In this experiment, you will explore the reaction between hydrochloric acid, an acid, and sodium hydroxide, a base. Be sure to use caution when handling these substances. In the event of a spill, immediately notify your teacher.

OBJECTIVE

- Describe a neutralization reaction and its products.

MATERIALS

For each group

- beakers, 100 mL (3)
- cylinder, graduated 50 mL
- eyedroppers (2)
- hydrochloric acid solution, 0.1 M
- magnifying lens
- petri dish
- phenolphthalein solution, in dropper bottle
- sodium hydroxide solution, 0.1 M
- stirring rod
- water, distilled

For each student

- gloves
- lab apron
- safety goggles

PROCEDURE

1. Put on protective gloves. Carefully measure 15 milliliters (mL) of hydrochloric acid in a graduated cylinder and pour it into the beaker. Rinse the graduated cylinder with distilled water to clean out any leftover acid.
2. Add three drops of phenolphthalein indicator to the acid in the beaker and use the glass rod to stir the solution. Record the color of the solution.
3. Measure 10 mL of sodium hydroxide in the graduated cylinder, and add it slowly to the beaker with the acid. Use the stirring rod to mix the substances completely.
4. Use an eyedropper to add more base, a few drops at a time, to the acid-base solution in the beaker. Stir the mixture after each addition of drops. Continue adding drops of base until the mixture remains colored after stirring.
5. Use another eyedropper to add acid to the beaker, one drop at a time, until the color just disappears after stirring. Be sure that the solution remains colorless for at least 30 seconds.
6. Pour the solution carefully into a petri dish and allow the dish to sit out overnight.
7. The next day, examine your petri dish. With a magnifying lens, study the crystals that were left. Identify the color, shape, and other properties of the crystals. Record your observations below.

____

____

____

____

____

____

Quick Lab continued

8. What was the purpose of using the phenolphthalein solution when you mixed the acid and base together?

____

____

9. What do you think the crystals are that were produced in this reaction?

____

10. What was the purpose of leaving the solution in the petri dish overnight?

____

____

11. Was the reaction between hydrochloric acid and sodium hydroxide a neutralization reaction? Explain why or why not.

____

____

____

EXPLORATION LAB DIRECTED Inquiry **AND** GUIDED Inquiry

Acids, Bases, and Fruit Oxidation GENERAL

Small groups

45 minutes, plus 10 minutes the next day

LAB RATINGS LESS ⟷ MORE

Teacher Prep — 2

Student Setup — 2

Cleanup — 2

SAFETY INFORMATION

Remind students to review all safety cautions and icons before beginning this lab. When students are describing the physical properties of the acids and bases, emphasize that they should not taste or touch any substances. Rather, they should fill in the table based on their experiences of having eaten a lemon, or salad dressing containing vinegar. Be sure that students wash and dry their hands after completing this inquiry.

TEACHER NOTES

In this activity, students will investigate how acids and bases affect the oxidation rate of apples. First, students will identify common household substances as acids or bases by describing their physical properties and using litmus paper. Provide each group of students with five paper cups, each containing one of the substances to be tested. After students have completed this step, slice the apples for each group using a knife or an apple slicer. Have students immediately place their apple slices in the cups and coat slices with the acid and base substances. Then, instruct students to set aside their apple slices for 24 hours. Be sure that groups place their cups in the same area to control for light and temperature. If apples are not available, other fruits that oxidize, such as pears or avocados, could be substituted.

Tip It may be useful to review the difference between physical properties and chemical properties before beginning this activity.

Student Tip What happens when a sliced apple sits out too long? What do you think could prevent this?

Skills Focus Making Observations, Drawing Conclusions

MATERIALS

For the teacher
- knife

For each group
- ammonia, household
- apple, sliced
- cups, plastic (6)
- lemon juice
- litmus paper, blue and red
- marker
- masking tape
- milk of magnesia
- paper towels
- spoon
- stirring rod
- vinegar
- water, distilled

For each student
- gloves
- lab apron
- safety goggles

My Notes

Exploration Lab continued

MODIFICATION FOR INDEPENDENT Inquiry

Explain that oxidation causes many fruits, such as apples and pears, to turn brown when the fruit flesh is exposed to the air. Challenge students to investigate how acids and bases might affect this process. Have students identify materials to use in their investigations. They should specify which fruits, acids, and bases they will use. Next, instruct student groups to devise procedures for the investigation. Students should be sure to describe how they will test the acidity/alkalinity of their acids and bases. Remind students to include a control in their experiment. Allow students to carry out their procedures once you have approved them. Finally, have students draw conclusions about whether acids or bases are more effective in preventing oxidation of fruit.

Answer Key for DIRECTED Inquiry

MAKE OBSERVATIONS

1. Accept all reasonable answers.
2. Results should show that lemon juice and vinegar are acidic, ammonia and milk of magnesia are basic, and water is neutral.

ANALYZE THE RESULTS

4. Sample answer: Acidic substances taste sour. Basic substances taste bitter and feel slippery.
   Teacher Prompt Lemons contain citric acid. How do they taste? Soap is another basic substance. How does it feel?

FORM A PREDICTION

6. Accept all reasonable answers.
   Teacher Prompt Which substances might slow or speed the rate of oxidation?

TEST THE PREDICTION

10. Answers will vary, but observations should show that apple slices coated in basic substances are browner than those coated in acidic substances. The apple slice coated in lemon juice should be the least brown.

ANALYZE THE RESULTS

11. Sample answer: The apple slices coated in acids seemed to experience less oxidation than the slices coated in bases or neutral substances.
    Teacher Prompt Which apple slices have changed the least since they were first sliced? Are any apple slices even browner than the control slice?
12. Sample answer: The data suggest that acids slow down the rate of oxidation. Bases and neutral substances seem to have little or no effect on the oxidation rate.
    Teacher Prompt Look for patterns in your data. Do apple slices coated in similar substances appear similar?

Exploration Lab continued

13. Accept all reasonable answers.

Connect TO THE ESSENTIAL QUESTION

14. Sample answer: An acid would be better for preventing oxidation. Our results show that oxidation happens more slowly when fruit is coated in an acid.
Teacher Prompt What effect did acids have on the oxidation process? What effect did bases have?

Answer Key for GUIDED Inquiry

MAKE OBSERVATIONS

1. Accept all reasonable answers.

2. Results should show that lemon juice and vinegar are acidic, ammonia and milk of magnesia are basic, and water is neutral.

ANALYZE THE RESULTS

4. Sample answer: Acidic substances taste sour. Basic substances taste bitter and feel slippery.
Teacher Prompt Lemons contain citric acid. How do they taste? Soap is another basic substance. How does it feel?

FORM A PREDICTION

6. Accept all reasonable answers.
Teacher Prompt What substances might slow or speed the rate of oxidation?

TEST THE PREDICTION

7. Accept all reasonable answers.
Teacher Prompt How can you compare the oxidation of apple slices coated in certain substances with the oxidation of uncoated apple slices? What variable(s) will you observe?

9. Answers will vary, but observations should show that apple slices coated in basic substances are browner than those coated in acidic substances. The apple slice coated in lemon juice should be the least brown.

ANALYZE THE RESULTS

10. Sample answer: The apple slices coated in acids seemed to experience less oxidation than the slices coated in bases or neutral substances.
Teacher Prompt Which apple slices have changed the least since they were first sliced? Are any apple slices even browner than the control slice?

Exploration Lab continued

11. Sample answer: Results show that acids slow down the rate of oxidation. Bases and neutral substances seem to have little or no effect on the oxidation rate.
Teacher Prompt Look for patterns in your data. Do apple slices coated in similar substances appear similar?

12. Accept all reasonable answers.

Connect TO THE ESSENTIAL QUESTION

13. Sample answer: An acid would be better for preventing oxidation. Our results show that oxidation happens more slowly when fruit is coated in an acid.
Teacher Prompt What effect did acids have on the oxidation process? What effect did bases have?

Name ______________________ Class ______________ Date ______________

EXPLORATION LAB DIRECTED *Inquiry*

Acids, Bases, and Fruit Oxidation

In this lab, you will first test whether common household substances are acidic or basic by using litmus paper as an acid-base indicator. Remember that blue litmus paper will turn red under acidic conditions, and red litmus paper will turn blue under basic conditions. You will then investigate how acids and bases affect the oxidation rate of fruit. Oxidation is a chemical reaction between oxygen in the air and another substance. Oxidation in fruit occurs when an enzyme in the plant tissue is exposed to oxygen. This process causes the fruit flesh to turn brown.

OBJECTIVES

- Describe the physical properties of acids and bases.
- Describe the chemical properties of acids and bases.

MATERIALS

For each group

- ammonia, household
- apple, sliced
- cups, plastic (6)
- lemon juice
- litmus paper, blue and red
- marker
- masking tape
- milk of magnesia
- paper towels
- spoon
- stirring rod
- vinegar
- water, distilled

For each student

- gloves
- lab apron
- safety goggles

MAKE OBSERVATIONS

1. Obtain the following test substances: lemon juice, household ammonia, milk of magnesia, water, and vinegar. Observe each substance and record its physical properties in the table below.

Substance	Physical properties	Litmus test results
ammonia		
lemon juice		
milk of magnesia		
vinegar		
water		

2. Dip a stirring rod into a solution and then touch the stirring rod to a piece of red and a piece of blue litmus paper. Record your results in the table in Step 1.

3. Repeat Step 2 for each test substance. Between each test, clean the stirring rod by dipping it in water and wiping it with a paper towel.

Name ______________________ Class ______________ Date ________________

Exploration Lab continued

ANALYZE THE RESULTS

4 **Interpreting Observations** Do the acidic substances share any physical properties? Do the basic substances share any physical properties?

____

____

____

____

____

____

ASK A QUESTION

5 Now you will investigate the following question: How do acids and bases affect the oxidation rate of apples? Discuss your ideas within your group.

FORM A PREDICTION

6 Form a prediction to address the question in Step 5.

____

____

TEST THE PREDICTION

7 Place a piece of tape on the sixth cup and label it "control."

8 Obtain freshly cut apple slices from your teacher. Place a slice of apple in each of the plastic cups. Coat each apple slice with the substance that matches the label on the cup. Do not apply any substance to the apple slice in the cup labeled "control."

9 Set aside your apple slices for one day.

10 The next day, observe your apple slices and record your observations below.

Test substance	Observations
ammonia	
lemon juice	
milk of magnesia	
vinegar	
water	
control	

ANALYZE THE RESULTS

11 **Analyzing Data** Which apple slices oxidized the most? Which slices oxidized the least?

12 **Identifying Patterns** How did the acidity or alkalinity of the test substances affect how the fruit oxidized? Did you observe a pattern? Explain.

13 **Evaluating Predictions** Do your results support the prediction you made? Explain.

Connect TO THE ESSENTIAL QUESTION

14 **Developing Conclusions** Based on your findings, would it be better to use an acid or a base to prevent oxidation? Explain.

Name ______________________ Class ______________ Date ______________

EXPLORATION LAB GUIDED Inquiry

Acids, Bases, and Fruit Oxidation

In this lab, you will first test whether common household substances are acidic or basic by using litmus paper as an acid-base indicator. Remember that blue litmus paper will turn red under acidic conditions, and red litmus paper will turn blue under basic conditions. You will then investigate how acids and bases affect the oxidation rate of fruit. Oxidation is a chemical reaction between oxygen in the air and another substance. Oxidation in fruit occurs when an enzyme in the plant tissue is exposed to oxygen. This process causes the fruit flesh to turn brown.

OBJECTIVES

- Describe the physical properties of acids and bases.
- Describe the chemical properties of acids and bases.

MATERIALS

For each group

- ammonia, household
- apple, sliced
- cups, plastic (6)
- lemon juice
- litmus paper, blue and red
- marker
- masking tape
- milk of magnesia
- paper towels
- spoon
- stirring rod
- vinegar
- water, distilled

For each student

- gloves
- lab apron
- safety goggles

MAKE OBSERVATIONS

1. Obtain the following test substances: lemon juice, household ammonia, milk of magnesia, water, and vinegar. Observe each substance and record its physical properties in the table below.

Substance	Physical properties	Litmus test results
ammonia		
lemon juice		
milk of magnesia		
vinegar		
water		

2. Dip a stirring rod into a solution and then touch the stirring rod to a piece of red and a piece of blue litmus paper. Record your results in the table in Step 1.

3. Repeat Step 2 for each test substance. Between each test, clean the stirring rod by dipping it in water and wiping it with a paper towel.

ANALYZE THE RESULTS

4. **Interpreting Observations** Do the acidic substances share any physical properties? Do the basic substances share any physical properties?

____

____

____

____

____

____

ASK A QUESTION

5. Now you will investigate the following question: How do acids and bases affect the oxidation rate of apples? Discuss your ideas within your group.

FORM A PREDICTION

6. Form a prediction to address the question in Step 5.

____

____

TEST THE PREDICTION

7. Write a procedure that will let you test your prediction. For best results, make your final observations after the apples have been left to sit out for one day.

____

____

____

____

____

____

____

____

8. Obtain freshly cut apple slices from your teacher. With teacher approval, carry out your procedure.

Exploration Lab continued

9. The next day, observe your apple slices. Create a table below in which you will record your observations.

ANALYZE THE RESULTS

10. **Analyzing Data** Which apple slices oxidized the most? Which slices oxidized the least?

____

____

____

____

11. **Identifying Patterns** How did the acidity or alkalinity of the test substances affect how the fruit oxidized? Did you observe a pattern? Explain.

____

____

____

____

____

____

12 **Evaluating Predictions** Do your results support the prediction you made? Explain.

____

____

____

____

____

____

Connect TO THE ESSENTIAL QUESTION

13 **Developing Conclusions** Based on your findings, would it be better to use an acid or a base to prevent oxidation? Explain.

____

____

____

____

QUICK LAB DIRECTED *Inquiry*

Determining pH Levels GENERAL

Small groups
20 minutes

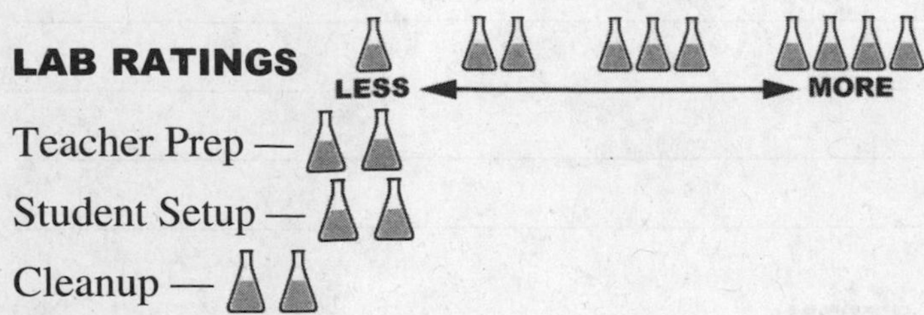

Teacher Prep —
Student Setup —
Cleanup —

SAFETY INFORMATION

Remind students to review all safety cautions and icons before beginning this lab. Some substances used in this investigation can cause eye or skin irritation, and they may also stain clothing. Aprons, gloves, and goggles should be worn at all times. Students should immediately use running water to rinse any skin area that comes in contact with the ammonia solution. All spills should be wiped up immediately. Keep paper towels on hand for wiping up spills. Have students wash and dry their hands after completing this inquiry.

TEACHER NOTES

In this activity, students will use litmus paper to determine whether substances are acidic or basic. Then, students will use pH paper and pH meters to determine a more precise pH measurement of each material.

Before the activity, prepare the baking soda solution by stirring 1 gram of baking soda into 500 mL of water. Then, calibrate the pH meters. Consult the pH meter's manual to determine the exact procedure for the model you have. Although students do not need to see the calibration process, you should explain the maintenance needed for a pH meter to work properly. If pH meters are not available, students can carry out the inquiry to determine what conclusions they can make by comparing the results they obtain from using litmus paper and pH paper.

Prepare the materials for each group by pouring a small amount of each substance into a plastic cup. (The substances include: ammonia solution, baking soda solution, lemon juice, milk, vinegar, and distilled water.) Students should receive two samples of distilled water; one will be used as a test substance and the other will be used to clean the stirring rod between tests. Label the contents of each cup with masking tape.

Tip This activity may help students evaluate methods of measuring pH.

Skills Focus Practicing Lab Techniques, Interpreting Data

MATERIALS

For each group
- ammonia, 20% solution diluted
- baking soda
- cups, plastic (7)
- lemon juice
- litmus paper, blue and red
- milk
- paper towels
- pH meter
- pH paper
- plate, paper
- stirring rod
- vinegar
- water, distilled

For each student
- lab apron
- protective gloves
- safety goggles

My Notes

Quick Lab continued

MODIFICATION FOR INDEPENDENT *Inquiry*

Challenge students to design an experiment that will explore different methods of measuring pH. Provide students with the measurement tools (litmus paper, pH paper, and a pH meter), but have them choose the test substances. Instruct students to develop their own procedures and methods of recording data. Once you have approved the procedures, allow students to carry out their investigations. Ask students to compare and contrast each method of testing pH.

Answer Key

2. Sample answers are provided in the chart below.

pH OF HOUSEHOLD SUBSTANCES

Substance	Litmus paper test	pH paper test	pH meter test
Ammonia solution	Turns red paper blue	12	12
Baking soda solution	Turns red paper blue	8	8
Lemon juice	Turns blue paper red	2	2
Milk	Turns blue paper red	6	6
Vinegar	Turns blue paper red	3	3
Distilled water	No color change	7	7

6. Sample answer: Ammonia and baking soda solution are bases. Lemon juice, milk, and vinegar are acids. The litmus paper test is the easiest way to observe this.

7. Sample answer: Lemon juice had a pH level of 2, so it was the most acidic substance. The pH paper test and the pH meter test show the pH levels of substances, so results from these tests allow you to compare different levels of acidity. The litmus paper test only shows whether a substance is an acid or a base. It does not allow you to compare pH levels of different acids.
Teacher prompt What information do you need to compare the pH of different acids? Which tests show the pH level of a substance? Which test does not?

8. Sample answer: The pH meter gives the most precise results. However, this test requires a special tool that may not be available to everyone.
Teacher prompt Which test gives the pH reading with the most significant figures? Does this test require any special tools?

Name ______________________________ Class ________________ Date ______________________

QUICK LAB DIRECTED Inquiry

Determining pH Levels

In this lab, you will use different methods to determine the pH levels of various test substances. The pH of a substance tells you how acidic or basic the substance is. Acidic substances have a pH less than 7, and basic substances have a pH greater than 7.

OBJECTIVES

- Identify different tools that can be used to determine pH.
- Measure the pH of a solution.

MATERIALS

For each group

- ammonia solution
- baking soda solution
- cups, plastic (7)
- lemon juice
- litmus paper, blue and red
- milk
- paper towels
- pH meter
- pH paper
- plate, paper
- stirring rod
- vinegar
- water, distilled

For each student

- lab apron
- protective gloves
- safety goggles

PROCEDURE

1. Collect the following test substances from your teacher: ammonia solution, baking soda solution, lemon juice, milk, vinegar, and distilled water. Be sure to collect two cups of distilled water. (You will use one as a test substance and one to clean your stirring rod.)

2. Put one piece of red litmus paper and one piece of blue litmus paper on a paper plate. Dip the stirring rod into the ammonia solution and then carefully touch the stirring rod to each piece of litmus paper. Observe the color of the litmus paper and record your results in the first column of the table on the next page.

Quick Lab continued

pH OF HOUSEHOLD SUBSTANCES

Substance	Litmus paper test	pH paper test	pH meter test
Ammonia solution			
Baking soda solution			
Lemon juice			
Milk			
Vinegar			
Distilled water			

3. Repeat Step 2 for each test substance. Between each test, clean the stirring rod by dipping it in tap water and wiping with a paper towel.

4. Repeat the process described in Steps 2 and 3 using pH paper instead of litmus paper. Record your results in the table in Step 2.

5. Test the substances again using a pH meter. Lower the tip of the pH meter into a substance. Allow the meter's reading to stabilize, and then record it in the table in Step 2. After each reading, rinse the tip of the meter with distilled water.

6. Based on your observations, which substances are acids and which are bases? Which method is the easiest way to test this?

____

____

____

____

7. Which substance was the most acidic? Which test(s) allowed you to determine this information? Explain.

____

____

____

____

8. Which test gives the most precise results? What is one limitation of this test?

____

____

____

____

QUICK LAB DIRECTED Inquiry

Investigating Respiration with Chemical Indicators GENERAL

Small groups
15 minutes

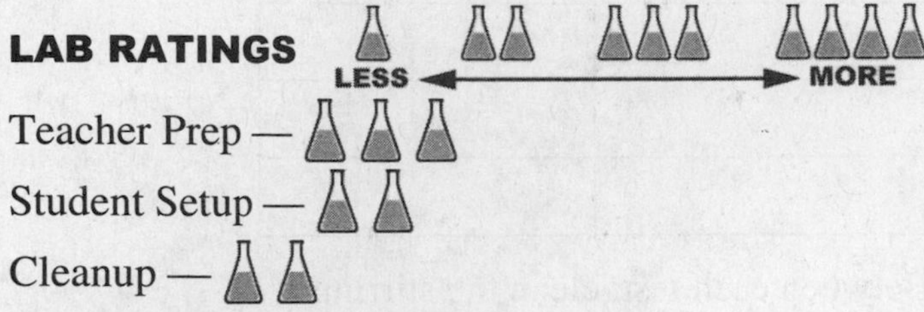

SAFETY INFORMATION

Remind students to review all safety cautions and icons before beginning this lab. Caution students not to ingest or inhale any of the liquids. Red cabbage extract can stain clothes; instruct students to handle it carefully. Have students wash and dry their hands after completing this inquiry.

TEACHER NOTES

In this activity, students will blow bubbles into an indicator-laced solution. As students blow bubbles, carbon dioxide will enter the solution, and students will observe that the solution changes color. They will then use a pH meter to determine whether the color change indicates a change to a more acidic or basic condition. Students will draw conclusions about how pH remains balanced in the human body. If beakers are not available, students may use small, clear plastic cups. If you do not have access to a pH meter, pH paper can be used instead.

To make red cabbage extract for six groups, finely chop 3 cups of red cabbage and add it to 900 mL of boiling water. Allow the mixture to cool, and strain the cabbage out of the liquid. Discard the solid cabbage and reserve the liquid.

Red cabbage extract diluted in distilled water takes on a bluish purple color. With four to five minutes of vigorous blowing into this solution, the color changes to a reddish purple. Students need to do side-by-side comparisons of a control solution with an experimental solution to see this color change; it is not dramatic but can be clearly observed using this side-by-side comparison method.

Tip Help students make connections between the pH of the solution they measure and the pH of the human body. Explain that humans can survive only if the pH level of the body is within a narrow range.

Student Tip Blow vigorously into the straw so that you produce large bubbles for at least two minutes.

Skills Focus Making Observations, Drawing Conclusions

MATERIALS

For each group
- beakers (2)
- cylinder, graduated, 100 mL
- drinking straw
- pH meter
- red cabbage extract, prepared, 2 tsp
- water, distilled, 200 mL

For each student
- lab apron
- protective gloves
- safety goggles

My Notes

Quick Lab continued

MODIFICATION FOR GUIDED *Inquiry*

Have students consider different variables that might affect the outcome of the pH change in this experiment. Students may want to vary the volume of water, the amount of time they blow into the water, or the amount of cabbage extract.

Answer Key

2. Sample answer: The solution is purplish-blue.

3. Accept all reasonable answers.

4. Sample answer: The solution turned from purple to a redder color.

5. Sample answer: The observation that the pH became lower shows that something present in our breath causes the solution to become acidic.
Teacher prompt Did your solution's pH increase or decrease when you blew into it? What does it mean when the pH of a solution decreases?

6. Sample answer: The respiratory system allows us to release carbon dioxide from the body. Without this system, carbon dioxide could accumulate in the body and pH levels could become too low.
Teacher prompt What does the respiratory system do with carbon dioxide? What could happen if carbon dioxide weren't released from the body?

Name ______________________ Class ______________ Date ________________

QUICK LAB DIRECTED Inquiry

Investigating Respiration with Chemical Indicators

In this lab, you will explore how pH relates to the human body. You will blow bubbles into a solution and observe how the pH of the solution changes. Remember that when you exhale, you release carbon dioxide from the body. Carbon dioxide is a waste product of cells in your body. It also has an important effect on pH in your body.

OBJECTIVES

- Observe pH changes in an indicator solution.
- Explore how respiration relates to pH in the human body.

MATERIALS

For each group
- beakers (2)
- cylinder, graduated, 100 mL
- drinking straw
- pH meter
- red cabbage extract, prepared, 2 tsp
- water, distilled, 200 mL

For each student
- lab apron
- protective gloves
- safety goggles

PROCEDURE

1. Measure 200 mL of distilled water into a beaker.
2. Add 2 tsp of red cabbage extract to the beaker. Observe and record the color of the solution.

   ____

3. Insert the tip of the pH meter into the solution and observe the pH of the solution. Record your observations.

   ____

4. Divide the solution by pouring half into another beaker. With a drinking straw, blow vigorously into one solution for four to five minutes. After four to five minutes, compare the color of the sample you blew into with the color of the original solution. Measure the pH of the solution using the pH meter. Record your observations.

   ____

   ____

5. What does the change in pH indicate about the composition of your breath? Explain your reasoning.

   ____

   ____

   ____

   ____

Quick Lab continued

6 Based on your observations, how might the respiratory system help to control pH levels in the body? Why is this control important?

____

____

____

____

____

QUICK LAB DIRECTED Inquiry

Investigating the Effects of Acid Precipitation GENERAL

MATERIALS

For each pair
- beakers, 50 mL (3)
- chalk (3)
- masking tape
- vinegar (5% acidity), 40 mL
- water, 35 mL
- wax pencil

For each student
- gloves
- lab apron
- safety goggles

My Notes

Student pairs
15 minutes for set up; 5 minutes per day for a week

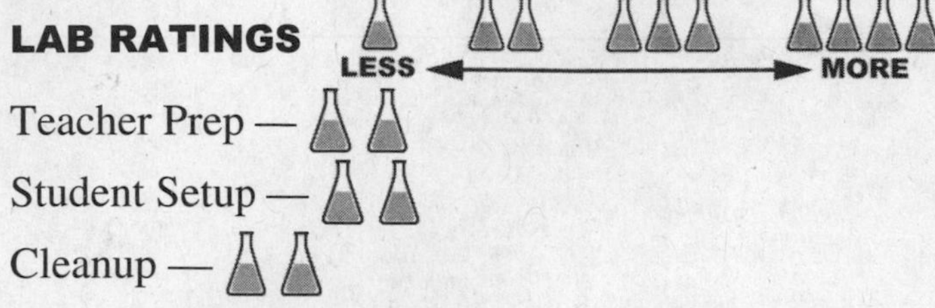

SAFETY INFORMATION

Remind students to review all safety cautions and icons before beginning this lab. Because students are handling an acidic substance, have them wear safety goggles and gloves. Lab aprons should also be worn. When students are finished setting up the experiment, have them thoroughly wash their hands.

TEACHER NOTES

In this activity, students will investigate the damage to building stones that acid precipitation causes. This experiment takes place over the course of a week. On the first day, students will set up the experiment. For the remainder of the week, students will observe their experiments.

Tip Because the vinegar is quickly neutralized by the calcium carbonate, you should have the students refresh the solution on day 4. Students should realize that days 1 and 4 represent precipitation days.

Skills Focus Making Observations, Drawing Conclusions, Applying Concepts

MODIFICATION FOR GUIDED Inquiry

Ask student pairs how vinegar, water, and chalk can be used to show the effect of acid precipitation on stone buildings. Have students design an experiment for you to approve. Do not approve experiments in which students only put the chalk in one type of solution. Then allow pairs to carry out approved procedures. Encourage pairs to discuss their procedure and findings with other pairs.

Quick Lab continued

Answer Key

1. **Teacher Prompt** Discuss with students what the liquid in the different beakers represents.
2. Accept all reasonable answers. Students should observe that the reaction was strongest in Beaker C. Students should observe that the highest amount of breakdown took place on day 1 and day 4. Students should observe that there was no visible change on day 3.
3. Accept all reasonable answers.
4. Sample answer: Stone monuments and buildings erode more quickly when they are exposed to acid precipitation because the acid seems to dissolve the stone.
5. Sample answer: The water becomes more acidic. The organisms that live in these waterways must adapt to higher acid levels in the water or they will die.
6. Sample answer: The soils also become more acidic. Organisms that live in the soil, such as worms and plants, must adapt to higher acidic levels or they will die. If the acidic levels are too far from the normal range, the organisms probably will die.
7. Sample answer: The trees and other plants could not quickly adapt to the high acid concentrations and they died.

Name ______________________ Class ______________ Date ______________

QUICK LAB DIRECTED *Inquiry*

Investigating the Effects of Acid Precipitation

Acid precipitation is a form of pollution caused by the burning of fossil fuels by automobiles and electric power plants, and by other industrial processes. During these processes, sulfur dioxide and nitrogen oxide are released into the atmosphere, where they combine with water vapor to form sulfuric and nitric acids. When this precipitation falls in the form of rain, sleet, snow, fog, or hail, it is acidic. In this lab, you will investigate the effects of acid precipitation on building stone. You will use different mixtures of vinegar and water to represent acid rain. You will use chalk to represent building stones.

OBJECTIVES

- Investigate the effect of an acidic solution on materials.
- Describe the effects of acid precipitation.

MATERIALS

For each pair

- beakers ,50 mL (3)
- chalk (3)
- masking tape
- vinegar (5% acidity), 40 mL
- water, 35 mL
- wax pencil

For each student

- gloves
- lab apron
- safety goggles

PROCEDURE

1. Label each **beaker** *A*, *B*, or C using the **masking tape** and **wax pencil.** Pour 25 mL of **water** into Beaker A. Pour 10 mL of water and 15 mL of **vinegar** into Beaker B. Pour 25 mL of vinegar into Beaker C.

2. Place a piece of **chalk** into each beaker. Observe what happens to the chalk over five days. Refresh the solution on Day 4. Record your observations in the chart.

Beaker	Day 1	Day 2	Day 3	Day 4	Day 5
A					
B					
C					

3. Based on your results, what is the effect of acid precipitation on building stone?

____

____

____

____

4. What do you think happens to stone monuments and buildings that are exposed to acid precipitation?

5. When acid precipitation falls into rivers and streams, what do you think happens to the water and the organisms that live in these waterways?

6. What happens when acid precipitation contaminates soils? What effect does this have on organisms that live in the soil?

7. In locations where the precipitation is very acidic, trees and other plants may die. Why do you think this occurs?